At the End of the Road

At the End of the Road

Nancy Peckinpaugh

ISBN: 0991456203
ISBN 13: 9780991456208
Library of Congress Control Number: 2015910893
Nancy Peckinpaugh, Sutter Creek CA

To My Family

"…young men will see visions, and your old men will dream dreams."
Acts 2:17

CHAPTER 1

Looking Back

As I DRIVE DOWN CHEROKEE Park Road I'm reminded of those early years spent tucked away within the eastern slope of the northern Colorado Rockies. It's a place where determination has always been essential to keep pace with everyday life. We were all too aware of how quickly tranquility could turn treacherous. Life here was a trade-off, yet the mountain folks chose it over a more comfortable and refined existence.

Looking through the dust-laden windshield has a way of taking me back to the all too familiar events that shaped my life; back to the day when Ma and Papa left the four of us kids with Gramps and Grandma while they drove to Ft. Collins for their much deserved anniversary celebration.

Ma had a real hard time getting herself into the truck. She kept going over the do's and don'ts, whys and why nots. Papa finally grabbed her hand and tugged her toward the rusty green pickup. Gramps eased her fears and promised he and Grandma would take good care of us, not to worry about a thing.

I'll always remember standing on my rough, calloused, bare feet with my toes burrowing into the loose gravel driveway. My arms were wrapped around Luke's pot belly as I elevated him off the ground. We were center front, with Eva on our right and Caleb on our left. Gramps and Grandma stood behind us and started waving goodbye. We all joined in, me waving Luke's little hand until the truck rounded the bend, losing sight of our parents, forever.

We didn't hear the sheriff's car pull in during the early morning hours. We didn't hear Gramps and Grandma as they held each other and wept. We were spared the loss of our parents a bit longer. Gramps and Grandma came up to the guest bedroom, devastation carved into their weary faces, as if to welcome in the new day. Only that day proved to be the beginning of a whole new life for us all.

Gramps wrapped his arms around Caleb and me while Grandma held Eva and Luke close to her chest. She mumbled, "Your Ma and Papa are finding comfort in the Lord's home." I found it hard to understand why the Lord felt Ma and Papa needed comforting. I figured they were pretty comfortable where they were, right here with us. Fact was, Ma and Papa's timing was all wrong; a brakeless cattle truck had no other place to go but into their pickup while trying to round a blind curve. Come to find out, a stubborn pine held firm and our unsuspecting folks were trapped in death's grip.

Ma and Papa were laid to rest on Gramps' ranch in the old family cemetery. There the aspens would show their fall splendor and drop their bright yellow leaves in time to protect them from winter's rage. Spring would then bring back new life, shading them with an umbrella of bright green foliage throughout the warm, wet, summer season.

After the funeral we helped Gramps and Grandma take all our clothes and the few handmade toys out of our home. Our new home would be with them in the big, old ranch house. Now we clung to our grandparents and them to us.

There would be no more fires blazing in the hearth while Papa played his guitar or told us stories of the mountains. No more humming by Ma as she set a big pot of elk stew on the table. No more. No more.

Although the log cabin Papa built was small, the perception I had was that of an expansive fortress that served as a barrier against hidden dangers of the outside world. It was the place of my birth, as well as those of Caleb and Eva. Luke was a few hours old when he joined us within our hand hewn walls. The land had been sectioned off from Gramps' large ranch when our folks were married. Ma was an only child and Papa had been one of Gramps' hired hands.

The rooms of my birthplace would stay furnished, yet they felt so empty and cold. We walked out onto the front porch, saying not a word as Grandma pulled the heavy plank door closed behind us. We knew we'd be able to come back to visit, but no one foresaw the desire. That's when Gramps reminded us of the promise he and Grandma made to our folks about taking good care of us. "A man is only as good as his word," Gramps uttered, "and we aim to do right by all of you." I knew they would work hard to do just that. Hard work was a way of life for them. They were thankful for the "get up and go" and appreciated doing it while living tucked away in some of the most magnificent of God's creative works.

We had always loved our grandparents' ranch. Once we had become full time residents, we hung out with Ol' Al and not-so-old Ben, the two ranch-hands. Ol' Al played a mean harmonica and Ben would focus hard to keep up on his hand-me-down fiddle. Evenings would usually consist of old time tunes coming from the bunk house or, on warmer nights, from the ranch house porch. During the day, chores kept Al and Ben busy cutting firewood, mending fences and buildings, haying, herding cattle or shoeing horses. Feeding the big livestock was a daily task. Gramps might have been their boss, but he pulled no rank when it came to working with them side by side. Grandma would feed everyone and tend to the house. Gramps always said he had the better of the deals when it came to who had the most to do, him or Grandma. She had her hands full.

The four of us did our share of the chores on a smaller scale. Along with house work, there were always chickens to feed, eggs to collect, mice to trap, vegetables to pick, kittens to love, and Betty, our dog, to play with once our chores were done. We shared a pony named Howdy. When I say shared, I mean we all rode him at the same time. He was a Welch pony, bigger than a Shetland but with a much better disposition. Howdy would turn his head around and patiently watch each of us climb the rail fence and stretch our right legs over his bare back until we were in riding position. Then, with just a halter on his head and the lead rope looped around his neck and hooked back under the halter, Howdy would carefully make his rounds with his precious cargo bouncing joyously.

Due to the loose hair and dirt Howdy would shed, we'd all end up looking as though we were wearing chaps between our thighs and our fannies instead of covering the front of our legs. Springtime was the worst. Howdy would get to itching so bad, with all that winter coat trying to fall off; he would roll around, kicking up dust fit to kill. Then, of course, we would all pile on and help Howdy rid himself of the loosened hair. All of our legs and bottoms would move simultaneously up and down, back and forth, left and right, collecting dirt, hair, and sweat. Sliding off was the grand finale. We could have filled a feed sack with the amount of residue that pony produced. Yep, we plum wore the winter hair right off of him. After each ride Howdy was always thankful. We older three would gather brushes and curry combs to brush down his chestnut coat and comb through his tan mane and tail. Luke kept him occupied by feeding him oats during the clean-up ceremony. He learned fast how to keep his little fingers flat so as not to confuse them with the molasses coated kernels. Howdy seemed to know Luke was new at all this and took care to eat cautiously. Most of the grain fell back into the bucket, but Luke would squat down to pick up handful after handful until every morsel was gone. There was no end to Howdy's patience.

Losing our folks was the heaviest blow God could deliver. Life had dealt us a tough hand, and I felt it my job, as the oldest, to watch over Caleb, Eva and Luke. Our lives with Ma and Papa had been shattered, but I knew Gramps and Grandma would pick up the pieces and do their best to keep us whole. We had to keep from being too much of a burden on them. I tried to make sure none of us got hurt and I was always reminding my sister and brothers to use good manners. Ma was a stickler on manners. Yep, there were manners for all occasions: "Excuse my boardin' house reach", "Yes Mam", "No Sir", "Pardon me", " I'm sorry", " Thank you", " No thank you", " Please", "God bless you…" The list went on in record proportions.

School would be starting up again in the fall. I'd be going back as a fourth grader and Caleb would begin second grade. The small country school was located near Livermore; you could hardly call it a town. There was just the post office, a gas station and the school, located down the road a bit. In good weather, traveling time by motorized vehicle took about thirty minutes one way. The county road, being packed dirt, extended a little under twenty miles to the nearest pavement. Once on solid road we made quick progress to the school house.

Eva, being only five, wouldn't enter first grade for another year. There was no kindergarten class offered then, so kids got to run wild an extra year before enlisting among the educational ranks.

Luke I worried about the most. Being only two and a half when Ma and Papa passed on, he didn't have much of a hold on recollection. I figured our folks might be gone from view, but I was beholden to keep their spirit alive in all of us. One morning, a few weeks after the funeral, I mustered up the courage to ask Gramps and Grandma why they wouldn't talk about our folks. Grandma looked down at her age worn hands and spoke meekly, "It hurts too much".

All was quiet.

Then Gramps' blue eyes showed some sparkle and he slowly said, "We need to heal the hurt, Anne. Ezra is right. We can't pretend they were never here. They gave us what they loved most. You and I shared a heck-of-a-lot more years with them than these youngins'. We need to give these kids all the memories we can muster up. They deserve at least that."

Well, that was about all it took. That and a lot of tears. Grandma had to open the floodgate so as to let some of her pain escape. Photo albums began to appear on the coffee table and soon became severely worn. Grandma even talked to Ma and Papa when she said our nightly prayers with us. She'd tell them about what each of us did during the day and how we all inherited Ma's loving ways and Papa's sense of humor.

Grandma was right. We sure did like poking fun. Papa always said, "Don't get mad, get even." We figured there was no limit to the word "even" as long as it was in good humor. We all got pretty creative with that "even" business.

Here I am, memories pouring through my mind as if I found the right wrench needed to loosen and remove a rusty gasket. Anxiously, I begin releasing details that have been carefully squeezed and forced into a protected chamber of my heart.

All the bits and pieces of my life that I have reflected on throughout the years are finally being connected into a long, overdue filmstrip in my mind. Yes sir, I can almost smell the bacon and feel the bed shake as Caleb's feet hit the floor, racing to the breakfast table. I vividly recall his keen sense of smell. His sense of taste came in a close second. It was his hearing that was selective.

The driveway to our homestead, leading to the cabin of our births, will be coming up just around the turn. I notice that the unusually wet spring did its part to grow record breaking weeds along the fence row. The cows seem overwhelmed with controlling the belly high grass inside the barbed wired pasture. They're taking their jobs seriously, not even permitting themselves a timeout to watch the intruder as I stop to unlatch the wire loop that holds the gate to the post. With the exception of an occasional tire crossing, the gravel road has been conquered by indigenous lupine, high waving grasses, Indian paint brush, and the spurred flowers of the columbine.

Shifting into first gear, I slowly accelerate to cross the cattle guard. No need to close the gate; it serves only as a human deterrent. The evenly spaced metal rails spanning the ditch will keep hooves from crossing the fence line.

Slowly, my pickup creeps along the driveway, rolling over stray meadow grasses and wildflowers. Scratching sounds echo dully under the fenders and undercarriage as the tall groundcover flattens beneath the tires. While crossing the large culvert I stop to watch as the high water wastes no time pushing its way through the circular metal funnel. I take a moment to acknowledge the unsympathetic force of the current, and then I step on the accelerator and inch forward, following the road as it veers right and parallels the swollen river.

Dense aspen groves thrive along the bank and mix with fir and pine trees to ascend up the mountain on the left, framing the graveled passage as if to keep me on track. The road appears narrower, perhaps the foliage is trying to reclaim its rightful due after years of human neglect. My trained eye is able to see antler rubbings and bear marks among tree trunks. They give evidence of the creatures and their size.

Our family tree skirts the outer fringe of the aspen grove. It will be one of the last large aspens before the tangle of trunks and branches open up to my cabin, alone on a knoll.

As I see the clearing approach, I stop the truck and proceed on foot, checking each tree until the one bearing our names appears. Moving a low branch, I'm awed and comforted to find six identifiable names preserved against years of punishment under Mother Nature's hand. Physically and emotionally my unguarded body reacts. Chills travel quickly throughout my torso and meet in full force beneath my hat's brim. My solid knees give way to weak joints and tears fill the reservoirs around my eyes.

Lowering my bereft body to a nearby log, I catch sight of the adjoining tree that has grown from the base of our family tree. On it were five more names etched neatly in Gramps' familiar slant: Gramps, Grandma, Al, Ben and Wedge. Yes, that old man had the last word. A smile widened my face as I thought how appropriate the additional names were in my life and to my family. Now I must find the little grave, freshly dug and covered with boulders to secure its content. It should be between here and the cabin.

"It's time to get a move on," as Gramps would say. Just a few more feet and the view opened up. There it stood. As a beacon upon the knoll, the cabin seemed to smile and welcome me with open arms asking, "What took you so long?" I felt such a tenderness of heart as I admired the home my mother and father built.

Without approaching, I turned my head and there, twenty feet or so from the road, were the boulders I envisioned stacked against the hillside. Chiseled into the highest rock was the name *WEDGE*. Gramps was right. Wedge was buried in a fitting location. This tomb will stand as an everlasting memorial. It will greet friends on their arrival and see them off on their departure. It can be viewed from the front porch and from within all the southern and eastern windows. He'll welcome in the day and catch the last of the sun's glow in the evenings. Most of all, Wedge will be here with me. I have come full circle. I'm home.

The family isn't expecting me for several hours yet. I allotted such time when planning this trip back. Courage for me now takes on a whole new definition. Looking over once again at the grave of my little dog, I made my way to the humble grave. It was no accident a log laid next to the piled boulders. I even detected evidence of a small mound of ash on the ground where Gramps emptied his pipe while keeping vigil over Wedge's remains. From the looks of it, Gramps must have ridden horseback over the mountain to spend quiet moments here.

Sitting down on the log I feel the need to talk to my little friend. "Well Wedge, I promised you'd be laid to rest on our own ranch someday. Gramps did a fine job making you comfortable. He seemed to know the exact spot I would have picked. I swear that old man can see inside my mind and understand my most concealed thoughts. I miss you, old boy.

"There will be other dogs, I suppose. But none will fill my heart the way you had. You made me strong when I needed strength. You made me love at a time when I feared love's pain.

"It was fitting that Gramps was with you in the end. At first I thought it should have been me. But it was Gramps and Grandma who showed wisdom when it came to your happiness. I was the selfish one. You see, it takes some people a lot longer to untangle all that goes into making things right. To keep you with me would have been a wrong I'd have a hard time justifying. Yeah, you would have put on a happy wag the hours we'd have together. But you always belonged here. These mountains, rivers and meadows gave you life. They unfolded a freedom seldom seen by most dogs. There are no regrets, no apologies. We were a good team."

Wiping tears with my shirt sleeve, I manage to finish what I came to say. "I'll be back here again soon. We have our ranch now, and we share it together." Turning, I head toward our home.

I begin walking up the knoll and onto the rocked steps, my feet climbing to the planked porch. The hollow wood sound follows my movement to the door. I find my hand shaking as it lifts the rusty door latch. Recently broken cobwebs sway along the upper frame as the heavy door swings open on noisy hinges. For a moment I stand as my eyes adjust to the dim room. Most everything is covered with a heavy coat of dust. The river rock, stacked and mortared into a fireplace, serve as a centerpiece between the two wood-paned windows.

Hesitation is immediately replaced by a familiar warmth pouring over my whole being. Everything is as it was, waiting to be acknowledged, loved and embraced. As I sit down in Papa's large leather chair I peer out the front window at my dog's grave. With a sigh, I lay my head back, put my booted feet up on the stone hearth and let all the memories flow unchecked.

CHAPTER 2

Pup Number Six

"Grandma, when do you suppose my shirt'll be done?"

"It won't be long now, Ezra. I'll put on these last two snaps and then it should be good to go."

Caleb was kicking up dust all over the living room with his straw cowboy hat hanging by the stampede strap around his neck, bucking and snorting as if the invisible bronc had no choice but to give in to such a skillful rider. Grandma's handy work was flashing before our eyes. Green and blue stripes would soon be tucked into my denim jeans. The hand-carved leather belt will be cinched together with a polished bronc buckle. Gramps had spent many late hours tanning and chiseling designs into each of the four cowhide strips and giving each belt one of our names across the back. He even went overboard, buck stitching around the edges. He knew Eva and Luke would soon grow out of their smaller belts, but he wanted them to feel just as important as us "big boys".

Eva wore her new belt hanging loosely around the outside of her sack dress. Ma's old buckle clasped the leather ends together and the stick horse Ma had made gave her a much smoother ride than Caleb's wild steed. Even Luke was getting in on the action. His uncontrollable horse left him in a staged heap numerous times. But he would mount up over and over again, make horse-like grunts and prove to all he was the stuff men were made of.

"Here, it's done. Now don't be going off and wearing it thin before you have a chance to show it off at school."

"Thanks, Grandma. Looks like you saved the best for last. Can I just wear it long enough to get the wrinkles worn out?"

"Why sure. You're growing before my eyes. I figure I might as well start cutting out the next size up. You'll be out of this soon enough. The good thing about you, Ezra, is that Caleb will be right there to jump into what you outgrow."

"You guys can pretend all you want. I'm goin' outside to ride Howdy," I shouted. Well, that's all it took. The household horses were abandoned and soon there were four decked out dudes galloping out the gate upon Howdy's back.

There's little more than seven weeks left before summer's freedom abruptly ends. Caleb and I will have to spend a good part of our days sitting at desks and "developing our brains", as Grandma puts it. School is a bit more than thirty minutes from our home on a good day. There's talk about a school bus coming out our way to pick up kids in our area and take us home again after school. But Gramps said it'll be a few years yet before our district can afford a bus. That's okay by me. I like the idea of Gramps hauling us to school in Henry, his 1950 Chevy truck. It's the newest automobile on the ranch, and it's Gramps' pride and joy. He used to take us in the morning and pick us up at the end of the day when Ma and Papa were alive. It was always a treat when Caleb and I would run out of the school house at the end of the day to find Henry sitting in the parking lot. Gramps would be behind the wheel reading the local paper with a strand of dry grass clenched between his teeth. That big cheerful grin would peek through the side of his mouth, with sky blue eyes dancing a jig the moment he saw us coming. He'd throw his paper on the seat, jump out of the cab and swallow us up in his massive arms.

We settled in at the ranch easy enough. Caleb and I took over the guest room after the second month. Eva and Luke had a hard time separating from us until that point. Back at our log cabin they had shared Ma and Papa's room while Caleb and I slept up in the loft. Grandma had said there was no hurry for them to make the move across the hall into Ma's old room. They played during the day in Ma's room and slept next to us at night. Gramps had rigged up a mattress on the floor near our beds for them to sleep. This went on until they decided, with both bedroom doors open, they could handle the partial isolation. They shared Ma's double bed, an old brass heirloom that had been in the family for three generations. Caleb and I were old enough to handle bunk beds. Since I was the oldest, I had dibs on the top. That was fine with Caleb. He tacked cowboy pictures all over the plywood above him that held up my mattress. He had his own little refuge while I had the perch I wanted.

I remember thinking when Ma and Papa were alive how come the six of us had a small, one bedroom cabin while Gramps and Grandma lived in a two story home with three bedrooms. Didn't make much sense to me. But then again, the Good Lord had no way of explaining these things early on. It all came together by and by.

Seems the days passed as fast as the trout in the river. Mornings began with Tonto, the old Rhode Island red rooster named after the Indian who helped the Lone Ranger get the bad guys. He'd crow his head off before the sun even had a chance to stoke up its fire behind the mountains. The hens even seemed annoyed by his hypertension and his desire to disrupt everyone's sleep. Well, we felt no need for alarm clocks. Tonto had a way of setting the wake-up call, and he needed no winding.

Caleb and I took turns feeding the chickens and collecting the eggs right after breakfast. We agreed on weekly shifts so we'd get seven days off every other week, starting on Sundays. The hen house was a busy little shed during the spring and summer. Those hens clucked up conversations nonstop while laying their brown shelled gifts. Eggs popped out as if they were on an assembly line. Eva and Luke didn't like putting their hands beneath the hens to collect the eggs. But Caleb and I loved sneaking our hands under their soft downy bodies. On cold mornings we'd gently wiggle our fingers between the straw bedding and their relaxed bellies to instantly warm our hands. Hens would sometimes get pretty protective and peck at us trying to steal their goods. Caleb and I got used to their moods. We felt pretty brave taking on the pecks they'd deliver. The real excitement came when we happened to check under a hen while she was dropping an egg. The shells come out soft. Within seconds the outside covering hardens. That sure makes laying eggs a lot easier for those poor hens, and it makes collecting the eggs a lot more exciting for us. We got pretty good at detecting which clucking noise meant an egg was "dropping down the shoot".

Eva and Luke would sometimes go inside the fenced chicken yard to scatter feed. Rarely did they do it without Caleb or me there to kick Tonto away. I never figured out why a creature so small would attack people, even little people, when they were out there giving him food. I suppose we gave him the wrong name. After all, we were the good guys and he was the outlaw, that is if you don't consider taking their eggs as stealing.

Grandma had no trouble selling or trading extra eggs to folks up and down the county road. Most ranchers didn't want to mess with chickens. They aren't the smartest animals and they are extremely defenseless when it comes to predators. For many stalkers, "chicken" was their favorite meal.

Howdy is a great companion, but our constant shadow is Betty. Betty has slowed down a bit since her belly is full of puppies. She's a working red heeler who Gramps says is on maternity leave for a while. A rancher up in Wyoming left his blue heeler here for a week to become the daddy of these pups. The deal was that the rancher, a Mr. Olson, would have the pick of the litter.

Heelers are great dogs. They're as smart as you'd want a dog to be. Cattle ranchers depend on them to move and control their cattle. One good dog can take the place of several men on horseback. Gramps figured he'd have no problem selling the pups to ranchers in Colorado, Wyoming or Montana.

Grandma says Betty is bagging up and will become a mom soon. The time it takes a dog to have pups, or the gestation period, is about nine weeks. And she's right on schedule. Betty seemed anxious all afternoon. She finally settled down for the night and we were all shuffled off to bed. Her whelping room was ready. We added some flour sacks to her bed in a dark corner of the mudroom right off the kitchen. She seemed pleased with the arrangement. It sure beat her boxed-in bed on the side porch.

Secretly, Caleb and I decided we'd take turns sneaking down during the night to check on Betty's progress. I took the first shift right after I could hear Gramps snoring to high heaven. I figured there was no way Grandma could hear me tiptoe down the hall over all his ruckus. There are times she joins in, making a snoring duet of amplified proportions. That's when it's time to get up and shut our bedroom door. But tonight only Gramps' rhythmical baritone, then deep bass snoring, competed with the chirping of the crickets outside the windows. I hung down over the top bunk and, whispering, told Caleb I'd head down to Betty and be back in an hour.

The moon was even cooperating. There was no need to flick on any lights as I followed the hallway to the staircase. Slowly I descended the wooden steps. Once on the lower floor I moved more freely to the mudroom.

Betty was in her bed. I knelt down and gently pet between her eyes and under her chin. "You'll be okay, girl. Caleb and I will be coming down all night. We'll help you if you need it. We've never delivered pups before, but we've seen a lot of calves and a few colts born. Gramps says you're sure to have at least eight pups. We figure you'll be so busy pushin' all those babies out that you won't be able to keep up with the cleanin' of them. That's where we come in. We got ourselves a whole bucket of rags. Together with warm water, we'll clean them right up so you can just concentrate on gettin' them all out."

Betty had never been a mom before and she looked a bit nervous. After telling her our plans she seemed to relax a bit. She laid her head in my lap and let out a big sigh. "I'll stay with you for about an hour. Then I'll get Caleb to come down so I can catch a little shut-eye. We won't be much good if we're too sleepy to help. Caleb will wake me when his time is up. We'll make sure someone is with you all night. I'll keep my eye on the kitchen clock. Don't you worry none. If it looks like we can't handle it and you need more help, we'll fetch Gramps and Grandma."

It seemed the hour would never end. Caleb met me on the stairs wondering if I fell asleep with Betty. I told him she's awake and is starting to make little moaning sounds. "Don't forget to keep checkin' the time. You need to get me up around two o'clock."

I knew Caleb would keep his eyes on his watch, all right. He had been learning how to tell time all summer. For his birthday Grandma and Gramps gave him a stainless steel pocket watch they had bought at the hardware store. It hooks to his belt loop with a chain. That's all he needed. He felt it was his duty to pester every living creature on this ranch with minute-by-minute time updates. Even Tonto was told what time it was one morning as Caleb hung out the bedroom window yelling, "It's only 5:05 and there's folks up here tryin' to sleep. So you hush and go on back to your perch."

I climbed up the end of the bunk and crawled under the covers. I swear I just closed my eyes when Caleb, standing on his mattress, poked his head up by my pillow and shook my arm. "It's your turn," he said. "Betty won't sleep and she seems mighty miserable. Her belly is hard as a rock. I'm all tuckered out. You can keep watch until three o'clock."

As I started down the stairs I noticed Grandma had joined in on the snoring chorus. No need to worry about moving around the squeaky floorboards or skipping the noisy stairs.

Betty was a lot worse off than I thought. She was moaning something terrible and didn't pay any attention to me. I began talking to her, but she wouldn't even look my way. Then I noticed her bedding was all wet. I've seen enough birthing to know a water sac, holding a baby, had broken. I could tell her contractions were strong when her lower belly became hard as a rock under my caressing hand. Seeing how tense she was, I knew she was working real hard to push her babies out. I ran to the kitchen and grabbed some matches and the kerosene lamp we used when the electricity went out. "That electric light bulb on the ceiling would be too bright for you, girl. But I'm goin' to need more light to see by."

Caleb must have heard me running about because he was down on his knees next to me before I could blink twice, and just in time too. Puppy number one was squirming and doing its best to learn how to breathe air. Betty began licking her newborn, quickly cleaning it of the clear coating that had protected it in her womb. She began chewing on the umbilical cord. That was my cue to sterilize the scissors from Grandma's first aid kit and cut the remaining cords for her. I knew it was best to cut them a couple of inches from the pups' bellies and tie tight strings around them.

No sooner had the first one been cleaned, another pup appeared. Caleb helped by keeping the newly arrived pups away from Betty's jerking back legs. We both realized at the same time that the pups were white with little black markings. That seemed a bit strange since neither Betty nor the dad dog were white.

"This is so much better than Christmas," Caleb said.

"I'll say! We don't know how many of these little presents we'll be gettin' and each one is different," I whispered.

All was going well without any help from us until pup number six came out still. Another followed immediately. Betty gave her attention to the seventh pup after sniffing number six. Caleb and I looked at each other in shock. "I'm gettin' Al!" Caleb insisted with a panicked voice.

I picked up number six. His little body was no bigger than my cupped hand. I used a clean rag out of the bucket to wipe the wet mucus away from its head. As I rubbed him, warm tears began falling on my hands and rolling off onto the pup's limp body. "Come on boy, breathe!" I felt a faint pulse in the attached umbilical cord.

Suddenly, two large hands covered mine as the soft voice of Ol' Al said, "Let me have the little feller, Ez". Carefully, he took the lifeless pup from my trembling hands and did something I'd never seen before. Ever so gently, he turned the pup on its back and, with his thumb and pointer finger, he separated the pup's tiny lips. He opened the little mouth and breathed short, quick breaths into number six. For the longest seconds of our lives Caleb and I knelt there, wide eyed and mouths gaping, as Al blew life into the pup. Caleb was sobbing and saying, "Please God."

The feet, that looked way too big for the pup's body, began twitching. Al stopped, smiled over at us, and said, "Well boys, looks as though this little feller likes it here." Number six made small whimpering noises as he took his first gasps of air.

As it turned out, Ol' Al was on his way up the back steps when Caleb ran into him. Caleb was so emotional he just grabbed Al's callused hand and hurried him through the back door. A minute longer and number six would need to be buried and my life would have taken a different turn.

Luckily, Al never could sleep straight through a night. He noticed the lamp on in the mudroom and figured Betty was having her pups. What he didn't figure on was finding Caleb and me alone with her.

Betty ended up with nine pups. After four intense hours she was plum tuckered out. But Caleb, Al and I were wide awake and laughing at all the fannies lined up along Betty's belly for breakfast. It wasn't long before we heard Gramps and Grandma running down the stairs to check out what the commotion was all about.

"Well I'll be. Betty sure had a heap of babies tucked away all this time," Gramps chuckled.

Grandma smiled as she knelt beside us. She gently stroked Betty's muzzle while saying in her soft voice, "You did a fine job, girl. Just sleep awhile. Your babies don't need you awake in order to eat."

"Talk about eating, Grandma, I'm half starved," said Caleb.

"Well, you best clean up and take those soiled jammies off. I could sure use some help fixing breakfast," yawned Grandma.

"You bet, Grandma. It's now, hmmm, 5:22," said Caleb, glancing down at his watch.

"You best clean up too, Ezra," Gramps mumbled as he rubbed his hand around the top of my head. "You boys, Al included, have a hearty breakfast comin' your way. I just happen to know that Grandma has dough ready to make cinnamon rolls this mornin'. Throw those on top of all the other vittles and there will be three napping bodies on the porch before Caleb can say, 'It's seven o'clock'."

CHAPTER 3

Wedge

CALEB AND I WERE ABOUT to bust a gut when I put pup number six on the pillow between Luke and Eva. His muffled, squeaky noises were enough to open their eyes and push smiles beneath their dimpled cheeks. They both sat up oohing and awing. Eva picked the pup up and cradled him in her arms. They both began rubbing his little tummy and fingering his oversized paws.

"Betty had her baby," giggled Luke.

"She had her baby and eight more," I responded.

"Oh my goodness!" Eva exclaimed. "That means we can each have one and Gramps can give one to Mr. Olson. Is that all of them?"

"Nope, that leaves three more. I suppose Gramps and Grandma won't want one cuz they got Betty. But Al and Ben might take a couple," I answered.

"I heard Gramps tell Al he wants to sell all of 'em," Caleb chimed in as he leaned over and kissed the pup on the head.

"No, no they mine!" cried Luke.

"Don't get all worked up, Luke. These pups aren't goin' nowhere for six weeks or so," I assured him. "Now you guys gotta get up and hustle down to breakfast. Grandma made cinnamon rolls with a mess of sticky goo and nuts on top."

Eva's big round eyes got even bigger as she jumped to her feet and sprang off the bed. We could hear her yell all the way down the hall and stairs saying, "I'm comin' Grandma, I'm comin'!"

Caleb carefully picked up the little whelp and held number six close to his chest, protecting him with both hands. Luke realized the pup's eyes still didn't open and he asked with concern, "What's wrong with his eyes? Can't he see?"

"No, he can't see yet. All the pups have closed eyes. They'll open up a little at a time till they get used to the light," I informed him. "Al told us it'll take about a week to ten days."

"Okay, I'm a puppy too and I can't see. My eyes are closed tight. You gotta give me a piggyback ride, Ez," begged Luke.

I sat on the edge of the bed while Luke climbed onto my back. With his hands clasped around my neck and his knees locked into my elbows, we followed Caleb down to the kitchen.

"I'm a puppy, Grandma. See my eyes can't open yet 'cuz the light will hurt'em," whined Luke.

"Well, I guess you don't want any of this food. Pups only want milk. Ez, just put that big pup down over there on the floor and I'll give him a bowl of warm milk," teased Grandma.

"No, no! It's just me, Grandma. Look, it's Luke. I was just pretendin'," hollered Luke.

"Oh, thank goodness. I was afraid poor Betty would get stuck with another pup, and a mighty big one at that," laughed Grandma.

Pup number six went back to nursing while we all wasted no time cleaning our plates. The cinnamon rolls never even had a chance to cool down. Ben came in after milking good ol' Bossy and we all sat around the long farmhouse table talking about how the night of birthing went. Al said Caleb and I were just what Betty needed. But we all knew pup number six would not be out in the mudroom, nuzzling his way into the chow line, if Al hadn't blown life into his little body.

Al was what Gramps called "a modest man". He rode broncs up in Cheyenne and down in Denver during his early cowboy days. He was one of the best. Ranchers from all around these parts hired him to break their wild horses. I remember Ma telling me how Al had been broken more than a few times himself. She said bones are bound to stop mending properly after a while. Ol' Al's body grew old fast. He walked with a gimpy leg for as long as Ma knew him. But it never stopped him from hard work, and he never complains about the pain that forever burdens him.

Al had been married once, for a short time. He never made mention of it to any of us kids. He seemed happy enough living his days out here on the big ranch. He'd comment every so often about how life here with Gramps and Grandma was about as good as it'd ever get for him. "What with Grandma's cookin', havin' a warm bunk, and livin' here tucked in the bosom of the Rockies, a man don't need to go anywhere else."

Caleb and I felt pretty important after helping Betty deliver her pups. Our egos were filling us up when Gramps said, "I best be gettin' down to the feed store and pick up two more cowboy hats, seein' how your heads are expandin' at such a quick pace." Everyone laughed.

Breakfast dishes were taken to the counter, and we all headed in the direction our chores took us. No one was exempt from work. Eva and Luke scrambled upstairs to change clothes and make their bed together. They helped Grandma by drying dishes and hanging up wet laundry on the lowered clothes line. All the big stuff Grandma hung up high. Gramps had lowered one of the lines so "the little people" could clip up the small items like: socks, hankies, undies, and our smaller clothes.

Then Eva and Luke spent the rest of the morning smiling over every sound and movement those pups made. Betty finally got up and waddled into the kitchen for some well-deserved food and water. Getting her fill, she returned to the mudroom to check out her brood. Appearing content, she walked past all of us and her sleeping pups. She used her nose to push open the screen door and headed down the back steps. A few minutes later we saw her turning herself around and around in some high grass, preparing her bed for a restful nap.

The four of us had a big job naming all those pups. They all looked similar, but to our trained eyes we could find markings that made each one a little different from the other. There were only two boys, way outnumbered by the seven girls. Mr. Olson said he wanted a boy. Number six was one of the two boys. Caleb and I took a real liking to that particular pup since we figured, with Al's help of course, we saved his life.

All the puppies were white with black markings on their lower backs. Al says they are found on all heelers. They each had other small black marks, giving them their own identity. Because Betty is a red heeler and their daddy is a blue heeler, some pups will be either blue or red or a mix of both colors. Even though they're born white with black markings, the color they'll end up being is visible at birth in the pads of their paws and on the roof of their mouths.

Now just because they are called blue heelers doesn't mean they are blue. Their coats are a mixture of white, brown and black hair, giving them a grayish blend, kind of like a roan. Al knows all about the heeler breed. He says some guy from Australia bred dingoes and collies together to make good herding dogs. They're intelligent, tough, protective, loving and hard-working dogs. Their coats have two layers, making them dense and weather resistant. That comes in real handy around these parts.

We named all the pups that first day, starting with pup number six. He had a little pie shaped black spot up on top of his shoulder blades and he was mighty pushy, wedging his way between the other pups to get his share of chow. "I think Wedge is a good name for this little guy," I suggested. Everyone agreed, and number six became "Wedge".

The next one named was a female. The little girl would hook onto Betty and fight gravity as it tried pulling her off. Whenever Betty wanted time to herself she would stretch, get up and slowly walk over her family with that one pup still hanging on. Eventually this determined little pooch would drop off, with a squeal, a few feet from the rest of the pack. We decided "Magnet" was the perfect name.

Eva played with Ma's Shirley Temple doll and insisted on calling one of the pups Shirley because she said it had the curliest hair and was the cutest one.

Caleb found another favorite. It was a girl, but he insisted on calling her Goober. None of us knew why other than he just liked the name.

Luke couldn't decide between two of the pups. He was hooked on both of them with equal affection. One was the girl runt he named Yodel, just like the sound Ol' Al makes when he sometimes gets to singing. It was the darnedest thing to hear little Yodel when she got excited. Luke also favored Yankee, the other boy dog. Gramps had told us a few stories about how families fought against each other about ninety years ago. The Yankees were fighting for the North and the Rebels were fighting for the Confederacy. We'd call him Yank for short.

If there was going to be a Yankee, then we needed a Rebel. The choice was easy. Yank was all over one of the unnamed sisters, who fought hard to keep her feeding position. Of course we named that little girl Reb.

We all sat there on our knees trying hard to come up with two more names for the remaining girls. Luckily, Al and Ben came in the back door just in time to name them Otis and Woody. For lack of better names, we agreed. Grandma said she hoped none of us, Al and Ben included, have little girls someday. They wouldn't have a chance in life if they had to live with such names. She was proud of Eva for having the good sense to call her puppy Shirley.

After the pups were all named and settled in, I asked Ben if he had heard anything about Gramps wanting to sell them. He said, "Sure, you can't keep all those dogs. This is a cattle ranch, not a kennel."

"Are we goin' to keep any of them?" I asked.

"Now don't be gettin' too attached to them pups, Ez. They'll bring good money from the cattle ranchers around these parts. Your Gramps put ads in the Denver paper as well as ones up in Wyoming and Montana. He's received some phone calls already," answered Ben. "There might be a chance of keepin' one, but the two boys will be the first to go. Mr. Olson gets first pick, you know."

That was just about the hardest news I could swallow. I turned away from Ben so he couldn't see my chin quiver as tears welled up in my eyes. I walked behind the barn and climbed on the top rail of Howdy's corral fence. He stopped eating the hay Caleb had thrown to him earlier that morning and walked over to see if I needed a ride. It's funny how animals seem to know when things aren't right. They do what they can to lift your spirits enough to get a smile from you. Howdy kept rubbing his big head against my leg. He just about knocked me right off the rail.

"Okay, okay. Stop using me as a fence post, you over-stuffed excuse for a pony." I slid off the rail onto his wide back. His legs seemed a lot shorter this summer compared to last year. "Maybe I'll be ready for a regular full-sized horse pretty soon," I told him. But right now Howdy was the perfect length for me to just lay on him, back to back, with my legs dangling under his neck while he went on eating his hay. "I could probably fall asleep right like this, with my hat shading my face," I told him.

I think I actually did doze off for a few minutes before Grandma rang the mid-day dinner bell.

Usually there's way too much time between meals for me. I can't seem to fill my stomach enough to last until the next table setting. Gramps always laughs about how much food it takes to fill my hollow leg. The full bowl of fruit on the hutch is there to help us "hold ourselves over" until dinner, but, of course, it's the cookie jar we raid first. Once the baked goods are gone, we start in on the fruit. To save us time going into the house, we often "make like rabbits" and feed on snap peas, green beans, radishes and tomatoes fresh out of the garden. But today my appetite has been tangled up. My stomach has no more room in it because of all the knots.

I rolled off Howdy and headed for the outdoor eating area we use on nice summer days for the noon meal.

Grandma wasted no time noticing how little I ate. "You feelin' okay, Ezra?"

"Yes, Mam. I'm just not real hungry is all," I said.

"Well, you better eat more for supper. I don't want to hear you rummaging around in the refrigerator in the middle of the night because your hunger button switched on," Grandma lectured.

After dinner Caleb and I started slowing way down. Grandma said our eyelids were working overtime trying to stay open. So we figured we'd join Betty out on the porch for a little nap. I stretched out on the padded bench and Caleb fit perfectly on the porch swing. He just grabbed a cushion off one of the outside rocking chairs to use as a pillow and was fast asleep before I even got settled. All I can say is being a vet sure saps the life out of a guy.

We must have been beat, because we slept right through until supper. Eva and Luke were told by Grandma to wake us up. I'm just glad Caleb had the swing. Eva and Luke thought it was great fun to toss him out of his slumber.

Supper didn't prove to be any tastier than the big mid-day dinner. I could tell Grandma was a bit concerned. When I'd look over at her she'd be watching me with that worried look in her eyes. I finally mustered up a smile and she winked at me as though she understood what I was feeling.

After patting Betty and all her babes good night, the "younger generation" headed up to the big clawfoot tub. It was a lot easier, and much faster, for the four of us to wash off the film of the day at the same time. The old water heater took too long to heat up one batch of water after another, and no one wanted a cold bath. So, as long as we all fit, we jumped in together. Grandma said it won't be long before they'll have to get a better water heater.

Once we finished our baths, Caleb and I always joined Grandma, or sometimes Gramps, on Eva and Luke's bed for a few minutes of story reading. We loved the old books that Grandma and Gramps read as children. Grandma usually read more than Gramps, but no one could compete with his dramatic touch. Grandma said he got us too riled up and made sleep harder to come by. Having less shuteye was a good trade off when it came to hearing and watching that old man exaggerate a story. He could transform a tear jerker into an outright comedy. Grandma would almost always have to come upstairs and "give him the boot" in order to calm down our belly laughs and put us back into a calm state of mind. When that happened, Gramps always put on his beaten dog look as he'd kiss each of us good night and shuffle out of the room.

Then our knees would all hit the floor for prayers. We would say one small memorized prayer and then talk to God from our hearts. Each of us, including Grandma, would contribute thoughts. That night we all thanked Him for the nine pups. I gave special thanks for letting Wedge live. Grandma tucked Eva and Luke in, turned off the lamp, and walked with Caleb and me to our room.

Now that Caleb and I had our own room, and because we were older, Grandma and Gramps would allow us to stay up a bit longer. We'd talk about that day and about what we planned to do tomorrow. On this night we got on the subject of how lucky we were to have Ol' Al and Ben around. They seemed like part of the family. We knew a little about how Al hooked up with Gramps and Grandma, but we were a bit sketchy on how Ben showed up. Grandma sat in the overstuffed chair next to the bedside table as she reflected back on just how Ben came to live here.

She told us, "Al got mighty huffy when Ben was hired on. It had been years since Al had to share a bunkhouse with your papa before he and your ma were married, and it just didn't settle right with him to give up any of his space. He said Ben was 'wet behind the ears' and just got in his way. But Gramps knew your papa was getting busier with his own spread and growing family. He couldn't keep askin' him for help on the big ranch, and Ol' Al would kill himself tryin' to keep up with all the work. So blond haired, blue eyed, seventeen year old Ben became Ol' Al's new roommate."

Grandma confided in us that Ben didn't have much of a family. "He's the nephew of one of our neighbors. He came down from Montana early one spring to help his uncle, and he never went back home. Gramps met him at one of the roundups. His flat hat was a sign to all he was cut from Montana stock. He's a natural around animals and Gramps wasted no time hiring him.

"He turned out to be an eager learner. He worked hard and was quick to fix any mistakes he made, and he didn't make excuses for why things went wrong either. You gotta love his toothy grin too. He's got the biggest smile a face can hold and a personality cheerful enough to blast Ol' Al's attitude all to pieces. When Al pulled out his harmonica one evening, Ben ran and got his fiddle from under his bunk. It surprised Al when Ben rosined up his bow and played right along with him. Al played faster. Ben sped up. Al picked up the pace. Ben stayed right with him. Finally, the squinty eyes in Al's red face met the crystal blue gaze from Ben. 'Dang you, Ben!' gasped Al. Then both men broke out laughing and slapping each other on their backs. Music in these hills went up a few notches from that night on."

Grandma yawned and slowly got up to tuck us in.

"Ben said we can't keep any of the pups," I said after a short silence.

"We have a good working dog, Ezra," Grandma responded. "Animals on a ranch have to have a purpose. We can't be having extra animals we don't need. They become pets with no real use. I know you kids would love to keep them all, but even one would be one too many. I'm afraid your grandpa has his mind set on selling all of them. We could sure use the money they'll bring, and we'll make sure they all go to good homes."

"Don't you think Betty would do better with a little help from another dog? She probably gets pretty lonely without a friend too. You know if Wedge didn't pull through like he did, we'd have one less pup. And Gramps wasn't figuring on her having that many to begin with."

"You've given this some thought, haven't you Ezra? Well, I think you're right, about everything except Betty being lonely. She has four kind and loving kids sharing their lives with her. I'd say she's pretty lucky. Keeping one puppy might not be out of the question. I'll see what I can do. But for now, you need to get some sleep and show me a hearty appetite in the morning. I kind of figured these pups had you worrisome today."

As Grandma kissed us good-night, Caleb rolled over to hide his tears. She knelt down and turned him toward her. "You know Gramps would do anything for you kids if he thought it was in your best interest. Whatever he decides, we must all stand with him. Now dry those tears and dream happy pup dreams. They're all ours for almost two months, so let's enjoy them."

I just laid there on my top bunk looking at the dark ceiling for a long time after Grandma left the room. I kept thinking about all she said and about the long night of delivering puppies. I told myself that Wedge was just another puppy. But I couldn't get past seeing him so helpless and limp when Al took him from my hands. It was as if he wanted to live. He wanted to breathe and be a part of our family. I could almost feel his warm little body wiggling under my chin again as he made his tiny grunt noises while he moved his mouth around looking for the milk sack that wasn't there.

Grandma was right. We don't need to keep any of the puppies. Betty is enough for all of us to love and she has proven to be quite capable of managing her work on the ranch. It's just that she belongs to Gramps and Grandma. Our family dog died last winter right after Christmas. Hefty was Papa's dog for sixteen years and had just died quietly in his sleep. Ma promised we could pick out another dog to replace him, but of course we didn't have a chance to do that.

Now, there's nobody who loves their grandparents as much as we love ours. But Gramps is about the most stubbornness old man I've ever run across. He never makes hasty decisions but, once he sets his mind to something, everyone knows there's no use badgering him. Grandma is the only one who can sometimes get him to take a second look at whatever he bows his neck against or digs his heels into. I just hope she can work wonders with him over keeping Wedge.

A bit of a breeze blew into our dark room. I tossed and turned until I ended up wrapping the pillow around my head and dozed off.

Wedge was a fighter from the start. He was the first to open his eyes in the morning and the last to fall asleep during nap time. He looked gawky before he was even able to move awkwardly. His ears were twice the size of any on the other pups, and his paws seemed way too big for his legs to maneuver. He loved to be loved, but he had a real independent streak. He was a solid little guy and alert to what was going on around him. I never thought I could feel this way about any animal. He seemed to sense my feelings and would nibble at my earlobes while softly sniffing in my ear. I'm sure it was his way of letting me know I was his buddy.

Betty was the perfect mom. She loved all of them unconditionally. All her babies were fat, clean and content. She spent a good part of her day feeding them while twisting and stretching her neck around to lick each one thoroughly. All nine puppies grew quickly. The only runt in the litter was Yodel. She might have been born small in stature, but her tummy kept right up with the others.

Grandma commented a few times on how she couldn't understand how one mom could care for nine babies all at the same time. Betty never seemed to complain though. The first week she left them only to eat, drink water, sneak in a short nap and take care of her "outdoor business". Then she'd be right back in the mudroom feeding nine pushing bodies trying to nuzzle their way to her teats.

By the time the pups reached two weeks old all their tummies looked as if hard boiled eggs were hidden under their stretched skin. Their eyes were all wide open as they began scooting around the mudroom showing off their distinct personalities.

We spent a good part of each day taking the pups out into the sunshine and onto the soft green grass. Betty got a bit worrisome the first couple of times we moved them outdoors. But, she didn't take long to get use to the idea of us babysitting while she had some quiet time to herself.

Ben went to work putting together a make-shift pen under the large blue spruce. The fence was low enough for Betty to leap over but too high for the pups to climb. It gave the noisy nine fresh air and space to exercise a few hours a day.

CHAPTER 4

The Hideaway

EVA WAS BOUND TO BE a tomboy with all us brothers surrounding her. If she wanted to play with someone she had to play boy stuff. Sometimes she'd break away and play with imaginary girls. Once in a while Luke would pretend the part of her little sister. He'd take on the name Lucy. Eva would put her dresses on him, tie a satin ribbon in his hair, or cover his ginger locks with a bonnet. They'd carry on like that for hours in the little tree house, drinking tea from the tiny cups and teapot that were once Ma's. Grandma would make them downsized sandwiches and miniature cookies served on the little coffee saucers. Luke went along with just about anything so long as he got fed.

That's when Caleb and I came into the picture. We'd sneak up wearing our cowboy hats and hiding all but our eyes under kerchiefs, making us pert near unidentifiable. With our bandit attire in order, we would burst into the treehouse. The only line we ever used was, "This is a hold up. Give us all your food and nobody gets hurt."

One time they wouldn't hand over the goods, so we tied them up and ate all their food in front of them. This was no easy feat, since we had to keep the kerchiefs hanging over our noses and mouths as we scarfed down the food. Well, that set them to crying and it set Grandma to whoppin' us with her fly swatter. We ended up in the kitchen making them a whole new round of those puny sandwiches and sitting at the supper table that night watching everyone but us eat strawberry shortcake. Grandma didn't put up with our shenanigans. She was a firm believer in making the playing field even, especially when it came to Caleb and me harassing Eva and Luke.

Caleb and I didn't always pair up together. It's a good thing there were four of us. No one was ever odd man out. Eva and I loved hiking the mountains surrounding the ranch. As long as we were within calling distance, Gramps and Grandma were comfortable with our exploring. Luke and Caleb were content to stay put and play cowboys and Indians or cowboys and bad guys around the barn and sheds.

One day, while tromping around, Eva and I came across a small cave hidden behind some thick brush. We were sitting on some large rocks to catch our breath when Eva noticed some cool air creeping up her back. We spread the branches of the dense fir tree behind her just enough to spot a dark hole hidden amongst the boulders. We looked at each other with wild anticipation in our eyes.

"Do you think it goes in very far?" she questioned.

"My guess is it's an old mine shaft given up on. I'd love to check it out, but we're gonna need some kind of axe to clear the brush and some light once we get inside. It's sure in a steep spot, and we'd be seen pretty easy if someone came out behind the barn and looked up this way."

"Do you think Gramps knows about this?"

"Probably. He knows these mountains like we know each of Betty's pups. His whole life has been spent walkin' and ridin' this ranch and up into the national forest bordering it. Nothin' gets past his hawk-eye gaze."

"I suppose we should tell him we found it," said Eva.

"Not just yet. I think we can clear the back side of the bush so we can walk into the opening and still have the cave hidden with the brush up front. I'd like to explore it a bit before lettin' Gramps in on our find. Knowing both Gramps and Grandma, they'd put Al to dynamiting it closed if they knew we'd go inside."

"Are we goin' to tell Caleb and Luke?"

"I'm all for tellin' Caleb, but I think Luke might spill the beans if he knew."

"Luke will be goin' in for his nap pretty soon. We can go down and tell Caleb and grab the hatchet from the kindling box to cut away the back branches," Eva suggested.

"Yep. That'll give us about an hour before we'll be needed to do our afternoon chores. Let's go."

Eva and I slid and stumbled down the steep embankment hurrying our way to the barn. We found Caleb standing over a dead outlaw sprawled out on his back, loose hay serving as his deathbed. It was always funny how Caleb would deepen his voice and talk like a tough guy while Luke laid motionless, paying for his crime. Luke's closed eyes and still body never stayed lifeless long. His nose crinkled up as his mouth broke character, laughing. The shoot'em up scene was over just as Grandma called Luke in for his nap.

"Dang it! Eva don't have to have a nap anymore. How come I gotta go in? I'm no baby. Why, I just robbed a bank," whined Luke.

"Naps are good for you," I insisted. "All of us had to have them. That's why we are so big and strong."

"Yeah, and if you take a nap I'll let you be the good guy and I'll be the bad guy when you wake up," promised Caleb.

"Okay, but you gotta do it today. And you gotta slow down so I can catch you and haul you to jail."

"We gotta a deal, partner," Caleb agreed. "Now mount up and get goin'."

Luke jumped onto his stick horse and galloped to the back porch where he hooked the reins onto the end of the hitching post. There his wooden and fabric steed would wait for him until his nap ended. With his cowboy hat hung over his back by its stampede strap, his little boots stomped up the back steps, where he soon disappeared behind the screen door.

"We found a cave or maybe an old mine shaft," I blurted out.

"What!" exclaimed Caleb, as his round hazel eyes popped out from under his dark eyebrows. "Where is it? Can we go there now?"

"You wouldn't believe how close it is. We walked past it a bunch of times and never noticed it," I said. "We can even see it from the back corral fence. So we'll have to make sure nobody's out there when we crawl behind the brush. They might spot us and that'd be the end of our hiding place."

"Come on. Let's show Caleb where it is," insisted Eva.

After grabbing the axe and wrapping a gunny sack around it, we headed out to the back corral. We ran through the aspen grove that grew along the north fork of the Poudre River.

Years ago Gramps and Ol' Al cleared a wide trail through the trees and built a bridge big enough for the farm truck to cross over the narrow river. The plan was to rough in a road to the open meadow beyond the mountain. That spot became Ma and Papa's when they married. It's where our folks often rode horseback and where Papa asked Ma to marry him. That probably explains why it's the place where our cabin stands now.

Well, the road never got finished. Gramps said it got too rough to even rough in. The tree stumps were too massive and the boulders unyielding. They got as far as the pines and let it fade back into the original trail. We still use that old weedy path when riding horseback to our cabin. Of course, we aren't allowed to ride that far from the main ranch without having Gramps, Al or Ben along.

Caleb, Eva and I took this cattle trail around the base of the mountain and stayed on it as it wound its way up the slope. It was a longer route, but it wasn't as steep as a direct shot. We also didn't want to mark our destination with three sets of tracks heading straight to our secret hideaway.

Bristly crocus grew all along the mountainside. Spring blooms late, but it seems to last all summer long here. Thunderstorms have a way of keeping everything alive and blooming until the frigid fall nights arrive, killing the floral and green carpet that spreads over the mountains.

We knew we'd have to hurry if we were to get back for chores and supper. Halfway up we all stopped to catch our breath and looked back over the aspens to the barnyard and house. We could see Al and Ben with their rumps sticking out on either side of the tractor. The engine flaps were up, covering their heads and shoulders. Gramps was high on the seat trying to turn the engine over while Al and Ben worked to give it life. Grandma pushed the back screen door open with her full laundry basket heading for the clothesline.

"They're all busy. Let's hustle," I insisted.

We got our second wind and made it directly across from the cave. I told Caleb and Eva to split up. We would all work our way over using different routes. "There's no need to beat down a path so as to mark where our cave is. Stay on the rocks as much as you can."

There was plenty of brush to hide all of us while I hacked away at the backside. Soon I had a nice tunnel cleared to the cave's entrance. The boulders were far enough apart for all of us to stand and walk in side by side.

"Holy cow! This is neat," Caleb's voice echoed off the smooth walls.

"Look. Those are crossbeams. This looks like a cave that was turned into a mine shaft. I bet it's been here a long time," I said.

"Do you suppose snakes live in here?" came Eva's frightened voice.

"I would if I were a snake," Caleb piped up.

"Let's not go in anymore," Eva whispered as she pulled the back of my shirt toward her.

"You're right, Eva. We'll need some kind of light to go in any further, and it's gettin' late. We'll head back and come up again tomorrow when Luke is nappin'. You and Caleb wait in the tunnel I just cleared out until you see that I'm back on the trail. Eva, you go next. Look down to see that nobody's watchin' and make a run for it. Caleb, you'll go when Eva is on the trail with me."

The thickness of the brush was perfect to camouflage us as we peered down onto the ranch. I saw my chance and bounded off. Eva and Caleb were soon with me heading down the trail. As we reached the bridge we heard Grandma yell for us, a common practice to locate where we're playing. We answered her immediately and ran into the yard in time for the afternoon chores.

Caleb and I agreed to help each other so we could talk and plan what we'd do to our fort. We decided it would need a table and chairs for starters. We could build some kind of door to keep the larger critters out. Now that a passage was cleared in the back of the brush, bear and mountain lions might consider it an open invitation to a pre-made den.

"Yep, this is goin' to be a lot of fun. Ben would help us with some of the sawin' if we asked him," said Caleb.

"Naw, we can't take a chance he'd keep quiet. Besides, he's kept too busy workin' around here," I put in.

"When do you suppose Luke can know about it?"

"Let's get it all done first and then see if we think he can keep a tight lip."

"Don't you think Gramps would fly off the handle if he knew we were doin' this behind his back?" Caleb asked as he pitched hay into the manger.

"Maybe if we get it all nice lookin' he would be okay with it. There's no way he'd let us play in that mine shaft the way it is now. In the meantime, I don't want you lookin' directly into Gramps' and Grandma's eyes. Ma always said she could tell you were up to somethin' by the way you looked at her. Remember she use to say, 'Those eyes are dancing to a mischievous tune'."

"I can't help the way my eyes let out secrets. If they were smaller I could get away with a lot more."

"There's the chow bell. We best finish up and get down to the house. I'm plenty hungry. What do you bet Gramps, Grandma, Ben and Al play cards tonight? If they do, we can go up to our room and start plannin' on what we need to make for the fort."

"Sure. There's so much stuff layin' around behind the tractor shed we can use. Gramps won't even miss them," chuckled Caleb.

Supper was always eaten in the big kitchen. The late afternoons tend to bring out the mosquitoes. If a person wasn't swatting them away, they were competing with them for their meal.

Grandma insisted years ago for Gramps to take out the wall separating the kitchen from the dining room. She said she liked visiting with everyone while she cooked. The wall kept her penned up and alone with her pots and pans. Now the kitchen houses the long plank table Al built, long enough to seat a dozen full-sized eaters propped up along the benches on either side with wooden high-back chairs at each end.

Luke had used the old wooden highchair that Gramps, Ma and all of us sat in as babies. But he refused to sit in it when he heard it referred to as a baby chair. After several minutes of hearing Luke's stubborn refusal, Ben agreed he was a big boy and deserved a big seat. He left the kitchen and returned carrying a narrow wooden milk crate along with two large clamps. He proceeded to flip the crate over on the end of one of the benches. He used the cut out handle holes to accept the clamps that held the crate to the bench. Now Luke sits proudly on his booster seat eating side by side with all the other "big boys and girls".

Eva still sits on her knees. Ben offered to make her a raised seat, but she would rather use her own legs to boost herself up.

Supper takes care of all the leftovers from our noontime dinner. Grandma says it's better to end the day with a lighter meal. We eat the big meal early on to give us the energy we need to work hard all day. She sliced up the roast and put out all the fixings needed for some mighty big sandwiches. Nothing could beat sandwiches made in the small, loaf shaped rolls Grandma baked several times a week. Just smelling the yeast heating up in the oven sent everyone's mouths to watering. I swear those bread vapors push their way clear out of the house and as far away as the barn.

It was Eva and Luke's turn to help Grandma clean up after supper. Everyone was responsible to set off their own dishes and eating utensils, placing them on the countertop. After doing our part, Caleb and I wasted no time running to the mudroom. We both laid on the floor next to all the little, wiggly, warm bodies. As soon as the pups realized we were there, an eruption of noise filled the room. Grandma walked over to the doorway and told us to keep those little dog tongues off our faces. "I'm about ready to get those pups a salt block. You kids seem to get a real kick out of them licking you to death," she scolded.

As soon as she went back to cleaning the kitchen Caleb and I gave those pups free rein. Half the fun is feeling their tongues on our necks, ears, and yes, our mouths. Grandma probably never let a pup kiss her before. Otherwise she'd be down on the floor with us, letting them swarm all over her.

Each time we played with Betty's brood I would watch Wedge's actions. No matter who was in the room he would always gravitate to me. It made me wonder if he had a keen sense of smell and remembers me from the night I held his limp body in my hands. Or does he just know how much I love him. I've heard tell that animals can sense a kindred spirit. Dogs are especially smart, and blue heelers top the smart chart according to Al. Whatever the reason, Wedge always ends up on me. Sometimes he even rolls up into a ball and falls asleep on my lap.

Eva and Luke joined us after finishing their kitchen duties. It wasn't long until Betty came in, circled around on her bed, and settled down for the night. Well, there's no replacing a good mom. All the pups began their journey back to the protective and loving body that nourished them. Even Wedge never looked back when he left me for Betty's soft, warm belly.

"I guess it's time to let them be," Grandma said while leaning against the doorjamb. "You kids have time to play a bit before taking a bath and hitting the sack. Looks like Ben and us old timers are about to put together a card game."

Caleb and I shot each other a glance. We cheerfully got up and said we'd play in our room. As usual, Eva and Luke said they wanted to play with us. I quickly touched Eva's shoulder and told her Caleb and I were going to be drawing sketches. She caught on to my wink and, looking at Luke, said they would rather play school in their room.

Once in our room, Caleb and I began writing a list of things we could make. Luckily, Gramps didn't throw much away. There were piles of old lumber, wooden barrels, metal wheels and rotten tools heaped up behind the tack room and tractor shed. It was a carpenter's paradise. We figured we were just about as skilled, and certainly more creative, than most builders. It wasn't long before we had ourselves a plan of all the furnishings needed to make our fort mighty comfortable. The small wooden nail kegs would make perfect seats when turned upside down. We'd need four of them so Luke could join us when the time comes that we think he's up to being sworn to secrecy. The big wooden water barrel will make a sturdy table. We decided we could always put boards across it to make the top bigger.

Caleb insisted on building a gun rack to hold our wooden play pistols and rifles Ben had made each of us last Christmas. "Anyone who's anyone knows you can't live out here without some kind of protection," Ben had said when we tore off the newspaper wrappings he had bundled them in. Ma was a bit concerned about us having such an arsenal. But she had to admit they would bring us hours of enjoyment. It was obvious to everyone that Ben put in a heap of time making the rifles, complete with small pipe scopes. Ol' Al was the one who made us leather holsters that held the pistols Ben had cut and sanded out of old fence boards.

By the time Grandma yelled up for us to run our bath water we had a long detailed list of items we'd need to furnish our mine shaft. Our floor plan was drawn up. Our vision was put into motion.

We got a real surprise when Ben showed up after our bath to tuck us all in for the night. He said he was all washed up with playin' cards. He couldn't win a hand to save his life. "Those geezers cleaned out all the coins in my pockets." So he figured he'd head upstairs and tell us a few bedtime stories instead. Grandma made him promise not to tell us anything that would spook our dreams. He kept his promise when putting Luke and Eva to bed, but Caleb and I convinced him that we were made of stronger stuff.

Ben got a little wilder with our bedtime story. He told us about Montana's back country and the wolves that did their hunting in packs. He put Caleb and me in the story, making us the prey. It sprang to life in our heads. We could visualize the wolves pursuing after us with the full moon spotlighting their bodies. They moved quickly. We could see them slink behind trees and boulders, their bodies in contrast to the illuminated granite. To make us even more edgy, Ben began to howl softly.

Caleb's eyes were about to pop out of their sockets, and my smile was slowly turning into a fearful grin when Ben decided we were probably scared enough. He ended the story with us stumbling across Howdy grazing in a meadow. We jumped on his back and galloped away to safety.

Grandma came in right when Ben was messing up our hair with his rough hands and saying good night. We got the scary story we wanted and Grandma was no more the wiser.

CHAPTER 5

The Deal

EARLY THE NEXT MORNING CALEB and I were first to hug Grandma in the kitchen and offer our services so as to hurry breakfast along. Eva agreed to play with Luke after the morning chores, giving Caleb and me a chance to rummage through the storage area in the back of the hay loft. I found a small stool and threw it down onto a pile of hay below. We tied a rope around an empty, wooden nail keg and lowered it down the loft's ladder to the center of the barn. Our new treasures were hidden in an empty stall before we headed out back to check on some potential furniture pieces in Gramps' junk pile. I came up with an old five gallon milk can with its lid tightly rusted on. Caleb confiscated a metal wheelbarrow wheel and found a few nice pieces of wood in the scrap heap. He suggested we use the rusted spokes on the wheel to hang pots like the one Grandma has in her kitchen. I told him we'd never be able to cook in our fort since the smoke would be a dead giveaway. We agreed to take it just because it was neat. If nothing else, it could lean against a wall for a rustic touch.

It wasn't long before several items were pushed into the corner of the stall and covered with empty burlap feed sacks. We figured once we hauled everything to the fort we could hammer and saw without fear of being heard. We knew moving everything up the mountain, one piece at a time, would be a challenge. Not getting caught would be a miracle.

Gramps and Al headed to town after breakfast the following day. Ben was busy re-roofing the chicken coop. The time was perfect for Caleb and me to start hauling our hidden stash. Lucky for us, Eva was giving Luke art lessons. She set up her small easel on the porch and had Luke using her water paints. Grandma was wise enough to spread an old sheet under his work area to minimize the damage to the wooden planks.

Caleb and I wasted no time exiting the back of the barn with whatever our arms could carry. We saved the last trip up the hill for the water barrel, since it took both of us to haul it. After four grueling trips our booty was relocated and the horse stall returned to its empty past.

We were exhausted. Our limp bodies were eventually roused from the porch swing when Gramps and Al drove into the yard. Grandma came out to gather the mail they brought from our box a half mile away on the main county road. She told Gramps that Caleb and I needed more work to keep us busy, claiming that most of the food we'd consumed was used to energize our hiking habit.

Gramps just smiled and said, "The way I see it they do plenty to help out. If there's enough energy left after all they do, then more power to them. They'll be hard at work most of their lives. The free time together now will make for happy memories later."

Our secret project was off to a great start. From now on Eva could join us during Luke's nap time. She would be an ideal spotter, watching for anyone looking or coming up the mountain while Caleb and I sawed and hammered away inside the fort. It was our perfect set-up for several days.

We always knew when Sunday came 'round. Grandma brought out the butch wax and would line all three of us boys up along the bench at the kitchen table. She'd comb in a part on the top right side of each of our heads, dip her fingers into the thick goo and then slick our hair down. I have to admit, we did look mighty fine. An inspection would follow, moving our ears around in case there were any "dirt patches hidden out back".

Eva was spared the wax. Her torture took the form of a hairbrush as it worked its way through the knots that accumulated in her auburn hair. Grandma took special pride in braiding, pony-tailing, barretteing, ribboning and just all around decorating Eva's long locks. It seemed Eva's dimples were a heap more noticeable with her hair all done up. We'd all pass around the hand mirror to check out Grandma's handy work. Heaven help any of us if we messed up our hair or dirtied our clothes before taking our seats in church.

Timing was everything. Gramps would back the station wagon, Ma and Papa had bought, out of the car shed and park it alongside the hitchin' post. We'd all clamber down the steps and pile into the car. Ben usually went with us, but Al would have none of the church-going business. He said he did his prayin' best right where he was. Besides, he did all our outdoor chores while we were gone. Now, it takes a real saint to do that as far as I'm concerned.

Luke used to sit on Ma's lap up front. Now that so many people go in the car, he gets in the back seat with the rest of us kids. Gramps drives with Grandma next to him on the bench seat and Ben rides shotgun next to the front passenger door. Caleb and I have to sit by the two back doors with Eva and Luke between us. Grandma is still afraid they might accidentally open a door and tumble out when going around a curve. Luke ends up standing on the seat with his arm around either Caleb's or my neck so he can see the road better.

I can't ever remember taking the car for any other reason than our Sunday trips to church and then to the grocery store. Usually, when we all traveled together and were not dressed in our Sunday best, we'd just pile into the back of the truck with strict orders to stay put.

Grandma always had a piece of paper tacked on the inside of the pantry door. Throughout the week, she'd jot down items used up or getting low. That list was the last thing she'd stuff into her purse as we headed out the door each Sunday morning. Grandma often said we were real lucky because most stores were closed on the Sabbath. But a couple would stay open a few hours for folks like us who usually go to town once a week for church services and supplies.

I swear church seemed to take up half our day. Gramps insisted it never lasted more than an hour. Caleb and I thought he was off his rocker, but Caleb's new watch confirmed Gramps was right as usual.

Grandma usually separated Caleb and me during the services. We weren't real good about sitting still and listening. Eva was a lot better at that. I suppose girls have more patience or they want to be recognized as angels earlier on.

Ben and Gramps took turns holding Luke up. It was worth carrying his weight so he'd be quiet and could see the front of the church. His little fingers were always twisting and moving about on the head of whoever held him. Gramps and Ben would have to smooth down their tangled hair, using their own fingers as combs once they handed Luke off. Gramps often said the only day of the week he wished he was bald was on Sundays.

When Ma and Papa were alive we always sat in the last pew on the left side of the church. That way Papa could get up and pace the back of the room with whatever baby he was trying to keep quiet. Gramps and Grandma would be there with us to help when needed. Grandma refuses to sit anywhere else now. Other folks must have sensed how she felt because, even if we're running a little late, the back pew is always vacant when we shuffle through the door. Grandma said she felt Ma and Papa's presence in that back row.

The store was the treat of the day. If we were well behaved in church we each got a penny to buy a gum ball or a piece of candy. Once I saved my pennies for five weeks so I could buy a big candy bar. It was sure good, but it wasn't worth the three sets of envious eyes staring at me while I ate it. After that I went right back to buying one piece and eating it without the guilty feeling that came with a candy bar.

Car radios were extra when Ma and Papa bought our station wagon. Since having a radio wasn't an option anyway for those of us who lived beyond the air waves, we didn't have one. We pretty much had to entertain each other. Ma used to sing to us, but now with Gramps driving we listen to stories of his childhood with some mighty tall tales thrown in. We knew Gramps' creative juices flowed too thick when Grandma and Ben would look at each other smiling. Then there were times when they'd just plain bust a gut laughing at the old man's stories. But on this Sunday Gramps got our attention real quick-like. He talked about finding an old mine shaft when he was a kid and fixing it up. It became his hideaway.

Well, you can guess how fast Eva, Caleb and I perked right up, straining our ears from the back seat so as not to miss a word.

"Yep, I had me a fine place to go, rain or shine. No one knew about it for almost a year until my ma followed me one day. It scared her half to death when she saw how old those timbers were that held up the earth over my head. I got me a good scoldin' and it wasn't long before my pa was up there blocking the entrance. To pacify me Pa built a treehouse, the same one you kids play in. But it just wasn't the same."

I happened to look up and caught Gramps looking in the rearview mirror. Those blue smiling eyes were looking right at me. Then I'd be darned if he didn't wink. He went on looking down the road and never looked back in the mirror again.

Dang it anyway! How does he do it? He never seems to be lookin', but he sees everything. He never seems to be payin' any attention, but he knows everything we think and do.

I looked over at Caleb and whispered, "He knows".

"No way. How can he? What do we do now?"

With both palms up and a shrug of my shoulders, Caleb knew I had no clue.

Gramps continued rambling on about the "to do" list on the ranch. Ben would nod in agreement and offered suggestions while Grandma inserted a few of her own.

Luke weighed heavy on me. I realized he had fallen asleep as soon as his head had dropped onto my shoulder. I carefully scooted him down, laying his head on my lap and stretching his little body across Eva's legs. We had all become accustomed to the jolting motion brought on by the rough county road. Our bodies bounced and swayed in unison. I kept going over in my mind our secret plans and the way we covered up our tracks. I'll be darned if I knew how Gramps found out about our discovery.

Once home, Gramps carried Luke up to his bed while the rest of us unloaded the groceries from the back of the car. Al greeted us with his half grin and opened the gate that held back our nine anxious puppies. They all ran to the car yipping their pleasure at our return. They followed us back and forth from the steps to the car until the back was emptied of its cargo.

While carrying the grocery bags to the kitchen table, we all heard a loud squeal. Caleb stepped on a pup's front paw under the bench. There was only one fellow on which that oversized paw could be attached. Wedge's unexpected pain caused a little accident. I was the one who volunteered to clean up the puddle he left behind. Grandma shook her head, "I can't believe Wedge climbed those back steps. We'll have to keep the screen door closed from now on. Those other pups will soon figure out how to get in the house too, and then we'll have ourselves one heck of a mess."

After helping Grandma restock the pantry, Caleb and I changed our clothes and headed straight out to the barnyard. We figured since Gramps was on to us we'd stay clear away from our fort.

Al and Ben were saddling up their horses to check fence lines beyond where the truck could navigate. We asked if we could ride along. Al was quick to include us if Gramps and Grandma gave the okay. Coming up behind us, Gramps responded, "You best ride Moses, Ez. The weight of you and Caleb together would make Howdy's trek through the mountains a bit rough. Besides, your feet are bound to hit ground goin' up even a slight embankment."

This was the first time Caleb or I rode a horse solo outside the barnyard. With our saddlebags packed with elk jerky and dried apple slices and our canteens filled with water, we fell quickly in line behind Al and Ben. I brought up the rear so Howdy wouldn't fall behind as he tried tirelessly to snip at the tall grasses along the way. Caleb looked back at me when we rode past the cut-off to our fort.

It wasn't until we were near the top that we heard coyotes yipping among some trees close to the trail we had just ridden. Al pulled up on his horse and, turning around in his saddle, looked intently on the lower path. "Well, I'll be a monkey's uncle if we're not being followed by one of those pups. Ez, you're goin' to have to head on down and pick that pup up before he decides to fall into the coyote's trap. My money's on it being Wedge. His curiosity's goin' to get the best of him some day."

Turning about face on such a narrow trail was easily handled by my seasoned horse. I gave him his head and Moses stepped cautiously down the steep, rocky slope. Sure enough, standing atop a flat boulder, Wedge was trying to decide whether to continue up after us or run over to check out all the wild barking noises. Seeing me helped him with the decision making process. In his excitement he was caught off guard and gravity pulled his roly-poly belly tumbling down the boulder onto the steep path, stopping short of my horse's front hooves. Moses stood perfectly still when I dismounted to pick up the little hitchhiker.

"You can sure be a numbskull at times. Looks like you'll be checkin' fences with us for a few hours. Hope you like jerky and water." I stuffed the fat little fur ball into my shirt. With only his head peering out between two snaps, we soon joined the others and continued to the top of the mountain.

Wedge turned out to be a good little traveler. His steep climb wore him to a frazzle and he was soon sleeping soundly. I pushed his head into my shirt to shade him from the afternoon sun. It wasn't until the second fence fixin' that I got off Moses to stretch my legs. That's when Wedge woke up and decided it was romping time again. All four of us relaxed under the shade of a tall pine while we ate and drank from our canteens. I broke some of my jerky up into small pieces so Wedge's sharp little teeth could gnaw them down. The only bowl for him to drink water from was my upturned cowboy hat. It served two purposes. The makeshift bowl also soaked the brim enough to cool down my overheated noggin.

After stopping to mend several broken or stretched out barb wire sections, we headed home. Wedge followed Moses and me for a spell, but the terrain was a bit rough for the little fellow. It wasn't long before I scooped him up again and gave him back his old spot in my shirt, where he fell right to sleep.

At the base of the mountain Ben challenged Caleb and me to a race ending at the corral. There was no way we could compete with Ben and his brute of a horse. Howdy could practically walk under Ben's Belgian. He stood seventeen hands tall, no match for Howdy's mere twelve hands. Moses was close to fifteen hands, but his portly body was enough to slow down even the longest of legs. Not only was I riding an oversized barrel, but the snoozing pooch tucked into my shirt was a handicap too.

Ben wasn't one to wait for a response. He was kicking up dust before Caleb and I put heels to our horses' ribs.

Howdy was up to the challenge. His little legs were almost mechanical the way they moved, like a locomotive at full throttle. Caleb's hat flew off within seconds, allowing his dark curly hair to spring up all around his head. The lost hat was enough of a distraction to cause Caleb to pull up on the reins and allow Moses to pass Howdy, keeping me in second place all the way to the corral gate. The jolting motion had awakened Wedge and he fought the enclosure of my shirt the entire distance of the race. Fortunately the snaps held tight.

Gramps was there to hold the gate open as we sped through. Ben had already dismounted and was leaning against the fence with reins in hand. "So, did you find another fence to fix? It sure took you long enough to get here."

"Real funny, Ben. We didn't have a chance against you and Rio."

Howdy pulled up a close third. Caleb couldn't stop laughing throughout the entire episode. You would have thought he came in first to see him in such an excited state.

Wedge's pawing, yelping and squirming just about wore my chest raw. I eagerly unsnapped the front of my shirt to release the frightened pup. Swinging my right leg over Moses' rump, I stepped down from the stirrup and set Wedge free. He ran under the fence rail as fast as his little legs could carry him to join Betty and his siblings near their pen. I'm sure he had plenty to tell them.

Al finally rode into the corral, "Now that you three worked your horses up to a lather, you can take off their saddles and spend a little time walking them. After they cool down you'll need to water, brush and grain them. One of us didn't lather up his mount. So I guess I know who will be sittin' down at the supper table before any of you hot shots."

Eva was standing on the stool Grandma kept on the porch and ringing the metal triangle. Supper was ready. We hurried the horses along. Caleb used his cool down time leading Howdy back to retrieve his hat. Each of us unsaddled, walked, watered, grained and brushed our horse. Al was really the winner. He and Gramps headed to the house long before any of us had the feed sacks hung around our horses' snouts.

Once in the mudroom, Caleb and I took turns removing each other's boots by straddling one leg at a time as the other sat pushing with their other foot against the rear of the straddler. All boots and hats never made it past the mudroom. Surface grime on our hands, arms and faces were removed there too. Grandma made it clear that she had no desire to pick up after those who could pick up after themselves. She also set a fine table and wouldn't be insulted by a dirty crew.

Grace was always said aloud on the Sabbath. The rest of the week we sat with hands clasped for a moment of silence. This way we could show our thanks in our own way without anyone but God hearing. Ma and Papa started this tradition. Gramps and Grandma thought it was worth continuing.

All the stops were pulled out for our Sunday meal. After a big breakfast we'd have a snack when we got back from church, and then a large supper would end the day. It was the only time, other than birthdays, holidays and occasional cookie baking, that Grandma served dessert. Sometimes she would make the special treats on Saturdays and leave them in the pie safe for all to see and drool over until the next day's meal.

On this particular Sunday Gramps wanted Caleb and me to tell him all about riding our own mounts. Al praised how well we handled our horses and Ben suggested we take over fixing all the fences from now on. I just about choked on my piece of steak, but Caleb was all for the idea of riding out on our own. We realized it was meant as a joke when Ben's wide smile broke into an uncontrollable laugh.

It wasn't long before the topic got onto Wedge. Gramps saw his round rump high-tailing it up the ravine, hot on our trail. He tried calling the little runaway back, but Wedge seemed focused only on letting the dirt fly under his mighty paws. "I figured he had a fifty-fifty chance of catchin' up with you. If he didn't, those coyotes were bent on havin' him join them for dinner. By the time I got Gus saddled and across the bridge I saw Ezra pickin' Wedge up and headin' back to the rim. So, how did the little cuss do taggin' along?"

"He slept in my shirt half the time. The climb plum tuckered him out. He really had no complaints and was no trouble."

"I'd say he has takin' quite a shine to Ez," Al commented. "He didn't leave Ezra's sight and pretty much stayed underfoot when Ez wasn't on Moses. We hardly knew he was around once Ez stuffed him in his shirt. The little guy pulled his head in like a baby kangaroo traveling in his mother's pouch."

I caught Grandma and Gramps looking at each other in the way they do when they're concerned about something. Grandma wasted no time changing the subject from Wedge to the strawberry-rhubarb pie she made for dessert. My last mouthful of food seemed to drop full force to the pit of my stomach. I knew Grandma and Gramps had had words about Wedge and the love I felt for him. No one was more aware of time ticking away than me. Six weeks go by mighty fast. Mr. Olson was due to show up in a little more than a week. I couldn't imagine him not choosing Wedge. He was big, strong and outshined all the others in the smart department. And he was a male.

As if that wasn't enough to ruin my appetite, Gramps looked right at me and asked if I had stumbled across a new hideaway lately. Knowing full well I couldn't lie and feeling all eyes on me, I glanced over at Caleb. Now that was one of the stupidest things I'd done in a long time. His eyebrows had shot up and his eyes were dancing to the tune of "we are guilty". Eva practically dropped her chin onto her plate and started picking at her piece of pie, avoiding all eye contact. As I looked back at Gramps I realized he was not backing off. His slight smile didn't trick me into thinking he was joking.

"As a matter-a-fact, Eva and I did find a little hole in the hillside the other day. Then we took Caleb up to check it out."

"How come you didn't take me?" Luke cried out.

"That so-called 'little hole' wouldn't happen to be behind a fir tree, now would it?" Gramps questioned.

"Yep, that's the one," Caleb blurted out.

"If I remember right, that's no small opening, Ezra. It's an old mine shaft. My folks knew it was dangerous when I was a kid and prohibited me from going in it. We count on you to help watch over your younger brothers and sister. I'm concerned about you showing poor judgment and endangering all of you."

With a pang of hurt jolting throughout my body, I meekly responded, "None of the timber looks weak or rotten. I figured it was safe enough for us to make into a fort. We were planin' on fixin' it up and then surprise you and Grandma with what we had done."

All this took Al by surprise. "Where is this here mine shaft? I never noticed one and I thought I've been over every square foot of this ranch."

"Oh, it's right under all our noses, about halfway up the eastern slope above the back bridge in the clearing," Gramps answered solemnly.

"I'll tell you what I'm goin' to do. All you kids need to listen to me closely. Al, Ben and I have a few days we can spare. We'll go up and check out the condition of the mine. If it's fixable, we will shim it up and make darn sure it won't collapse. If it's beyond repair, I will use dynamite to keep anyone from ever entering it again. I recall the mine goes in quite a distance. There's no reason for any of you to wander that deep into the hillside. If Grandma and I allow you to use it as a fort, I will close off the tunnel leading from the main chamber."

"You mean you'll help us build our fort?" Caleb asked.

"Only if it's worth repairing," Gramps corrected. "I was one disappointed boy when my folks blocked the entrance with boulders. I rolled the huge rocks down the mountain after the ranch became mine and allowed the sapling to grow and spread in front of the opening."

"Some kids never grow up," Grandma finally chimed in after sitting quietly in a dumbfounded sort of way. Looking straight at Gramps she questioned, "How come today is the first I ever heard of this cave?"

"It was just one of those things a fella wants kept to himself. I don't mind sharing it with all of you youngins now, but it has to be safe."

"How soon can we get goin' on it?" Ben enthusiastically asked. "I'd like nothin' better than checkin' it out right after swallowin' this last bite of pie."

"I go too! I go too!" shouted Luke.

Gramps suggested all of us head up together. "Finish up what you're eatin' and set your dishes off. I'll get a lantern, hand saw, and the large clippers and wait for you on the backside of the barn."

I inhaled what was left of my meal, cleared off my plate, and ran out to get Wedge. I took Caleb's suggestion and put Wedge in one of the pouches of a saddle bag. With the other pouch slung over my shoulder and resting on my chest, Wedge was comfortable facing backwards. Everyone met Gramps behind the barn where we began the trip up to our fort.

I swear older folks can never get out of low gear. Luke even gave in and rode the last half of the climb on top of Ben's shoulders. Grandma was in tow behind Eva. Ben was on our heels as Caleb and I kept yelling encouragement back to our elderly stragglers.

Once everyone gathered by the fir tree and caught their breath, Ben began snipping away at the branches until the massive trunk was exposed. Our fort's opening was no longer hidden. Gramps seemed to take pleasure in sawing the thick core at its base. The tree's lifeline was soon severed and Gramps heaved what remained of our natural shield down the mountain.

Grandma gasped at the size of the entrance. Looking at Gramps she said, "No wonder your momma panicked when she saw where you had been playing."

Gramps, Al and Ben stood at the opening. "You know, it don't look all that bad," remarked Al. "Some of the timbers could use replacin' and a few more added for extra support."

Ben was as excited as us kids. "I would have loved to have a fort like this back when I was a kid."

"What do you mean? You're still a kid," Al commented as he rolled his eyes and shook his head. "It'd be okay with me if you moved all your belongings here and set up house."

"No, it my house," cried Luke.

"It's nobody's house," Gramps informed all of us. "You kids stay out here with Grandma. Al and I will take Big Kid Ben inside with us to check this place out."

Grandma got all of us to sit on our fannies while we told her about all the stuff we hauled up to our fort. We could hear the three voices echoing inside the mine's cavity as they discussed possibilities.

After several minutes the three of them came out into the fading sunshine. Gramps was doing his best not to grin, Al showed no emotion and Ben's eyes were wild with excitement. "We get to keep it!" I smiled looking straight at Ben.

"I knew I should have kept you out here with the kids," Gramps mumbled while eyeballing Ben.

"Okay, this is the plan. We will reinforce all the beams first. Then close off the back tunnel. The last thing we'll do is build a stout door to keep out unwelcomed critters."

We all shouted and jumped around like chickens with their heads cut off. Gramps led Grandma and the rest of us back into the mine. "This is not the first time that nail keg has been in here. You kids must'a built up a few muscles draggin' all this stuff up from the barn. I was a might older when I did the same thing. My folks made me haul it all back down when they found out what I was up to. We'll move it all into the tunnel and out of the way while we work on this main room. Then we'll put it back before blockin' off the tunnel."

"Are you sure this is safe?" Grandma questioned.

"It'll be fine once we get done workin' on it," Gramps assured her. "Then you kids can fix it the way you want."

Luke and Wedge ran around in circles on the hard packed dirt floor. Eva, Caleb and I hugged Gramps and thanked him over and over again. "Let's get back to the house," Gramps suggested as he released all of us from his arms. "We have a busy few days ahead of us. You kids will have to stay clear from here until we're done. The more chores you do for Grandma and us, the more time we'll have to work on your fort."

CHAPTER 6

Helping Hands

THE ENTIRE HOUSEHOLD WAS UP at the crack of dawn. We hustled through breakfast and ran out to offer assistance with Ben and Al's chores. Gramps came out of the house with plans he had drawn up for a pulley system. The massive timbers needed to add support would be too hard for a horse to haul up the steep embankment. With the use of Moses, the thick beams could be raised with two large pulleys attached to a tall pine above and slightly to the left of the mine's entrance. While he made a slow progression diagonally down the hill, heavy ropes fastened to the sides of his harness would enable Moses to drag timbers up the mountain.

We all sat on the fence railing watching as our three laborers loaded beams, tools, pulleys, ropes and a bucket of bolts onto the flatbed trailer. Once all the items were accounted for, Gramps put the tractor into gear. The trailer jerked into motion with Ben and Al straddling the building materials for a free ride.

"I sure wish we could go up there and watch," said Caleb.

"Well we can't," I responded. "So there's no use wishin' to do somethin' else when we got plenty to do here."

Eva and Luke agreed they could handle Caleb's and my chores while we took on the morning work usually done by Al and Ben, starting with moving the cows and calves.

Betty kept an eye on us as we started down the driveway. She soon followed as if to offer her services. She must have figured we were two greenhorns incapable of pushing the cattle down to the lower pasture. It was the first time she showed an interest in working since delivering her pups.

Betty hadn't lost her touch. I raised my arm and pointed saying, "Go get'em girl." My sendoff was simple. Her response was amazing. She darted around and through the herd relying on the maneuvering skills bred into her. She nipped the unsuspecting heels at breakneck speed, always in control and hitting her mark every time. She never went after the calves. As long as the cows were moving, their offspring would follow.

After the entire herd was in motion I realized our blunder. Without a moment to spare, I began running as I yelled at Caleb that we forgot to open the lower pasture's gate. The lead cow and calf were trampling down the grass not ten feet from the fence by the time we got there. We slid the metal bolt out of its slot and quickly jumped up on the bottom rail, riding the gate as it swung wide open. Dust billowed up from hundreds of hooves as they funneled into the newly opened space.

The last of the herd was upon us when I heard a calf bellowing. Its mother was in a fighting stance and bent on killing herself a small dog. There was the culprit nipping at the heels of the calf. Wedge must have witnessed Betty at work and thought he wanted to have a shot at it. Caleb and I jumped the fence lickety-split. With our hats gripped in our waving hands and hollering our heads off, we were hopeful we'd distract the cow long enough to rescue the little tyrant. Betty outdistanced us and began working on the mama cow's heels. I ran in, grabbed Wedge by the scruff of his neck and headed for the nearest fence. Caleb was a few steps ahead of me. With us safely straddling the boards, Betty backed off and allowed the stragglers to reunite with the herd.

Caleb offered to close the gate while I sat catching my breath. Holding Wedge up to where his eyes were level with mine, I scolded, "What am I goin' to do with you? You can't keep leavin' the barnyard. One of these days you're goin' to get yourself into a heap of trouble and no one will be there to bail you out."

Our three fort contractors came down for the midday meal displaying a heap of enthusiasm. They were like three chums, patting each other's backs on what a great job they were doing. They blurted out ideas and how they would go about doing them. Caleb and I stood by as if invisible, listening to how our fort and our plans were reconfigured into some kind of big boy club house.

They agreed Caleb and I would be of some use in a few days. We could become their "gofers". Al was quick to define a gofer as someone who "goes for this and goes for that". We were okay with having the gofer status, anything to hurry the building process. We could run up and down the mountain fetching things they would need. It was agreed Grandma would pack food in a bucket for their mid-day meal. Caleb and I would haul it to the fort each day, starting tomorrow, so they wouldn't waste time walking down to the house and then back up after eating.

"I figure", Gramps said, "all the new beams will be in place in three more days. Then we'll drag your furnishings into the big chamber and block the back tunnel. Al will frame in the entry and Ben can make the door down here in the barn. We also decided a cemented threshold dug deep under the door will help keep the creepin' and slithering type critters out. Hangin' the door will be the last thing on our list before it's a done deal."

Smiles plastered our four small faces. "We wouldn't have been able to fix the fort up half as nice as you," I admitted.

"That's a fact," Gramps responded. "And I didn't do such a good job myself when I took it over as a kid. My folks probably saved my life by stoppin' me from playin' in it. I guarantee the place has seen better days. We'll make it safe. I figure you kids wouldn't mind if we earned the right to relive our childhood up there too."

"Since when do we have free time to go traipsin' off to play in a cave? It'll take us a month to catch up on all the things we're not doin' now," whined Ben.

"Quit your snivelin'," Al retorted. "For such a young buck you sure know how to complain. Maybe if you didn't spend so much time shoveling food in that trap of yours during every meal you'd have more time to be the kid your mind never outgrew."

"You know Al, I think you've gotten so old you can't even remember what it was like being a kid," Ben smiled as he grabbed his hat from the peg in the mudroom. He placed it on his head and tipped the brim toward Al before turning around and disappearing through the door.

"I can tell you one thing," Gramps looked at the rest of us chuckling, "those two won't be spendin' much free time buddy bonding up there in the fort."

"You got that right," muttered Al.

Gramps kissed Grandma and thanked her for the meal before heading out the back door on the heels of Al. "We'll be back when we hear the dinner bell," he yelled over his shoulder. "You kids help Grandma."

With Luke napping and the rest of us having a few hours to play, the three of us spent the warm afternoon with the pups. We would lay with our bellies flat on the ground and our faces hidden in our hands as they squirmed and nibbled at our live carcasses. We pretended they were vultures feasting on dead cows. Except these dead cows couldn't stop wiggling and giggling as the little paws and mouths climbed and sniffed their way around all our nooks and crannies.

You haven't lived until wet noses, warm tongues and grunting mouths work their way under your armpits, around your earlobes, over your head and down your back. It's the bare feet that sends me into a frenzy. Once the pups discover your toes, it's all over. You would have thought they found a bowl of milk the way they lick the bottom of your feet.

Poor Eva took to screaming when Otis got tangled in her hair. It took both Caleb and me working together to release the frantic pup and return Eva to normal, minus a few strands of her curly locks.

The wind began to stir and thunder clouds were forming over the mountains. Grandma came out to the porch and yelled for us to get the doggies inside their shed before the distant thunderstorm was upon us, frightening and scattering the pups.

Luke swung open the screen door behind her and hit the stairs running. Grandma always said naps have a way of rejuvenating a person's body. He's living proof. Luke wasted no time joining us as we rounded the pups up and ran for cover. Caleb and I hauled the last four of Betty's puppies through the shed's door. The timing was perfect. We all joined the mutts on the carpet of straw just as the deafening thunder clapped overhead. The small glass windowpanes rattled and the building itself felt as though it would be shaken from its rock foundation. The intense bolt of lightning sent shock waves through our bodies. The pups went berserk. Every one of them yelped as they began digging, thinking their flimsy straw caves could offer protection against the storm's wrath. Rain started pelting the tin roof, making the volume so loud we had to yell at each other in order to be heard.

Several minutes went by before the shed's door opened, silhouetting a very wet Grandma. Somewhat breathless and laughing, she asked, "Is there room for one more?"

"Sure," we all replied.

Closing the door behind her, Grandma proceeded to get down on her knees alongside us. "I knew you couldn't hear me holler to come up to the house. This shed is like being entombed in both a snare and a base drum. It looks like our little buddies don't rightly know what to think of all this commotion. It might be their first storm, but it definitely won't be their last."

Luke and Eva were caught up in the excitement until Grandma showed up. As the storm peaked overhead, Luke and Eva's enthusiasm began to diminish. It wasn't long before they both flung themselves into Grandma's arms with their hands cupped over their ears. Grandma hugged them close while stroking their heads.

Moments later the door was being attacked from the outside. Caleb and I got up to investigate. As we approached the door we could hear a dog crying and then it barked several times. We unlatched the door to let an upset and soaked Betty join her family.

"The poor thing," said Grandma. "She must have run all the way down the mountain when the storm started. She wants to make sure her babies are safe. Why don't you two get a couple of those gunnysacks stacked over there and dry her off."

Caleb and I each fetched a burlap sack and went to work mopping up Betty's wet coat. We grabbed a few more sacks and worked our way down her legs and around her dripping ears. Her body was trembling as she looked around for signs of her cowering brood. By the time we rubbed most of the moisture from her, the bulk of the storm had moved on. Eva and Luke eased away from Grandma and the pups began jumping all over Betty.

"My guess is Gramps, Al and Ben are high and dry in your fort. Betty could have stayed with them. She should have known you kids would take care of her pups," Grandma said smiling as she patted Betty's head. "She's an exceptional dog."

"How about we head up to the house and make some hot cocoa? This is a perfect day for it," suggested Grandma.

Well, we didn't have to be asked twice. All of us headed out the door hot on Grandma's trail. With a few raindrops left to contend with and dodging the small streams still flowing down the eaves, we all made it to the mudroom fairly dry. Of course our bare feet looked as though they were wearing mud socks. We took turns sitting two at a time on the rim of the large washtub that collected water from the washing machine. The warm water flowing from the faucet felt great on our cold feet. Within minutes we were all on our knees around the coffee table warming up in front of the fireplace and drinking hot cocoa.

It wasn't long before Gramps, Al and Ben shuffled through the back door. Gramps and Al poured themselves some hot coffee. Ben went for the cocoa. They couldn't stop talking about how snug they were up in the cave during the storm. "Why, it's the safest place to be when lightnin's flashin'," Al said.

"With a stout door the noise would be muffled too," added Ben.

"I assume Betty made it down okay. I tried to get her to stay put, but she would have none of it," said Gramps. "We figured she was in a hurry to get down to her pups and make sure they were all accounted for."

Looking at Caleb and me he went on to say, "We'll be needin' you two first thing after your mornin' chores. This project will be wrapped up soon."

The next day we became full fledged gofers. We deepened the path by running back and forth with food and building materials. Most of the big jobs were done with Ben's help. The sand, cement and necessary water can were each hauled up using Moses and the pulley system.

Within two days Ben had moved down to the barn to make the door. There was nothing flimsy about it. Two horizontal boards and one diagonal board were bolted into place over the vertical planks with three large hinges to carry its weight. A small window cut into the upper center and covered with a small hinged shutter was the finishing touch. Ben said it was so we could check out who was knockin' on the door before opening it. "You gotta be careful," he said. "You never know who might be up there tryin' to get into your fort." We helped him wrap the door with feed sacks and twine to minimize the rough trip it faced being pulled up the side of the mountain by Moses.

By the end of the week our fort was finished. Grandma, Luke and Eva joined Caleb and me in hauling up the last mid-day meal. Everyone sat on overturned barrels and crates inside the fort, eating and talking about how it all came together. The back tunnel had been sealed with rocks and cement, the sturdy new beams looked massive compared to the old ones, and the large door opening allowed ample light.

Then Gramps showed us how dark the fort became when he shut the door. The pitch blackness was a bit unnerving until Gramps turned on a flashlight. "That's where these will come in handy," he said.

Grandma wasn't all too thrilled when the light settled on the metal candle holders attached to two upright beams. "Now we can't be having these kids using matches and lighting candles up here," she objected.

"I have no doubt Ezra and Caleb can handle matches. There are only two metal candle holders and they are bolted on. Al worked overtime designing and welding them to be as safe as possible. They can't keep the door open all the time and there is no other light source."

There was no arguing with Gramps on the subject of lighting. He put a lot of faith in us, and we wanted nothing more than to prove he was right.

CHAPTER 7

A Shot in the Dark

WEDGE HAD RUN UP THE mountain chasing every critter that flew, ran or hopped. There, alongside the trail and propped up in the shade of a boulder, he sat panting and resting until I caught up. The sun was going down, casting shadows from the large rock formations onto the meadow speckled with millions of multi colored wildflowers. Clouds were starting to come between the land and the blue sky.

"It sure looks like a thunderstorm brewin'," I told Wedge when I caught up to him. "We best be gettin' home before those clouds knock into each other and start spillin' rain. We'll just climb up this mountain and follow the ridge's backbone home. It's a heap quicker than goin' back the way we came."

Wedge wagged his tail and began dancing around as if to say, "I'm with you". His quick wet tongue reached out and slicked up my mouth real good. I sat beside him for a little breather and offered him a piece of my jerky, which he gladly swallowed without the formality of chewing. Feeling pretty rested, we began the steep climb up, around and between massive granite boulders. My legs were straining and my lungs screamed at my body to stop. Wedge's hind end didn't seem to know that they were supposed to follow his front legs and he began to lose his footing. I had to lift his awkward little body up several times to place it at a higher level in order to continue the ascent.

About three quarters of the way up I stopped to give us both a rest. Wedge laid his head on my leg and closed his eyes. "Don't be goin' off to sleep now, Wedge. I don't think I can carry you and my own body to the top."

Just about then a flash of lightning lit up the whole valley below. I began counting and, sure enough, a clap of thunder roared over us just three seconds later. If you divide the seconds you count by five, you can determine how far away the lightning struck. I figured it was a bit more than a half a mile away. Wedge figured it was too close for comfort. His oversized paws sprang into action and shot him down the mountain. His little body moved faster than his legs, causing him to lose control, tumble and freefall until I could no longer follow his downward trek to the bottom of the steep incline.

"Wedge! Wedge! Stop! Wedge, where are you?"

I couldn't believe my legs wouldn't move and I was shaking uncontrollably. I kept yelling and trying to see where Wedge ended up. My voice was calling Wedge's name and Gramps was calling mine.

How did Gramps get here? He kept saying, "Ez, Ez, open your eyes."

He's right, I thought. I need to open my eyes. I can't find Wedge unless I open my eyes.

As my eyes opened, the shaking stopped. There, on his tiptoes reaching over and holding my shoulders, was Gramps calmly trying to ease me out of my nightmarish adventure. "You're okay, Ezra. Wedge is okay too."

It felt so good to know I was safe on my bunk and Gramps was there holding me in his firm grip with Grandma standing behind him. "Think you can slip on back to sleep and look for a happier dream?" he asked.

"Sure, Gramps. Sorry I woke both of you."

"No problem, Ezra. Tonto has already declared it a new day," Grandma yawned. "It's about time to start breakfast anyway."

Gramps hugged me and kissed my forehead, prickling me with those stiff old whiskers he has right before he shaves each morning. "You just turn over and get in a few more winks. I'll make sure you're up for breakfast," whispered Gramps.

Rolling over seemed to settle my mind just right. No sooner did I doze off than the chow bell rang. I dropped to the floor and noticed Caleb was already up and gone. Everyone was sitting down and heaping their plates with food by the time I slid to my place on the bench.

It seems Caleb didn't hear me yelling last night. How that guy sleeps through noise and a shaking bed, I'll never know. Why there could be thunder, an earthquake and a tornado all rolled up into one and you wouldn't so much as get a half opened eye out of him. But if a whiff of bacon finds its way upstairs, he's awake lickety-split.

"Sure hope I never depend on you if I'm ever yellin' for my life and you're snoozin' in the bunk right below me," I said while glaring at Caleb. "Gramps and Grandma could hear me from down the hall. You must have been dreamin' about eatin' a big ice cream cone and wouldn't let anything come between you and your food."

"That's not true. It was a hot dog. And I thought the shaking was caused by Howdy, cuz I was ridin' him while I was eatin' my hot dog."

The room exploded into laughter. "It looks as though Caleb and Ezra both had dreams about dogs last night," chuckled Gramps. "Only Ezra's dog was lost and Caleb's stomach found his."

"Speaking of dogs, Ben finished rigging up the shed and fenced-in yard next to the chicken coop for Betty and the pups," Grandma mentioned between bites. "It's ready and waiting for the new occupants. How about moving them sometime today? They're making a terrible mess and I'm afraid I'll flatten one out when walking through the mudroom with my arms full."

"Well, that settles that. The westward movement will take place right after breakfast. From now on, you kids are responsible to make sure all the pups are in their shed before nightfall. Coyotes, bear and mountain lions would like nothin' better than a plump little pup to line their stomachs," warned Gramps. "You remember what happened to Tucker's dog right before Christmas last year. That big ol' mountain lion came right over the fence, snatched his dog and sailed back over the rails before Tucker could fetch his gun layin' just two feet away."

"'Quick' ain't the word for it. The dog no sooner picked up the big cat's scent and let out about three barks before she was shaken by the neck and silenced. Tucker saw it all and couldn't believe how fast it happened." Al went on to say, "And that's another person interested in one of your pups. The lion took the younger of his two dogs. He'll be needin' another female. Seein' how there's no shortage of girl pups, I told him to come on over and check them out."

Shaking his head, Gramps said, "Sure, he's welcome to come see what we got. I think that lion's a bit too close for comfort. Tucker's only about a mile away as the crow flies, you know. Heck, a lion roams a territory of about 15 miles, and a lot further if food is scarce."

Grandma offered to clean up the breakfast mess if the four of us cleared the pups out and helped tidy the mudroom. Luke was first to jump into action. He ran to the pups' nursery and began pulling them from Betty. Caleb pushed past him, flying through the screen door to fetch the rusty wagon with the worn wooden sideboards. We used it during the winter to haul firewood to the house. I have to admit it was quick thinking on Caleb's part to gather all the pups at one time using the wagon. I put the ramp into place over the steps and helped Caleb pull it up to the back door. Eva came out with an armful of rags to line the wagon's bed. The pups were loaded in no time at all. I proceeded to grab the handle and steer the wagon in the direction of the ramp when Luke yelled his disapproval.

"That's not fair! You can't take all those puppies by yourself. You gotta share."

"Tell you what," said Gramps. "You get in the wagon too and make sure none of those pups tumble out. Ez can pull, Caleb you push, and Eva can run ahead to open the shed's door."

All of us went to work doing our assigned jobs. The pups wiggled over Luke's feet and under his raised knees. Their noisy little muzzles searched Luke frantically for the nipples that provide them with warm milk. Luke giggled with delight, throwing in a few hearty belly laughs when a pup hit a ticklish spot. All of us chuckled along with him as we made our way to the shed. Betty ran alongside the wagon, overseeing the mass exodus. She seemed pleased with the location and space of their new home.

Ben had generously scattered fresh sawdust from the small mill Gramps had set up under a pole barn behind the tractor shed. There was an endless supply of fine wood chips made from the lumber of diseased or downed trees on the ranch. Next to bread baking, I can't think of anything I like smelling more than sawdust straight from the mill. It's the heart and soul of a tree. Blended from spruce and pine, the flakes of wood gather in a large mound under the blade as it sinks its teeth into the slow moving logs.

The pups wasted no time rolling in the timber scented carpet. Betty found her large wooden box filled with clean bedding and did her usual circular turn routine before settling down. Along the side wall was a mountain of fresh straw. It would be the perfect play area for her nine feisty charges. The junk-room-turned-dog-shed was perfect. Gramps commented on how nice it will be to have all of them as neighbors instead of living underfoot with us in the main house.

Grandma had finished the kitchen cleanup and began throwing all the old towels and sheets that were used by the dog family into the wringer washing machine. I eagerly helped her and offered to wash the floor. That's when Grandma did her famous raised eyebrow trick and asked suspiciously what I had up my sleeve. I knew there was no beating around the bush, so I came right out and asked if I could keep Wedge.

Grandma got all serious looking. She put her arms out to me and said, "Come here, Ez." As I walked into her hold she went on to say, "I kinda figured you were getting attached to that little guy. He's only one of two boy pups. Mr. Olson wants a boy and he gets first pick. Why don't we wait until he chooses? You know we had no plans to keep any of them. Your Gramps is counting on the money they'll bring, since we have a lot more mouths to feed."

"I know, Grandma. All the pups are great, but I loved Wedge from the moment I saw his lifeless body in my hands. He seems to know me and wants to be with me too." No longer able to control my trembling lips, I began to cry.

"Listen Ezra, I'll talk to Gramps. He might go for keeping one pup. But he is a man of his word. He won't short-change Mr. Olson. Are you willing to compromise, Ez? Will you be satisfied with a pup, even if it isn't Wedge?"

"Honestly, Grandma, I only want Wedge. But one pup is better than no pup at all. Caleb, Eva and Luke would love having any of them."

"That's my boy." Grandma squeezed me as she kissed my forehead. She promised to talk to Gramps when he was in a good listening mood.

After unloading half my worrisome thoughts onto Grandma, I felt a heap better. Gramps always said that he has the muscle but that Grandma has the strength in the family. I sure hope he's right. Grandma will have to be my backbone on this one. When Gramps isn't going a mile a minute, he's deep in thought about ranch survival. There's always a problem with getting Gramps in a position where he wants to listen. But I figured there wasn't a lot of time left before the pups were old enough to sell. I suppose Grandma knows Gramps better than anyone. I put my trust in her, and by the way her eyes teared up, I hope it isn't too much of a burden.

The move to the shed proved to be just what the dog family needed. The whole litter seemed to double in size overnight and were running outside their enclosure and around the barnyard in no time. We were all on the lookout when any of the trucks or the tractor started up, making sure Betty's family was safe from the rolling wheels.

Each of the pups' personalities came out more too. Although Yodel was the runt, she had no problem keeping up with the others. She definitely had a bit of a short dog attitude. The hair along her spine would bristle as she growled her way between rumps to the long wooden trough that Al made to hold their puppy food. Now that they'd moved on to solid food, Betty had more time to herself. She'd hop up onto a bale of straw or the opened tailgate of the truck, out of their reach. It was her quiet time and she wasted none of it while she licked herself clean and stretched out to soak up the warmth of the sun. Just a few feet away, nine little rear ends whipped their tails back and forth as they greedily devoured the day's meal. It was another chore added to our list, but well worth the entertainment.

Although it had only been two days since Grandma and I had our talk, it seemed the hands on the clock were taking one step forward and two steps back. Every time Grandma and I made eye contact she would give me a slight smile and wink. I couldn't figure out if she had talked to Gramps or was still waiting for that perfect moment. When it got to the point where one more smile or wink would reduce my young manhood to that of a blubbering boy, Grandma took my hand and sat down with me on the porch step. I couldn't control all the "worry fists" punching away at the insides of my stomach.

Tears were beginning to form as Grandma put her arm around my shoulders. With a little squeeze she told me, "Gramps already knew how you wanted Wedge. He'd been wrestling with losing the pup to Mr. Olson too. However, he feels more troubled that you couldn't go to him directly with your request. He thinks it's never too early to face your problems head-on, no matter what the outcome."

I let that soak in for a moment. "I suppose he's right. I just don't want to look weak when he tells me what I already know."

"Ez, if crying is what you mean by weak, then no one here would have strength to face each new day. We all cry when our hearts are so full of love and something happens that crushes down on us. Having love attacked is painful. It affects our entire being and changes how we see things forever.

"You know, Ezra, I worry about people who have never had their hearts filled in the first place. They have little from which to draw true happiness. You have such wonderful memories of the life you had with your folks. We will never stop hurting because they are gone. But our hearts are slowly filling back up with the love we are able to share."

I put a lot of stock in what Grandma was saying. I knew if I wanted Wedge bad enough I would have to pull myself together the best I could and make my wishes known to Gramps. Maybe the two of us could work something out with Mr. Olson. At least she didn't say Gramps was unwilling to keep the pup.

"Ok, Grandma. I'll talk to Gramps."

"That'a boy, Ez. Talk about being full of love, I fear that old man's chest will burst with the tenderness he totes around. His prickly covering is protecting a very soft and vulnerable heart."

I looked up and kissed Grandma on her aged cheek. "Thanks, Grandma." Sliding off the step, I slowly headed down the driveway to where Gramps was digging fence posts.

Caleb ran to join me. I told him what I was up to and he decided he'd shift gears and join Eva and Luke. With a slap on my back, he quietly said, "Whoa, good luck." He made a quick U-turn and galloped his stick horse back to the barn. I guess he figured whatever they were doing would be a heck-of-a-lot more fun than where I was heading. I was on my own.

Crossing the bridge that spanned Sheep Creek and continuing down the long driveway, I spotted Gramps about ten fence posts ahead. His back was to me and his arms were hard at work lifting the wooden handles of the post-hole digger. With his hat covering his head and gloves protecting his hands, there was not a trace of skin to be seen. His shirt showed signs of perspiration between his shoulder blades. It dawned on me how young this man looked as he jammed the metal plates into the rocky soil, held the dirt by pulling the handles apart and then lifted the contraption up. The contents were released into a pile by pushing the handles together. This was done over and over again until the desired depth was reached.

Butterflies had multiplied to swarm capacity in my stomach. My feet felt as though they weren't controlled by me at all, but were robotically following each other down the road. The sun at my back gave me away as Gramps spotted my shadow coming up to join his.

"Well now, what brings you down here? Did you come to help an old man dig holes? By the look on your face, I suspect you're down in some hole yourself and wrestlin' with the best way to get out."

I decided to take my pa's advice and just get on with it. My mouth blurted out, "I came to talk to you about keeping Wedge."

Standing the post digger upright in the hole, Gramps said, "Yep, I kinda thought you were strugglin' with how you could hang on to him. I've been givin' this matter some thought myself. You see, Ezra, I got no problem with you takin' on a dog. I know you will earn his keep and train him proper so he can help out around here. But, as you know, I do have a real problem with a man who goes back on his handshake. Mr. Olson and I have an agreement, and I would sooner die than not keep my word. That is no different than lyin' and cheatin'. I want to like what I see in the mirror, even if it's weathered and beaten down."

"I know, Gramps. I just thought maybe we could talk to Mr. Olson and try to get him interested in Yank. With a little extra attention I could make him look like a good choice."

"That's a thought, but not a guarantee. Are you up to handin' over Wedge and wishin' him a good life if Mr. Olson makes him his choice?"

Looking down at my bare feet I mumbled, "I guess so".

"There won't be no guessin'. You have to know what's right and what's wrong. Wedge would be goin' to a good home, I can vouch for that. You'll have to take a likin' to another dog or go without. I'm compromising by allowing you to keep one. You'll need to compromise too."

"Okay," I answered.

"Look at me, Ez. Look into my eyes and shake my hand. Tell me we have a deal."

Squinting up, I removed my right hand from the pocket of my overalls and took hold of Gramps' extended palm. "We have a deal. I'll let Mr. Olson pick his dog. If it's Wedge then I'll wish him happiness and let him go." After the quick shake I pulled my hands up over my eyes and, leaning against Gramps' belt, I wept.

Gramps kneeled down and embraced me. I didn't look at him, but dug my face into his shoulder. For a long moment nothing was said. Then, in a slow deliberate voice, Gramps said he was proud of me and we best be gettin' on with the work that's always sittin' around starin' at us. He stood up and lifted my hat long enough to rustle my hair. I said goodbye and headed back up the dirt road.

Grandma met me at the bridge, holding Wedge. "I thought you might like to play with this little guy. He seemed to be looking everywhere for you."

The only thing I could muster up was a weak, "Thanks Grandma." Pressing Wedge against my chest and burying my face into his soft hair, I walked under Grandma's arm back to the porch. We sat on the top step and she listened intently while I mulled over what Gramps had said. Wedge had heard enough and wiggled his way to freedom, scampering across the barnyard to find happier playmates.

Grandma squeezed my shoulder and pulled me closer saying, "Well, I guess you have your work cut out for you."

Not knowing what she was getting at, I just stared into her soft hazel eyes.

"Don't you think Yank should get some of that attention you have been pouring onto Wedge? After all, Mr. Olson is looking for a smart and reliable dog. There's still a little time to polish up Yank's act. How can you ever forgive yourself if Wedge is taken and you did nothing to stop it? Like Gramps said, 'There's no guarantee'. But you have to try."

As usual, Grandma was right. I perked up, kissed her on the cheek, said I agreed, and headed for the barn. There I found Yank running in circles after Luke while the other pups were trying desperately to get up on the bales of hay that protected Caleb and Eva. Wedge ran over to me. I patted his head and said it was Yank I needed to spend time with right now. Walking over to Yank, I lifted him under his forelegs and, with our noses almost touching, I said, "You and me got ourselves some work to do. It's a shot in the dark, but at least I have a shot."

"What are you talkin' about?" asked Caleb.

"I aim to make Yank look like a better choice to Mr. Olson."

"How you 'spect to do that?"

"I'm goin' to start by pushin' his fanny down and sayin', 'SIT'. Then I'll work on makin' him STAY."

"We can help you," Eva volunteered.

"That's okay with me as long as we don't confuse the little guy. It might be better if you each take a pup of your own. Don't work with Wedge. The dumber he looks the better."

Luke picked up Yodel, Eva grabbed Otis and Caleb settled for Rebel. School was in session. Wedge looked on as the four pups were put through the drills. "SIT", we all demanded in unison while pushing down gently on their behinds.

At first we used bits of dry dog food as rewards. When they no longer seemed interested in that, I ran up to the pantry. I should have remembered how Grandma keeps a sharp eye on any activity taking place behind the pantry door. As I tried to make my getaway, Grandma's voice rang out, "Wait just a minute, young man. What's in the bag and where are you taking it?"

After a quick explanation and handing the bag over for her inspection, she scolded, "You are not stuffing jerky down the mouths of those mutts. Al would have your hide if he found out about this. It takes him a lot of time and effort to season and dry all that meat. I'll donate some stale crackers. They're lucky to get that."

Amazingly, Yank was receptive. After working with him for two days he began to respond to the "SIT" command with little effort. What surprised me most was when Wedge responded to the verbal command faster, although he was strictly a bystander and was never acknowledged or rewarded.

Feeling optimistic, I went on to include the second round of training, "STAY". Well, the one thing puppies don't have a hankerin' to do is stay in one spot while you walk away. This was about the time Eva and Luke tired of the whole dog training bit and left Caleb, Rebel, Yank and me to our own devices. Wedge was fine with looking on. I'm not sure if he just wanted to be with me or if he actually enjoyed the education. He was always first to catch on and patiently waited for Rebel and Yank to learn the drills. My heart eventually softened and I began to reward him for his efforts. We had to slide the barn doors shut to keep the other pups from causing mass confusion and gobbling up all the crackers. Within three days Yank and Rebel, and of course Wedge, were promoted to the rank of "Smart Dogs", a noticeable notch higher than "Crazy Puppies".

CHAPTER 8

New Accommodations

MY TOSSING AND TURNING GOT me nowhere closer to sleeping. I figured once everybody dozed off I'd quietly head outside to the dog shed and spend some time with Wedge.

As my feet felt their way down the stairs, I remembered going through the same motions just six weeks ago when the pups were first born. That was a night of excitement and anticipation. Tonight I felt the emotional pangs of loss. Grabbing my jacket off its hook in the mudroom, I made it out the back door undetected. The trace of a moon was enough to light my way across the barnyard.

I whispered to Betty so she'd know it was me and to keep her from barking a warning signal. Turning the wooden latch gave way to the high pitched grind of three rusted, metal hinges as I opened the door wide enough to squeeze through. I held my breath when the screech repeated itself through the door's closing process. What little light the moon offered was now completely shut off. Except for the thumping of Betty's tail, all was still. I shuffled through the sawdust toward Betty's welcoming sound. The pups were all asleep in one large heap, cuddled up against their mother. I found Betty's head and stroked her from ears to tail.

"I'm just goin' to stay out here a bit with you, seeing as how I can't sleep. Hope you don't mind a little company." I felt around to locate Wedge's big paws, but realized my probing was causing the whole brood to stir. The last thing I needed was a chorus of pup cries to wake Ben and Al just a few doors down. I had to settle for Wedge's entire family. It was enough for the moment. In the pitch black darkness I had little choice but to lay down head-to-head with Betty and complete the half circle she had made around her pups. I gently petted Betty's long nose and up between her kind eyes.

"You're goin' to have to let go of your babies soon, gal. That's goin' to be a tough thing for you to do seein' how much you care for all of them. There's a big chance I'll have to say goodbye to Wedge too. But right now they are all here. We'll spend all the time we can with them."

There was no point keeping my eyes open in such a dark void. After a few minutes there was movement among the pups. A few made annoyed sounds of resistance until one nuzzled its way under my chin. Reaching up I gathered an over-sized paw into my hand. With a smile on my face I felt Wedge turn around, curl into a ball, and sigh. We slept.

Tonto tipped me off to it being a new day. I straightened my legs and stretched my arms over the wooden sides of the dog bed. Wedge was still dozing by my chest. Betty was awake and seemed anxious to get moving. The early morning light filtered through the boards nailed outside the shed's framework. My idea of spending a few minutes with Wedge had extended to be a whole night. I knew Grandma and Al would be up soon, if not already. There would be no denying where I'd slept.

"Well Betty, I might as well tend to you now. I'll let you get a little fresh air and throw some food out for all of you."

The pups were scrambling through the door as soon as the sound of their dry food hit the trough.

"Since when do you do chores in your long-johns?" came a baffled voice.

With the bucket in tow, I looked up to see Al standing outside the fenced enclosure. His hands were resting on his hips, his hat pushed back on his head and his mouth stretched into a grin across his entire weathered face. "If this ain't the darnedest thing I've seen in a month of Sundays! Please tell me you didn't sleep with them dogs last night."

"I wasn't plannin' on fallin' asleep. I just came out for a little visit."

"Really? How'd you like the accommodations? Do you plan on staying for breakfast too?"

There come times when a fella has to bite the bullet and succumb to harmless ridicule. I quickly played along and tried to save what little pride I had left. "Naw, I think I'll head up to the house to see what Grandma's fixin'."

"Well now, I don't think you're as dumb as you look. I was just headin' up that way myself for a hot cup of coffee. Maybe she'll pour you some to help clear your head," laughed Al.

Grandma looked a might preoccupied when we walked into the kitchen. I could tell she had been expecting Al. His big coffee mug was on the stove waiting to be filled with the fresh brew. But she lit up when Al stepped aside and revealed me in my long-johns standing right behind him.

"What on earth were you doing outside in your pj's?"

"Oh, you're goin' to love this," chuckled Al.

"It looks like I made it down just in time," Gramps chimed in as he hit the base of the stairs.

With three sets of eyes glued to my face and Al doing his best to keep his gut from popping his belt wide open, I could feel my face and ears putting off heat. I stammered, "I couldn't sleep last night, so I went out to check in on the dogs. They were all warm and soft and comfortable. I thought I'd lay down with them for just a little while. But I guess I fell asleep, cuz the next thing I knew Tonto was blowin' off steam and it was mornin'."

All three of them looked back and forth at each other and, as if rehearsed, they all burst into a loud roar. It seemed to pick up speed the more they made eye contact. Finally Al turned to pour coffee into his mug. We could hear the pot bumping up and down off the lip of the cup as he tried desperately to keep his laughter in check. I have to admit, even though the joke was on me, I could do nothing but join in. Grandma's eyes were squeezing out tears and Gramps was bent over supporting himself on the table top with his extended arms. We were all just about out of steam when Ben entered. Then the three chuckling grownups took turns telling about my night in the shed.

"I thought you had to be married to be in the doghouse. You're way ahead of the game, Ez," laughed Ben.

"I'm glad you guys are havin' so much fun. You sure know how to make a fella feel stupid."

Ben shot back, "In this case, what you see is what you get."

It was no surprise to hear three pairs of bare feet racing down the stairs. "Looks like we woke up the whole house. Good morning kids," Grandma smiled. "How come you all slept in your own beds last night?"

"What's goin' on? Why's everyone so goofy?" asked Caleb.

"I fell asleep with the dogs last night. Get your laughing done so I can get on with eatin' breakfast."

I continued to be the topic of conversation. Then Wedge's name was thrown in for good measure. "Wouldn't it be easier makin' a bed for Wedge next to yours?" asked Gramps. "He's old enough to spend his nights away from the pack."

Shock and utter disbelief is a subtle way of describing how I felt. "You mean I can have Wedge sleep in our room?"

"Gramps has gone all soft. Since, since when do you allow a dog upstairs?" Grandma stammered.

"I figure I'd sleep a lot better knowin' Ez was in his own bed rather than curled up with all those varmints in the dog shed," Gramps responded. "And believe me, Wedge won't make it through the night without whining to get out for a potty break. It'll be up to you to lug the oversized rascal downstairs and outside. If he's like most pups you won't be given a heap of warning before all heck breaks loose. Let me add, only ONE dog will be permitted upstairs."

Everyone, except Luke, agreed. But no amount of begging could shake Gramps' decision.

I spent a good part of the morning building a box for Wedge's new bed. There were plenty of old boards in the lumber pile from which to select the perfect materials. I set up shop just inside the opened barn doors. The boards laid level across the sawhorses where they were measured, marked and cut. Caleb helped by sitting on the long ends as I set to work pushing and pulling the handsaw up and down along the pencil lines. The downsized tools Gramps and Grandma got me for my last birthday had never been used with such enthusiasm as they were for this project. With a few nails and a lot of sandpaper, Wedge's bed was complete. We marched up to our room, set it down next to the bunk and stuffed an old pillow in the custom framework.

Bedtime couldn't come soon enough to suit me. After sundown Grandma suggested I give Wedge a small bowl of warm milk so he'd sleep better. "He has only two days left before Betty will be totally separated from her pups. They're old enough to be weaned," she said.

After practically inhaling the warmed milk, Wedge settled comfortably in my arms while I transported him up to our room. There to greet us and sitting around the newly made dog bed were Eva, Luke and Caleb. "Can't a fella put a dog to bed without an audience lookin' on?" I asked a bit irritably.

"Well now, it's a big deal having a dog sleep upstairs in this house," Grandma answered from behind me.

"Okay, but Wedge needs to keep calm so he'll go to sleep," I insisted.

"Put him on his bed and all of you can give him a pat good night. I'll take Eva and Luke to their room, tuck them in, say prayers and read a short book to them," came the directions from Grandma. "Then I'll be back to read another chapter of *The Last of the Chiefs* to you two. By then things will be quieting down and Wedge should have no problem dozing off."

Once Eva and Luke finished patting and kissing Wedge, Caleb and I were alone to try and settle the confused little guy down. His full tummy kept him from getting too rambunctious and soon he curled into a ball. Grandma returned and, reading aloud in her soothing voice, soon put Wedge to sleep. She kissed us goodnight, turned off the lamp and left our door partially opened.

All was peaceful until Wedge woke in the middle of the night realizing he was not bedded with his mom and siblings. His mournful cry brought me clambering down from the top bunk. I quickly gathered him into my arms. He became excited and immediately cleaned my cheek with his warm tongue. Soon I felt more warmth as liquid soaked into my long-johns. "Dang it Wedge, look what you did!"

I grabbed a fresh pair of long-johns from my drawer and toted Wedge down the hall to do some cleaning up in the bathroom. After returning

Wedge to his bed, I climbed back into mine. Then began the sad whimpering. No matter how much I tried to console the little guy, he continued crying a heartbreaking tune. There were two options. I could return him to Betty, or I could put him in bed with me. Knowing he had to learn to be separated from his mother, I chose the second plan.

Back down I went and back up the ladder I hauled Wedge. It worked. He settled having me as a snoozing partner. Within a minute one of us was fast asleep and the other laid there wide awake, savoring the closeness we had to each other and that we might soon lose. Sometime before light began to filter through the windows, I fell asleep.

"Hmm, good thing you made a dog bed," was the comment I woke up to. There, standing next to my bed at eye level, was Grandma. And there, rolled up under my arm and partially covered with my blanket, was Wedge.

"I can explain, Grandma. Wedge..."

"No need to, Ezra. I heard the commotion last night and found evidence of a mishap hanging from the hamper. It looks like you had another rough night because of this little hairball. Maybe having him sleep up here wasn't such a good idea."

"He's just scared and a little lonely for his mom is all," I responded. "He has to get used to it sooner or later."

"Yes, I suppose you're right. Give him to me and I'll take him outside before he has another accident."

"What's goin' on?" yawned Caleb as Grandma left the room.

"Nothin' you need to worry your curly head about," I answered. "Go back to sleep until you smell breakfast."

I was now faced with the fact that Caleb's bed under mine would be a better spot for me to sleep for the time being. I'd be at arm's length to Wedge and in a better position to comfort him as well as rush him outside to do his business. Caleb has always been one to help others, and he'd jump at the chance to sleep on the top bunk. So it was quite a surprise when Caleb wanted to negotiate terms to my idea of trading beds.

"You can sleep in my bed only if you do all my chores for a month," was his reply.

"A MONTH! Wedge will only be here for about another week," I argued.

"Okay, two weeks and no less," countered Caleb.

"That's not fair!"

"Papa used to say, 'Life's not fair'," Caleb reminded me.

Standing with my arms crossed and the maddest, baddest glare I could muster up, I finally said, "We got a deal. But don't expect me to go easy on you when you ask for a favor."

The pups were just over six weeks old when Betty moved back into the house. Weaning had begun. Betty spent her days with Gramps and her nights in the mudroom. And Wedge spent his days with me and most of his sleeping hours under the blankets in my temporary bottom bunk. I had no problem keeping track of the little guy. During our meals he ate and played with his brother and sisters. Other than that, he shadowed me everywhere.

Conversation was becoming strained in a lighthearted way. Grandma talked a lot about school starting back up soon and Caleb and me getting to town for new pants. I would need a bigger jacket soon and pass my used one on to Caleb.

"It's a good thing you're older, Ezra. You keep your clothes in good enough shape to pass down to Caleb. There's no way I'd send Eva or Luke off in the clothes broken in by you, Caleb. They're pretty much done in by then."

Caleb spoke up saying, "Yeah, well I'm doin' them a favor. They get to pick out new clothes and not get stuck lookin' like Ezra."

"You probably wish you look like me in your dreams," I laughed.

"I'll tell you what, Caleb. You can pick out something that looks like you when Ez finds the jacket he wants," suggested Grandma.

"Okay, you gotta deal," agreed Caleb. "I'm gettin' a new vest, a dark one. Not no light colored one like Ezra's."

"That sounds like a good idea," came Grandma's response. "You have a little time yet to think about how you want to look. But you do realize, no matter what you wear, you'll always look like Caleb. You're your own person. No clothes can change that."

CHAPTER 9

My Plan

THE DREADED TELEPHONE CALL CAME during supper one evening well into the seventh week. Grandma's voice softened and her eyes met mine as she said, "Oh, hello Mr. Olson. How have you been? I'm very well, thank you. Yes, he's right here."

Gramps got up and took the receiver from Grandma. No one spoke while listening to the one sided conversation. Although Grandpa had his back to us, his hushed bass voice could be heard clearly. "Okay, we'll see you Friday afternoon". Gramps hung the handset back in the wall mount's cradle.

He slowly turned to face our seven sets of eyes. "We all knew the time was coming when those pups would be movin' on. It looks like either Yank or Wedge will be leaving on Friday. So let's get doin' what we do at the supper table. I'm not goin' to have you ruin my appetite for the next two days with all your long faces gawking at each other."

Looking at me he went on to say, "You've done a good job with Yank. No one has put money down sayin' your efforts would pay off. But then, to not try would give little hope."

I knew the next two days would zoom by. I didn't know if I should spend all my time with Wedge or double down on working with Yank. In desperation I decided to focus on keeping Wedge by drilling Yank. Caleb was a big help. Whenever Wedge and I went off to do chores I could hear Caleb pick up where I left off, giving commands to Yank. It was good knowing the little guy would respond to more than one person.

The hardest part was not wearing my emotions on my sleeve. With a lot of effort, I tried appearing somewhat cheerful. I knew the chance of keeping Wedge was a long shot and it weighed heavily on Gramps and Grandma. Al seemed a bit out-a-sorts too. There was no need for me to go moping around to make matters worse. One thing my early years taught me was that no matter how hard life comes slamming down on you, you pull yourself back up onto your feet, wipe yourself off and keep moving forward one step at a time.

That night I didn't bother starting Wedge out in his bed. He was asleep with his head on my pillow when Grandma showed up to tuck us in for the night. I knew sleep would be next to impossible. With a lot of yawning, I let on that I was as tired as Wedge when Grandma kissed me good night. After the lights were out, Caleb tried to talk to me about our fort. Figuring I was asleep when there was no response on my part, he gave up and turned over. I laid motionless. My eyes were fixed on the moon-silhouetted tree branches with their reckless leaves bumping into each other outside our window.

There were many times since Ma and Papa died that I just wanted to go home and sit in front of the fireplace, eat at our table and sleep in my bed up in the loft Caleb and I shared. But on this night the urge to be back in our old place was overwhelming. If only I could spend one night there, alone with Wedge.

I often imagined owning our parents' spread and working hard to finish the barn Papa had started. Recently, Wedge has been a part of that vision. He and I would be running Gramps' cattle through the large fenced meadows and mountains connecting our two ranches.

The longer I laid there thinking about my home, the more convinced and determined I became. Wedge had never been to my folks' cabin, and tomorrow night might be his only chance. I'd have to gather a few food items, since the canned goods still on Mama's shelf wouldn't interest Wedge. Everything else is in place. The beds are made and the firewood is stacked outside the back door, just like Ma and Papa left them the day they drove away to celebrate their anniversary.

I could sneak out after everyone falls asleep and hike the short distance over the mountains. The moon will be full and I should have no problem getting home. I'd leave a note on the bottom bunk and promise to be back by the time Mr. Olson arrives. I didn't dare mention my plan to Caleb. His mouth keeps great secrets. But again, it's those darned eyes that inform others that something is up.

With my plan intact, I fell asleep.

All morning Wedge worked hard at distracting me from Yank. He would wiggle his way in between Yank and me, much like he used to do on Betty's chow line. Once again Caleb took turns with me to insure Yank wouldn't have a lapse in memory. He gave me the extra time I needed to prepare for my overnight stay at our old home. Before the noon meal I had managed to hide a little dog food and jerky in a gunny sack and drop it into a metal grain barrel.

After eating dinner, Grandma gave all four of us free rein to spend a few hours in our fort. Each of us grabbed a pup and headed up the hill. Of course, Yodel didn't last long in Luke's small grip. So, with Wedge and Yodel hanging on for dear life, I became the caboose behind our slow procession up the trail.

Our fort was perfect. The stout door sealed out all the uninvited varmints. I lit the two mounted candles and left the door open so we'd have plenty of light. It worked out nicely for the pups too. They were in and out a bunch of times until they settled on a sunny spot just outside the door to curl up together and nap.

The work crew left us plenty to do. Gramps said it was only right that we clean up after them. All of us chipped in and threw all the scrap wood pieces in a pile outside. Grandma had donated an old broom. Eva and Caleb took turns using it to sweep the packed earth. Luke made himself busy by climbing on top of the table and shelf to give them a "once over" with his cleaning rag.

We were all surprised to hear Grandma asking permission to enter. She had hiked up with a basket slung over her arm. "Look what Goldilocks brought the four little bears."

"You too big to be Goldilocks, and there only three bears," corrected Luke.

"Okay. I guess I'm in the wrong place. I'll just head on out-a here and see if I can find them," Grandma said as she turned to leave.

"No, no!" Eva, Caleb and I shouted.

"Hmm, I guess you three have better noses than that little bear. Maybe he doesn't want any cookies and milk," Grandma responded looking at Luke.

"I smell cookies too," insisted Luke.

"Well, looks like I'm in the right place after all."

Grandma set the basket on the table and pulled out a large cloth napkin full of warm chocolate chip cookies. The cold milk made the trip safely in a large glass milk bottle. She took out five small tin cups and a damp towel to wipe our grubby hands. We all gathered around the table, sitting on our mismatched stools or wooden nail kegs.

"Happy Days!" Grandma cheered as she raised her cup of milk to our extended cups. We wasted no time wiping out the unexpected treats. It wasn't long before four furry bodies came waddling in for a tasty morsel. Grandma agreed they could each have one small bite-size piece.

"This place is looking great," Grandma complimented.

"I cleaned table and shelf," bragged Luke.

"You did a fine job, Luke. Do you think you could skip a nap today and help some more?"

Luke's eyes looked almost as big as Caleb's when he blurted out, "Oh yeah, Grandma. They need me here."

"In that case you can all stay for another hour. I'll take this stuff back home to clean. Don't forget to blow out the candles and close the door tight when you leave."

With the treat to energize us, we had the fort in tiptop shape in no time at all. We blew out the candles and shut the door. Each of us picked up a puppy for the downhill trek. I decided Yodel would live to see another day if, instead of Luke carrying her, I did. He had a hard enough time staying on his feet without anything else in his hands. I'd say he usually did about half the journey down the mountain on his fanny. Surprisingly, he didn't wear his britches out enough to reveal skin on his chubby backside.

Caleb and I got right back to training Yank once we were in the barn again. I had Eva take Wedge in the house with her so he wouldn't interfere. Caleb commented on how we could work with Yank again in the morning before Mr. Olson got here. I didn't say anything. Agreeing would be just like lying to him.

That evening I was surprised that everybody contributed to the conversation around the supper table. There was no mention of Mr. Olson or the prospect of losing Wedge. We talked about our fort and how Grandma joined us with cookies and milk.

Caleb and I went right to work washing dishes, pots and pans. Thursday was the night we had picked to clean the kitchen when Ma and Papa were alive. We continued the household task with Gramps and Grandma. On this night it gave me the chance to snatch up some leftovers. I wrapped a couple of pieces of sliced cheese and two freshly baked rolls in one of my clean hankies. I hid the small bundle in my coat pocket, hanging on the mudroom wall. It would be easier to grab on my way out the door later that night.

Everyone went quietly to their spots in the house. Gramps settled in his large leather chair with the light from a floor lamp shining over his shoulder onto the newspaper he read. Grandma sat across the room mending clothes. While sprawled out on the living room rug, Eva tried teaching Luke how to play the *Old Maid* card game. Caleb and I finished kitchen duty and headed outside to round up the pups. Once they were all fed, I grabbed Wedge and shut the others securely in their shed.

Darkness rushed in, blacking out our little valley. It wasn't long before the four of us were bathed and jumping into bed. Once again Wedge was snoozing alongside me when Grandma came in to read and say prayers. She made no comment, and she even pecked the top of Wedge's head when she handed out the bedtime kisses to Caleb and me. "Things always seem to work out, Ezra. Sweet dreams," she whispered as she hugged me.

I was afraid to doze off and miss my chance to take Wedge home for the night. Caleb tried to talk, but I told him I needed some sleep.

Gramps and Grandma turned in for the night about an hour later. Much like the night the pups were born, I waited for the snoring down the hall to break the still silence.

Carefully, I crawled out of bed. Caleb and Wedge didn't even twitch as I pulled my pants and shirt on over my long-johns. Wedge let out a small grunt when I slowly pulled him from the bed and pressed him close to my chest. By covering him with another shirt I had hoped he would be content enough to continue sleeping soundly. After heading out the door into the hallway, I stopped short and retraced my steps. I returned to my room and, out of a book on top of the chest of drawers, pulled the note I had written earlier. Quietly I placed the paper on the lower bunk.

Walking along the edge of the hallway was almost a guarantee the wooden floorboards wouldn't sound off. The stairs were tricky too, but I remembered the places to avoid from the up and down sneaking Caleb and I did seven weeks earlier.

Betty jumped up to greet me when I entered the mudroom. Her presence was enough to wake Wedge. I quickly took the hanky of food from my coat and coaxed her to lay back down with one of the dinner rolls. Once we squeezed our way out the screen door I took in a lungful of night air and scampered down the steps. Wedge was wide awake by this time. He seemed to sense my urgency and remained mute.

The moon was right on time. It had just cleared the top of the mountains to the east. I didn't dare stop until entering the barn where I could put on my boots and jacket. Everything was going according to plan. My last stop was the grain barrel. I reached in and grabbed the gunnysack. With the lid back in place, Wedge and I started on our way.

CHAPTER 10

Going Home

I DECIDED I WOULD CARRY Wedge all the way home. He was still small enough to ride up front under my jacket. I rigged my belt around the outside of the coat to keep him from slipping down and to allow my hands freedom to carry our food sack. The top two buttons were opened to give Wedge headroom and fresh air.

My heart was pumping double-time. Every bone, muscle, brain cell and nerve told me I was doing the right thing. As I climbed the corral fence and swung my right leg over the top rail, a shadow moved away from the back of the barn. Al's voice brought everything to an abrupt halt. "And where do you think you're goin', young man?"

I sat silently straddling the fence with Wedge's head hanging out of the partially buttoned jacket. My mind was numb and my eyes were frozen on Al's uneven gait as he walked toward me in the moonlight. He said no more until he was standing in front of me. I looked down from my elevated position into those kind old eyes set in among weathered creases. Al put his hand on my knee and asked quietly why I had Wedge and what was I planning on doing.

Trying to muster up courage, I decided to tell Al about my plans for the night. He listened intently without interrupting. When I was finished he spoke. "I can't let you do this, Ezra. There are all kinds of varmints out there just waitin' for a helpless creature to cross their path. In this case there are two of you. Wedge is in danger too."

"Please let me go. It might be the only chance I'll have to show Wedge my home. I left a note, and besides, I'll be back tomorrow in time for Mr. Olson."

"No sir, I can't do that. But, we can saddle up Dolly and Moses. I'll take along a rifle for protection. It'll be faster and safer, givin' you more time alone with Wedge at your place. You can keep Moses with you in the corral for the night. It won't take you long to hightail it back here by noon tomorrow. That'll give me plenty of time to convince your grandparents you are safe and calm them down a might. It makes a heap-of-a-lot more sense than turning my back and lettin' you walk there by yourself."

Al was right. Holding back tears I said, "Okay, let's saddle up."

Within minutes we were mounted and heading up the trail. There was a bit of a chill in the air, but Wedge's warm body was better than a hot water bottle snug against my chest.

Al whistled and talked most of the way, which was out of character. He said, "You never want to sneak up quietly on a wild animal. They hate surprises. Give them a little warnin' and they'll head in another direction."

The moon radiated its glow as far as the eye could see. The bark of the aspen trees looked as though they were sources of light. Water flowing from the stream gave the impression of millions of small, metal disks catching the reflection from the bright night sky as they moved on their way down between the soft, overgrown banks.

"You sure picked the perfect night to go horseback ridin'. This is right up there with a few of my most memorable rides. You'd be hard pressed to find a more beautiful sight." Al did his best to make conversation. I started feeling grateful for his presence and realized my initial plan was not wise.

Moses and Dolly made their way around boulders and up steep paths without any reining. It seemed as though they were in no hurry, but I could see we were making good time. As we reached the flat area beyond the first ridge, the horses instinctively wanted to run. It was the straight-a-way where we often galloped, and flat out ran our horses, when Caleb and I rode double with Ma and Papa. It was kind of traditional to let your mount kick up their heels at this spot. Gramps said he always had a rip-roarin' time here. Fortunately, Al was in the lead and kept Dolly at a walk.

In less than an hour we looked down and spotted the moonlight being cast back from our cabin's tin roof. Al turned his shadowed face toward me and spoke softly. "Your ma and papa sure did right buildin' their home at the end of the road. And I don't blame you for wantin' to be here."

Wedge had fallen asleep long before we reached the ridge. Al guided Dolly to a side and told me to lead the way down the embankment. Moses didn't hesitate. I was confident our sure footed horses would deliver us safely. I gave him his head and he carefully picked his way between the rocks and through the trees. Wedge woke up during our descent. He poked his head out and reached up to lick my chin. After hitting level ground, Al trotted alongside us. He chuckled when he caught sight of Wedge. "That dang dog still looks like a kangaroo ridin' in his mama's pouch. His ears even look the part."

"Yeah, well he'll grow into them along about the same time his body catches up to his feet."

Al and I stepped down from our saddles and flipped the reins around the hitching post in front of the porch. I took Wedge and the food sack into the house. Al followed. He located the wooden matches, lit the kerosene lantern on the mantel and took a quick look around. "I best be headin' back. There's still a chance I'll grab me some shuteye before Tonto blasts off. It looks like you have everything you'll need for the night."

"Thank you, Al."

I set Wedge down and went to shake his outstretched hand. After taking his firm grip I wrapped my arms around his belt line and hugged his thin, half crippled body. "You be careful gettin' back. Tell Gramps and Grandma I'll be there in plenty of time for dinner."

He gently squeezed me and then gave his eyes a quick wipe with the top of his hand. After patting my back he turned and walked out the door. I closed Wedge in the house and stood on the porch while Al mounted Dolly.

"Get Moses tended to and build yourself a nice fire. I'll see you tomorrow." After taking a few steps he turned in his saddle and said, "And Ezra, try to get some sleep."

CHAPTER 11

Our Time Alone

Moses wanted to go with Al and Dolly. He danced around a bit and pulled against the reins as I held firm and led him in the opposite direction. The pond water satisfied his thirst and was enough to calm his nerves. Turning, we continued on to the barn. Papa had figured two more days would have been enough to finish it. Now, as I walk toward the dark structure, I'm reminded of a time not so long ago.

The small stack of hay that was once outside the corral was now gone, thanks to the deer, elk and moose roaming the area. Fortunately, there would be ample hay inside the barn, protected from freeloaders by the large hinged doors. Moses walked willingly beside me. He had spent many days and nights in our corral when my folks were alive. He entered through the wooden gate and stood motionless as I released the cinches on the safety and girth straps. The sawhorse was waiting inside the barn ready to receive the saddle and blanket. I returned to Moses and gently removed the bridle over his ears and out of his mouth. Once it was hung on a peg next to the saddle, I fetched a large armful of hay and dropped it on the ground in front of him. I found a curry comb on a horizontal two-by-four inside the barn and went back to Moses to brush him down as he ate. "Thanks for the ride home. I'll leave a stall door open for you in case you want to sleep inside tonight. We'll be headin' back tomorrow. See ya in the mornin'."

The closer I got to the house the better I could hear Wedge yapping. He was beside himself being left alone in a strange place. He ran out the door as soon as it opened. "You're okay, Wedge. Go take a look around. This was my home, the one I've been tellin' you about. It's the place I want us to have and work on together some day."

We spent a good half hour outside while he marked his territory, ran after shadows and sniffed every nook and cranny on the porch and foundation. The night air was getting pretty chilly and we were losing moonlight quickly. "Come on Wedge. It's time to haul a little wood inside and start a fire."

It had been a while since I'd built a fire here. There was plenty of old weeklies and seasoned wood available. After opening the damper, I went right to work bunching up paper and creating a teepee around it with kindling. We soon had a blazing fire. Wedge settled for a meal of jerky and dry dog food. I passed on eating. Nothing sounded good and my appetite was at a standstill.

Wedge had enough excitement for one day. He licked himself the best he could and curled up next to me on the rug in front of the hearth. I laid there petting his soft coat and thought about how wonderful it would be to move back home someday. I knew it wouldn't be for quite a while. But the desire to finish what my folks set out to do, and to live in the place I love most, was a force to reckon with. There was no doubt in my mind that Wedge would be the luckiest dog alive if he could stay in these mountains with me and end his days right here.

We warmed up in no time at all, one of the fringe benefits to having a small house. Looking up I noticed the loft's door was open. All this heat would soon engulf our sleeping area. There's not much in the way of head room up there. Papa made a raised short frame for our mattress. All our clothes were kept in shallow wooden boxes we slid under the bed. The two crates that hold our toys at Gramps and Grandma's house used to be pushed against one of the low, side loft walls.

It felt natural laying on the familiar floor once again and watching the flames in the fireplace dance to sparks snapping and embers falling. Surprisingly, I was at peace, even though in a few short hours there was a good chance I'd have to hand Wedge over to Mr. Olson. The likelihood of him choosing Yank over Wedge was slim to none. Dwelling on that possibility would help no one. Instead I continued to stroke Wedge's small body and tell the sleeping dog about my dreams of the future.

"If I get to keep you I would do whatever I could to finish this place. We could live here and help Gramps enlarge his cattle ranch. I'd even try to get electricity brought in."

I got up to put more wood on the fire and place a screen in front of the opening to prevent sparks from jumping out. I blew out the kerosene lantern. With only the light from the flickering flames, I held Wedge in one arm as I climbed up the ladder to my old room. When Caleb and I used to turn in for the night Papa often said, "You can't climb the ladder of success with your hands in your pockets." I never gave those words much thought until now. I'm willing to fall at times, grab hold with both hands and then climb, using all my strength in order to reach my goal. I aim to run this ranch someday. Doin' it with Wedge would be a dream come true.

I found Caleb's and my bed the way we had left it months ago. Ma always insisted on us making the bed before eating breakfast. My side always looked tidier. Maybe it's because I'm older with more experience, or it could be that Caleb was always in a hurry to get down to breakfast. I'm not sure, but my guess is Caleb's stomach urged him to do bare minimum until he filled it with food.

I closed the small loft door behind me and, holding Wedge, crawled into my side of the bed. He made a few grunts but showed no sign of waking. The paned window over my head allowed a little light to spill down over us. My head laid comfortably on my pillow. Once again, I could gaze up into the massive starlit heavens.

Like I had done here so many times before, I said my prayers. "Please God, have Mr. Olson choose Yank. Don't let him take Wedge from me. I will always take good care of him and train him to earn his keep. I can't imagine handin' him over."

After my heartfelt plea I did something I thought impossible. I fell asleep. Exhaustion can be one's closest friend. I didn't have enough energy to even muster up a dream, at least one I could remember. Then, the next thing I knew, my eyes opened to a bright new day, with my hands still clasped together in prayer. Wedge began pushing his little paws against my side as he stretched himself awake.

"This is our big day. Do your best not to show off to Mr. Olson. Let Yank strut his stuff. He looks pretty good as long as you aren't there to show him up. I figure we'll feed Moses and eat breakfast before headin' back. Hopefully, Al will have had time to smooth over any rough edges with Gramps and Grandma. At least they know we're safe, thanks to Al."

Wedge ran around outside the cabin. He stopped shortly by the pond to dab his feet and quench his thirst. Then he raced past me to the barn. Moses was waiting patiently by the gate for his morning meal. Wedge showed no hesitation entering the barn once I opened the doors. With a pitchfork I jabbed some loose hay and threw it in to Moses.

"Good morning, Moses. How was your night? We'll be headin' back in a couple of hours. Eat up."

"Come on Wedge. I'll fix us a good breakfast and show you around."

I fired up the cook stove and checked Ma's small pantry for something to eat. There were still two jars of Ma's homemade jam on a shelf. I also found one lone can of Spam, which would go nicely heated up with the cheese and remaining roll I brought. In no time at all Wedge and I had consumed a delicious meal. While he did his best to lick himself clean, I tidied the kitchen.

We had a bit of time left before having to saddle up Moses. Wedge was always in for an adventure, so we headed off to the far side of the pond. There were fresh moose and elk tracks. Papa used to take Caleb and me out by the pond to point out the variety of prints left in the mud by our thirsty neighbors. We got pretty good at identifying what animals visited during the night.

Next, we tried our luck climbing the steep rock outcropping behind the barn. After getting about a third of the way up I decided it wasn't the wisest thing to do. Wedge couldn't stretch his little body far enough to get a good footing and I needed both my hands to pull myself up to the next level. If I should fall and get hurt, it would be a while before anyone would come searching for me. And if Wedge got hurt I would never forgive myself, not to mention how Gramps, Grandma and Mr. Olson would feel.

Slowly, I inched my way back down the jagged rocks. I'd get about shoulder level with Wedge when I would pick him up and set him down by my feet. Repeating this process, we worked our way back to solid ground.

It was time to gather up the few things I left in the house and saddle Moses. Wedge was eager to get back to the cabin. He followed me as I picked up my belongings and made sure the fire in the stove was out and the damper shut. He seemed very much at home, so much so that he looked surprised and confused when I called him and turned to head outside again. I slung my coat over my shoulder, took one more look around and closed the door.

We sat for a few minutes on the top step as I ruffled up the soft hair between his ears. "Hopefully you'll be comin' back here with me soon. And, hopefully, this place will be ours someday. We best be gettin' back before everyone drives up lookin' for us."

The tears couldn't hold on another moment. They let go and fell one after another onto Wedge's head. His ears tried flicking them away, but they kept falling with precision. I pulled him up and kissed his wet ears. "Please let this be one of those perfect days."

I did my best to dry Wedge off with the front of my shirt. Then we headed for the barn.

Moses was waiting by the gate as if to say, "I've been ready for a long time. Let's get goin'."

Standing on a small wooden box, I was able to lift the saddle to its rightful place atop Moses. He took the bit into his mouth easy enough as I raised the leather straps of the bridle back over his ears. Once again, Wedge settled snugly into my jacket's makeshift carrier. With a little nudge from both of my heels, Moses started back up the trail.

CHAPTER 12

Headin' Back

IT WAS A BEAUTIFUL AUGUST morning. All the day creatures seemed to come out to bid their greetings and farewells. Halfway up to the ridge, flies were already settling over bear scat left a few hours earlier. Moses laid his ears back when we approached the scent. I spoke softly to him as I rubbed the left side of his thick neck, urging him to keep moving.

Once we climbed the first mountain I turned Moses and stopped him for a breather. Wedge and I took in the view. My eyes combed over the near-by mountains and slowly gazed down at three meadows divided by a small stream and clusters of mixed trees. The cabin sat on higher ground overlooking the grassy field closest to us. Ma had always said she felt as though our cabin had open arms, welcoming us back after being away. It now seemed to wave a friendly goodbye and invite to come back soon.

"I guess we should get a move-on before we see dust billowing up on the road behind Gramps' pickup." Nudging Moses with my heels and reining to the right, we proceeded southeast along the familiar cow path.

We took a short break after crossing the high mountain stream. Moses drank a little water and clipped a few blades of tender grass while I set Wedge down and took off my much unneeded jacket. The day was already heating up. Luckily, I had enough water left in my canteen to reach the ranch. I forgot all about refilling it at our cabin.

"You're goin' to have to ride in the saddlebag, little boy. I'm not puttin' you in my shirt this time. Your nails are enough to scar a person for life."

The saddlebag was a perfect solution for our travel needs. I tied the flap up so Wedge could look out and I stuffed my jacket in the opposite bag. I set it up and around the saddle horn so as to keep an eye on my little partner. A fallen tree became my boost up to the stirrup. We were on our way once again.

The closer we got to the ranch the more butterflies joined the swarm in my belly. My hand holding the reins was shaking and my chin began to quiver as Moses stood motionless, allowing me time to peer down onto the ranch.

After a few minutes, I clicked the roof of my mouth with my tongue and gently pushed my heels into Moses' sides. He was eager to return to the corral. I did my best to keep him from picking up speed as we made our way down the steep slope. Halfway marked the location of our cave. I looked to my right to see if, by any chance, the door was open, indicating Eva and Caleb being there. I knew Grandma would never allow Luke to play in the fort without me. The door was closed.

I have to say, by the time we reached level ground I was a total wreck. No one was in sight. I had no preconception on what to expect. But I didn't expect the ranch yard to be empty of all two legged creatures. The animals had been fed and were content in their designated areas. Betty ran up to greet us as we crossed the bridge. Her tail was wagging as her front feet danced the two-step. Wedge was whining to get down and Moses was bitin' at the bit to get the customary grain treatment and rubdown.

I rode to the nearest fence and slid onto the top rail. Wedge practically jumped into my arms as I raised them up to take him from the saddlebag. I led Moses through the opened corral gate, tied him to a post and immediately started taking his saddle off. Wedge followed my every move. He helped me fill the grain sack and was at my feet as I hung the sack's rope behind Moses' ears.

Moses chomped away on the kernels as I brushed the patch of sweat that had formed under the saddle blanket. Every few minutes I would look around to see if Al, Ben, Gramps or anyone was around. It was unnerving. I couldn't remember another time when at least one person wasn't out working on something or one of us kids out playing. It wasn't even Luke's nap time yet. Where was everyone?

I put Moses in to graze with the other horses. Looking down at Wedge I said, "Well, looks like this is it. Hopefully you're too tired to make much of an impression on Mr. Olson."

We headed for the house. An unfamiliar truck parked under a tree caught my eye. That's when my heart sunk to its lowest level. Wedge, Betty and I started up the back steps.

"You two stay out here. I'll face the music alone." I squatted down and, holding my hands on each side of Wedge's head, I kissed him on his noggin. He looked at me as if to say, "What's with that?"

Quietly I opened the screen and entered the mudroom. I hung my hat and pulled off my boots. Although I'm usually reminded to wash my hands, I did it then without prompting. Anything to waste time.

I could hear muted words coming from an unfamiliar voice in the living room. Suddenly there was laughter and the talking multiplied.

"Here goes nothin'."

I opened the door to the kitchen and all the speaking stopped. Every eye turned my way. Caleb, Eva and Luke sat on their knees around the coffee table protecting their glasses of milk and a dish filled halfway with muffins. Al and Ben were on the stairway. They had each chosen their own step to sit on and were leaning against opposite banisters. Gramps and Grandma sat comfortably in their large chairs on either side of the fireplace. Sitting on the couch were a man and a woman. I took them as being Mr. and Mrs. Olson.

"Hi, Ezra. Come on in. How was your little trip back home?" asked Gramps.

"Pour yourself some milk and join us for some fresh baked muffins," Grandma suggested.

I glanced quickly at Al. His eyes told me to calm down. Ben just had a stupid grin, revealing only the teeth on the right side of his mouth. I then looked at Gramps. His blue eyes showed no anger or agitation. Grandma was no surprise, with her sweet, nonjudgmental smile. Luke turned to eat more of his muffin while Eva and Caleb just sat there grinning at me. Mr. and Mrs. Olson looked like any couple stopping by for a friendly visit.

Letting my breath escape slowly, I walked over to retrieve a glass and poured myself some milk.

"Sit here," Caleb said as he scooted closer to Eva and opened up a spot at the coffee table.

I walked over and set my milk down in the offered location.

Looking at Mr. and Mrs. Olson, Gramps said, "This is my oldest grandson, Ezra."

Mr. Olson stood up and extended his hand. I reached over, offering mine. We shook hands and looked into each other's eyes. He held my grip firmly and said, "I'm glad to meet you, Ezra."

I heard only warmth and sincerity in his deep voice and saw a gentle quality in his dark brown eyes.

"Glad to meet you too, Sir," I lied.

"This is my wife, Mrs. Olson," he said, nodding at the woman to his left.

Because she didn't extend her hand, I only nodded to her and said, "Pleased to meet you, Mam."

Her smile was contagious. I smiled back and then lowered myself to the floor next to Caleb. I tried to appear unshaken and cordial. I reached for a muffin and took a bite.

"Mr. Olson was just telling us about his eleven grandchildren and how they all go to their ranch a few times a year." Grandma went on to say, "He has a grandson your age who loves dogs too. It sounds like they are all a bunch of characters like the four of you."

"Let's pray they're not," Ben laughed. Everyone but me joined in.

"As soon as you kids finish your milk and muffins we can take the Olson's out to meet the pups," Gramps said as he stood with his coffee cup in hand.

As if on cue, Al and Ben got to their feet, placed their cups on the counter and exited through the mudroom. It was then I realized my blunder. I should have put Wedge in with the other pups so as to not draw attention to him. I quickly gulped down my milk and, surprising Caleb, put the rest of my muffin on his napkin. I think my hat and boots were on before the Olson's even got up off the couch.

Faithful Wedge was waiting for me right outside the screen door. "Come on, Wedge." We ran to the enclosed dog yard and I pushed his defiant little body through the gate.

There are times when things don't go according to plan. This was one of those times. Wedge threw a raging fit that beat all others. He barked, jumped up on the wire fencing, ran around yapping as though he'd sat in a hornet's nest and began digging under the fence's frame. The other pups looked at him like he'd gone plum loco. I thought about taking him back out until I looked behind me and saw Gramps, Grandma, Eva, Caleb and Luke heading my way. With them were Mr. and Mrs. Olson.

CHAPTER 13

Losing Two Pups

"LOOKS LIKE THAT LITTLE GUY wants out right now," Mr. Olson laughed.

I decided to open the gate and let all nine pups have their freedom. Then maybe Wedge would blend in better. They all ran and yipped anxiously once they saw what my intentions were. Luke laid flat on his back to show how the puppies jumped on his prone position. Caleb was quick to point out Yank as being one of the boy dogs. He waded through the frenzied fury bodies and captured Yank for Mr. Olson's inspection. Mr. and Mrs. Olson squatted down to receive Yank just as Wedge decided to display his competitive spirit and rear up, planting his big paws on Mrs. Olson's lap.

"You look to be the other boy pup," she said.

"Yeah, you got both of them now," Gramps pointed out.

I stood there speechless and unable to move. Then Caleb said, "Let me show you what Yank can do. Put Yank down please, Mr. Olson, and I'll give him a couple of commands."

Mr. Olson set Yank down on all fours and Caleb gave the order, "Come". Yank was quick to respond. Unfortunately, Wedge obeyed the same order and reached Caleb first. With the second command, "Sit", they both sat in unison. Caleb's eyes shot up at me. I felt totally helpless and discouraged.

"What else can they do?" asked Mrs. Olson.

"That's just about it for now," answered Caleb. "Rebel is learnin' how to come and sit too, but she's not as fast. We're tryin' to get them to stay when we walk away. But, it ain't goin' too good."

"Really? Which one is Rebel?" Mr. Olson asked as he looked over at the gang of girl pups.

Luke sat up and lifted Rebel over his head for the Olson's to see. "This one is Rebel," he announced.

"Mr. Olson might be taking two dogs home with him today," Gramps said.

Could things get any worse? I stood there frozen in total disbelief, unable to move, talk, or think straight. How could Gramps agree to such a deal?

Al must have sensed my uneasiness. He came up from behind and patted my shoulder. Looking straight at me he whispered, "Hang in there, Ez."

Mr. and Mrs. Olson spent a lot of time checking out all the pups. Wedge scored points when he licked Mr. Olson's cheek. They would put each one down and walk away to see if any would follow. Otis and Rebel were right on their heels. Yank and Wedge were close behind. It was out of my hands. I wanted to walk away. If this was a circus side show, Wedge would definitely be the star clown. He was on a roll, drawing attention to himself and causing much laughter.

It was unbearable. I turned around and headed for the barn. Wedge was at my feet in an instant. "Call Wedge, Caleb," I yelled. Tears were streaming down my face and I didn't dare turn around for everyone to see my pain.

Ben strutted over and picked Wedge up. In a hushed voice he said, "Take it easy. It ain't over yet."

Once inside the barn I ran into an empty stall, slid my back down the wall, covered my face with my hands and wept. I could hear Wedge barking and trying to get back to me. Later I found out that Gramps had to use Luke's belt as a collar in order to control the little scamp.

I didn't want to hear what was going on outside the barn, but sound found its way through the old, gray boards.

"Let me see that little guy," came Mr. Olson's voice. "You're one smart little feller, aren't you? How did you come up with a name like Wedge?"

Then came Caleb's response, "Ezra named him because of the black wedge shape on the top of his shoulder blades. He also wedged his way in for milk right from the start."

"Hmm, I think he likes me. Or maybe he has a hankering for my shaving cream," Mr. Olson chuckled.

"Look at the size of those paws," observed Mrs. Olson.

"Yeah, he's bound to be a big boy," Mr. Olson said.

I couldn't take it. Between covering my ears and everybody walking toward the house, I didn't hear any more of their conversation.

It seemed as though I was alone in the stall for about a half hour before I heard Mr. Olson's truck doors slam shut and the motor start. Everyone shouted their good-byes as the old Ford was put into gear. The tires moved slowly over the gravel, making the familiar crunching sound. I heard the clanking of timber as it rolled across the bridge. I sat motionless, listening until no sounds could be heard except the routine barnyard noises. Getting up, I moved toward the opened barn door. Slowly, I walked out into the sunlight. Gathered before me, about twenty feet away, were Gramps, Grandma, Caleb, Eva, Luke and Ben. Stepping out from behind Gramps came Al, holding Wedge.

Everyone cheered while I stood in disbelief. Al set Wedge down and he mustered up the fastest run his little legs could travel into my waiting arms. He squirmed and licked at my salty tears. I laughed and cried without shame.

Everyone assembled around us and began talking at the same time. Eva told me that the Olson's took Yank and Rebel. We all knew they were going to a good home.

Once the commotion settled down, Al and Ben headed out back of the barn to continue their work and Grandma insisted on taking Caleb, Eva and Luke into the house to help with dinner. That left me standing there looking at Gramps with his no nonsense eyebrow raised.

"So you spent the night back at your cabin."

"Yes Sir."

"I don't need to tell you how glad I am that Al went with you."

"No Sir."

"Ezra, there are times you're goin' to have to listen to your common sense more than your heart. Emotions can get the best of you if you're not careful. I understand you needed to be alone with Wedge. I understand you wanted to be back home. What I don't understand is why you couldn't confide in us. We love you and only want happiness for all you kids."

Looking up at the sky and then back down at me he continued, "We'll let it go this time. But from now on we don't want to read a note about your intentions. We don't want to have Al tell us how it all panned out. We want to see you come to us and hear your voice. Together we'll work out the kinks. That's what family does."

"I'm sorry, Gramps. I didn't want to take a chance that you wouldn't let me go."

"This is your home now, Ez. This is where we all live, work and pray together. We'll call it the stepping stone between your past life and your future."

"I want my folks' place someday," I admitted.

"Well now, that's a possibility. Your folks wanted you kids to decide on your own futures, hopefully go to college so as to open more doors for careers. I don't believe in handouts, not for this family. My folks made sure I earned this ranch in order to appreciate it. Your folks were no different. They worked mighty hard for their section of land. They toiled relentlessly to build their cabin. What they really built was character. They were honest, hard-working people who stepped on no one to get to their goal."

"Do you think I can earn our ranch?"

"It's not just your ranch. You have three siblings who might have an interest in it too. Let's just say there's a good chance it can be yours someday. You have a long road to travel in the meantime, and your brothers and sister must be considered."

"Fair enough, Gramps. Right now I'm happy to have Wedge. And I'm happy to have you and Grandma raising us here at our new home."

When I looked up into Gramps' face it was obvious I struck a nerve. His blue eyes clouded over with tears. He bent over and we hugged until Wedge yelped at being sandwiched between us.

The dinner bell sounded and four sets of people legs headed for the house. Dogs were not permitted in while we were dining. It had something to do with sneaking food to them under the table.

When I entered the kitchen I noticed red circles around Grandma's eyes. Caleb told me after dinner that she had watched Gramps and me through the window above the sink.

It was announced that Wedge would be mine, and with him came responsibility. I had to take on extra chores to pay for his food and, with Al's help, train him to herd cattle. Al was an expert when it came to training dogs, but I knew Betty's example would go a long way.

We had quite a day. Wedge made no complaints when I placed him in his bed. He walked around in circles for the traditional dog-going-to-sleep ceremony and, without even attempting to clean himself, fell asleep.

Grandma came in to read the final chapter in *The Last of the Chiefs*. She then knelt next to the bed for prayers. Caleb always had plenty to say. It stood to reason why Ma and Papa called him "Short-story-long". Grandma added her thanks. Then I ended our prayers by thanking God for such a perfect day.

We kissed Grandma good night just as Gramps entered the room. He came over and ruffled our heads as he kissed each of our cheeks. "Good night you two, sweet dreams and don't let the bedbugs bite." Reaching down he patted Wedge's sleeping body.

The lamp was turned off and the door was closed enough to almost block the light coming in from the hallway. Caleb hung his head over the edge of the bed and asked how long I'd be on the bottom bunk now that Wedge is staying.

"He'll be potty trained soon. Then I'll move back up to the top bed," was my reply.

"You don't have to do my chores anymore. You have enough to do to pay for the food Wedge eats. I'll help you train him too, if you want."

"Thanks. And thank you for all your help with Yank. Wedge would have been a goner if you didn't draw attention to Yank today."

Then Caleb let me in on a secret. He said Gramps made a deal with Mr. Olson before I returned this morning with Wedge. Gramps told Mr. Olson he could take two dogs, Yank and a female, if he didn't take Wedge. It was still Mr. Olson's choice, but Gramps was trying to sway him by "sweetening the pot". "Mr. Olson understood how you felt about Wedge and said Yank would be enough, but Gramps wouldn't have it."

I whispered back, "Did you hear them talkin'?"

"Nope. Eva was settin' the muffins on the plate in the kitchen when she listened in on their conversation."

"I bet Al and Ben knew about the deal Gramps made with Mr. Olson."

"Probably," Caleb answered.

"We best get some sleep. I'll have another busy day tomorrow."

I leaned over to pet Wedge. Without speaking I promised him we would own our ranch someday and I would work hard to make Gramps and Grandma proud of both of us.

CHAPTER 14

Betty

After Mr. Olson got the pick of the litter the other pups were sold in rapid order, all except Yodel. She was an exceptionally smart dog, but people are funny when it comes to selecting the runt. I suppose the men who put up hard earned money for cattle dogs correlate size with quality.

Luke did his darnedest to convince Gramps we needed Yodel on the ranch. He badgered, pleaded, cried, pouted and stomped around while Gramps ignored, smiled, shook his head and walked away. As it turned out, Gramps was ahead of the game and had already decided to keep her. He could always recognize natural skills in animals. Yodel was the spittin' image of Betty as a pup. Gramps knew size didn't always equate to speed. Yodel had heart. She would prove herself worthy, alright.

One day Grandma had finally had enough. "Luke, stop that moping around. Does it look like Yodel is going anywhere? Has Gramps said he's selling her? Has anyone come and taken an interest in her?"

"What do you mean?" asked Luke.

"I mean we're all tired of your complaining and whining. Otis was the last pup that was sold, and that was over a week ago. Gramps is taking no more calls. Try asking Gramps, like a big boy, if Yodel is staying and see what he says."

With that suggestion, Luke ran outside to confront Gramps as he climbed down from the tractor. All of us followed.

Looking up into Gramps' face, Luke strained to appear big. With hands on his hips and his eyes squinted against the sun, he asked in his unusually deep voice, "Are we keepin' Yodel?"

Gramps had little choice but to smile. He went down on one knee in order to make the playing field somewhat level. He placed his hands on Luke's shoulders and simply said, "Yes".

We were all glad to hear it. As the three of us voiced our excitement, Luke leaped into Gramps' arms and kissed him. "Oh thanks, Gramps. Thank you so much. Don't worry, I take care of her. She can sleep by me too."

"Hold your horses. Who said anything about another dog sleepin' upstairs? And Yodel is not your dog. She belongs to all of us."

"That okay. We talk about that later," Luke said as he pulled away and ran to find Yodel, undoubtedly to give her the good news.

So we went from one dog to having three. It was decided that we would have no more pups. "Gettin' rid of those money makers is not worth dealin' with all the heartache and drama," announced Gramps. "Ben will be takin' Betty to town tomorrow to see the vet. The other two will be goin' in a few more months."

"You mean Wedge will have to go to the vet?" I stammered.

"That's exactly what I mean. It'll be easier on him than the two females, Ez. Wedge and Yodel need to be about six months old first," informed Gramps.

"Can I go with Ben?" I asked.

"Sure, but you might end up sittin' a while in the waitin' room."

"Nah, I got some business to tend to," said Ben. "Ezra can go with me into town to pick up some supplies. We can take your food list with us too," he offered, looking at Grandma.

"Can I go too?" asked Caleb.

"It's okay with me, but just you two," was Ben's response.

I was glad Caleb wanted to go. I felt pretty darn lucky to have a dog of my own. Each of us had our favorites. It made me feel awkward and downright guilty ever since Goober was taken from Caleb's arms. He had cried himself to sleep that night. The next day I gave back the bottom bunk so he could be nearer Wedge. Every night since then I would peer down and see Caleb's outstretched arm reaching to pet my dog.

Caleb never questioned the fairness of it all. He was happy for me and I was happy to share Wedge with him.

Eva was easier to console when Otis was taken to Tucker's ranch. He was our closest neighbor and Eva knew she could go visit Otis any time. She didn't hesitate to shake her finger at Tucker and demand him to protect Otis from mountain lions.

Caleb and I were up early the next day. We hustled outside to get our chores done before breakfast. Grandma put the list of needed items in my back pocket along with money to purchase them. "There's enough for all of you to stop by the drugstore for an ice cream cone," she offered.

"Thanks, Grandma," Caleb and I both responded.

"You two stay with Ben and mind your manners."

"They'll be fine, Anne," Gramps said as he entered the kitchen. "Betty is loaded up and Ben is anxious to get goin'. You'll be takin' the car instead of the pickup so Betty won't have dirt flyin' all over her comin' home after surgery."

"Can I take Wedge?" I pleaded.

"Why in the world do you want to drag Wedge along?" questioned Grandma.

"I just want him to get use to traveling."

"Are you sure you just don't want to be separated from him all day?" Grandma asked.

"If you plan on ridin' with me you two better get your little man boots in the car. I'm leavin'," announced Ben as he popped his head in the kitchen door.

"We're comin'!" shouted Caleb.

Grandma had packed us a lunch and filled our canteens with water. Caleb and I jumped in front with Ben. Grandma set Wedge on my lap as Gramps gave her a "What-the-heck?" look. I shut the door immediately. Soon Wedge's front paws were hanging out the rolled down window with his tongue dangling from his mouth. Betty had a bed made from old blankets in the rear of the station wagon.

"It looks like all the boys get the front seat," laughed Grandma. "The brains in the group has her own space to spread out and enjoy the ride in comfort."

"Can't argue with that," admitted Ben. "But what we lack in brains we make up in good looks."

"Yeah," laughed Caleb in agreement.

"Spare us the bad jokes so early in the day," Al retorted.

"See you at supper," said Ben. And with a smirk and a wink he added, "Thanks for pickin' up the slack while I'm gone, Al."

Al just shook his head, turned, mumbled something and headed to the barn.

Luke and Eva were excited to have the day to themselves. Grandma said they could help her put together some treats and eat them in the treehouse. "I hear tell those pesky bandits will be driven clean out of the territory today," she laughed, referring to our trip to town. Normally, Caleb and I would feel a little left out. But we knew ice cream cones were waiting for us in Fort Collins.

Everyone said goodbye. Ben got the usual "Drive careful", and we were on our way.

Wedge had never gone anywhere in the car before. He fit the tall order of riding shotgun to perfection. It wasn't long before his head was out the window and over the side mirror. I held his two back legs firmly to keep him from falling out. Wind blew his fuzzy hair back, showing small bald spots as it smashed his ears against his head. Once we hit level ground, Ben sped up.

"You might want to pull Wedge in, Ez. He's havin' a hard time breathin' in all that wind, and he might just bounce out."

Caleb grabbed his back legs while I reached out to yank his top half back through the window. Quickly, I rolled the glass up high enough so only his nose could fit through. Opening the small wing window allowed air to rush in and satisfy his need for wind in his face. He'd gasp, shake his head and go for more. He finally made his circle on my lap and settled down for a nap right before we hit pavement.

We headed straight for the vet. Betty looked fearful and was hesitant when Ben snapped the short lead rope onto her collar. "Come on, girl. You'll be okay." Betty jumped from the lowered tailgate and followed Ben into the vet's office. Caleb and I were close behind, along with Wedge in my arms.

"Put that dog in the car, Ezra. He needs to learn how to wait until we return. Just leave some windows open a good bit."

I knew Ben was right, but I didn't want Wedge out of my sight. Without a word, I took Wedge back and rolled two windows down enough he'd get air, but high enough to prevent an escape.

Wedge let the whole world, within hearing distance, know his disapproval. He howled, barked, whined, scratched, jumped and cried pitifully the entire time it took us to check our patient in and return to the car.

"Settle down, Wedge. You're goin' to be left in here a lot today. We have several stops to make before it's time to fetch Betty back," warned Ben.

Our first stop was the feed barn. It was a repeat performance by Wedge. Then we pulled over at the park to eat our lunch. Wedge was allowed out of the car to run and drink from the upright fountain. He had watched me gulp water bubbling up out of a hole in the center of a white porcelain ball. Then I held him up as Caleb turned the knob. The little guy had worked up quite a thirst. His tongue lapped at the cool water with a vengeance. He earned a corner of my sandwich and a small piece of meat from Caleb, which was a surprise and very generous of my food focused brother. We all sat and watched Wedge chase bird shadows and run squirrels up trees. After eating all Grandma had packed, we headed for the station wagon. Wedge was not going to be left behind. He passed us at full throttle and stood waiting at the car. I guess he saw how we left Betty and wanted no part of it.

We decided to stop for ice cream next. Store bought ice cream was practically unheard of in our family. We made our own by skimming cream that separated and floated on top of the milk and then adding sugar, vanilla and eggs. Grandma would pour the mixture into a metal tube with a wooden paddle inside, set the tube in the old ice cream bucket and then surround the metal with ice and rock salt. Everyone would take turns turning the hand crank attached to the tube and lid. The paddle on the inside was turned by the handle outside. The longer we cranked, the thicker the ice cream got. We always made vanilla because we could change it by adding fruit or chocolate syrup. The ice cream maker was pulled out every Fourth of July and then one more time, usually before school started up again in September.

The three of us stood looking over the ice cream counter trying to decide on our favorite flavor. There was vanilla, chocolate, strawberry and chocolate chip. Caleb and I agreed to disagree on flavors so we could share. I knew Caleb would choose vanilla, and he did. I guess I'm just as predictable because I asked for chocolate, although the chocolate chip was very tempting.

Ben was a good sport about letting both of us take first licks off his strawberry scoop. We jumped at the chance. Then we offered him to try our vanilla and chocolate. He said our eyes didn't seem to agree with the generosity spoken by our mouths. With a wink, he kindly declined.

I saved the pointed end of my sugar cone for Wedge. From the sound of it, he was adjusting to staying in the car alone. There were only a few dog noises coming from his direction.

When we went back outside we found his nose pushed through the wing window. His front paws began dancing around on the door's ledge when he spotted us walking his way. I wiggled the tidbit of a cone into his protruding mouth and pushed his head back into the car so I could open the door.

Grocery shopping went smooth enough. Caleb rode on the front of the cart while Ben pushed. I walked alongside while reading the list and throwing contents into the "food cage", as Gramps liked calling it.

Wedge was actually asleep on the front seat when we returned with the bags of groceries. "He finally gave up. I guess he figured we'll come back sooner or later," said Ben.

Our last stop was to pick up Betty. Ben warned us that she would have several stitches on her belly and would feel a bit under-the-weather. But nothing prepared us for what we saw. Ben carried her out to the car and placed her gently on the blankets in the back. She looked so weak and tired. Wedge sensed something was wrong and kept quiet and still.

"She'll probably sleep all the way home. By then she'll start feelin' the pain," said Ben.

Caleb and I hated to see Betty in such a sad state. But Ben was right. She fell asleep immediately and didn't open her eyes again until we pulled into our driveway.

CHAPTER 15

A Busy Schedule

BEN AND AL KEPT BETTY in the bunkhouse with them for a few nights so she didn't have to negotiate the porch steps to the mudroom. We all knew Ben would be of no help if she needed care during the night. Like Caleb, Ben could sleep through anything. Al would keep Betty close by and check on her periodically. His stiff joints kept him from long periods of sleep and his compassion for animals never took second place.

It was no surprise that Betty was a good patient. Within a couple of days she was getting around as if she never had surgery. Al gave her ten days and then removed the sutures. All of us kids looked on as he gently cut and pulled all but two of the small, knotted strings from her belly.

Looking up at me he asked, "How'd you like to remove the last two, Ezra?"

"Sure. I think I can do it."

Al handed me the miniature scissors and, kneeling down next to him, I clipped the last stitches. Gently, I pulled them from Betty's skin.

"Good job, Ez. You'll make a fine vet someday, if you choose to go on that path." And with that said, Al patted my back and slowly began his struggle up to a standing position.

Betty returned to the mudroom and Yodel seemed to find her way upstairs next to Luke's side of the bed.

"Gramps must be losing his edge," declared Grandma. "He never gave in to your ma, but you kids have put some kind of spell on him."

It wasn't long before Caleb and I began construction on another dog bed. We figured we'd give it to Luke for his birthday in early October. School was just around the corner and we knew that soon there wouldn't be much time for such precision work.

Our end of vacation time had been used wisely. After doing morning chores, we hiked up to the fort every day for the last two weeks of summer freedom. We knew once school started Eva and Luke would be confined to the main house, treehouse and barn. They seemed okay with that. Brave, they were not, when it came to venturing outside the barnyard without the protection of their older brothers.

Wedge and Yodel were big enough to lead the way up to our mountainside retreat. It looked great. We had all our homemade wooden rifles and hand guns leaning against the rock wall on display. Eva scrounged around and found mismatched dishes Grandma no longer needed. We made shelves from stacked wooden crates. As long as we were back down the trail and in the house to help with dinner, Grandma was patient with our need to play in the fort.

We used picks, crowbars, shovels and small trowels to cut away the hillside and create a walking path, about two feet wide, from the main trail to the cave's door. Caleb and I handled the larger rocks that were chipped from the high side and then moved, as support, to the lower edge of our project. Eva used a square shovel, with the handle cut down to a manageable length, to reroute all the loose dirt onto the path. Luke did his share of work using a trowel. He'd scoop up dirt and fill the two buckets that Caleb and I hauled and dumped wherever there was a low spot.

And so it went. Our summer ended, filled with planning and hours of cheap labor. Wedge was with me every step of the way, for the most part. He'd start out underfoot, but would eventually settle just inside the fort's cool doorway. He'd become an observer until the monotonous back and forth motion hypnotized him into joining Yodel in deep slumber. We would all be ready to call it quits by the time they'd wake with hunger pangs. Wedge's nonstop whimpering would cease once we headed for home. He and Yodel would run and tumble down the trail after us.

Ben came up to offer a hand every now and then when he had free time. It was his idea to spread wood chips on the top of our trail to keep it from eroding under heavy rain. Thanks to his manpower we were able to haul many gunnysacks of the shaved wood up to our somewhat level path. He truly enjoyed giving us his advice and muscle. I always felt bad that he couldn't spend as much time as we did just enjoying our fort, but he seemed okay with being a drop-in helper.

Walking up and down the mountain wasn't Al's idea of fun. He contributed in other ways. There were a couple of times when one of us would mention something at the dinner table, or just in passing, as being neat to have in our fort. Low and behold, Al would present it to us a few days later. The horseshoe gun rack was such an item. He welded it during one of his late, unpaid, overtime shifts. The idea came after Caleb had briefly talked about needing a place to hang our wooden rifles.

Then there was the time Eva had a hankering for a hutch in the fort. Within five days it stood, sanded and varnished, in Grandma's kitchen. Attached was a written order for Ben to haul it up to the fort.

Everyone had a part in our project. It goes back to the saying, "If you want something done, ask a busy person." We had always been around busy people, so working with our hands and keeping our minds active was something we understood. We got pretty creative making do with what we had and working hard if we wanted more. With that in mind, we valued and appreciated the time and things others gave us.

Betty began working once again with Gramps, Al and Ben. Lucky for her, we had Yodel to entertain Wedge. He'd chase, nip, pounce and harass poor Yodel until her growls turned into vicious snapping. Being the runt had no impact on her fearlessness.

"It's not personality, it's attitude," Ben insisted. "She's got one heck-of-a short dog's complex. Not even a brute like Wedge can take advantage of her size."

Yodel even scared Luke a few times when she turned on Wedge and Luke was in the mix. He learned to get out of the way and let her school down her larger sibling. It was comical how the smallest pup stayed on the offensive with the biggest. Wedge could have taken control, but he seemed to enjoy just getting a rise out of her.

The ice cream maker was pulled out for the second and last time that year. We were down to three days left of our summer vacation. School always started back up the day after Labor Day. Caleb and I had our starched and ironed shirts that Grandma made laying over new denim pants, waiting and ready for the first day of class.

There was never a question of who our teachers would be because they were the same ones who taught the same grades year after year. I guess, once they settled on teaching particular age groups, it was a life sentence. Two of them had taught our ma in the same rooms and at the same grade levels as we now found ourselves.

Come that Tuesday morning Gramps and Grandma decided to make a day of it. They took Eva and Luke along to drop Caleb and me off at school. They would head on to Ft. Collins and return for us in the afternoon.

Al held Wedge and had a firm grip on his collar as we drove away. Wedge fought hard to be released so he could follow our car. I had to turn my head to keep from watching his desperation. Spending all my time with Wedge had now come to an abrupt halt. He had been my shadow since he was old enough to walk. I swore to myself that someday we would do everything together. This was just one of the roads I had to travel on the map through life.

It was always fun seeing our old classmates again and, once in a while, there would be a newcomer. Our school was made up of three classrooms with usually two grade levels per room. Grades first through sixth were taught in the small building. Seventh graders and older had to go to Ft. Collins. We had swings, two killer slides, a dirt baseball field and a merry-go-round that Ma called a "death trap".

Of course, recess and lunch time were the best parts of the day. Even though Caleb was two years younger, he was in high demand when it came to kickball. Maybe it was the fact he inherited Ma's wide feet along with a squatty version of Papa's powerful legs that made him so explosive. I refer to him as being stubby, but Grandma always corrects me by saying he's compact. It didn't much matter. We were often on the same side, which rarely lost. Five kids were all we needed to make up a team. Naturally, we had to include girls when they wanted to play so they wouldn't whine to the teachers. Once in a while they'd surprise us with their hard kicks and speed. With a maximum population of thirty-five students in the entire school, we couldn't be too picky on team selections.

Each year the demands put on the poor souls who were forced to attend school were raised a few notches. Mrs. Murphy, my fourth grade teacher, was a doozy. I remember Ma telling me that old gal loved setting the bar high. I was afraid I'd be jumping all year long trying to reach it. But one thing for certain, if challenges keep life from being dull, it was shaping up to be a pretty exciting year.

Mrs. Murphy promised no homework on weekends unless we had assignments to make up. But, from the sound of it, she had no trouble piling it on during the week. You know when they say, "This too shall pass," well they didn't know Mrs. Murphy. All I could see was one long tunnel with no light at the end showing me the way out. Passing through it would take nine long months. If that first day in her class was any indication, I would be traveling at a snail's pace. That had to be one of the longest seven hours of my life.

The final bell broke my trance. I grabbed my things and was out the door, only to be stopped in my tracks by the long reach of Mrs. Murphy's right hand clasped to the back of my shirt collar. "Hold on there, Ezra. You can illustrate to the class how a gentleman holds the door open for all others to pass through first." Needless to say, I never attempted to make haste from class again.

I had to cool my heels once more when Caleb and I realized Gramps and Grandma were not waiting for us in the graveled parking lot. We stood peering down the paved road hoping to catch sight of the station wagon when a familiar sound came up from our rear. Sitting behind the wheel of his old black pickup and balancing a big eared pup across his lap and on the ledge of the window, was Al. As soon as he eased off the accelerator Yodel popped up from the passenger seat.

"You two look as though you might need a ride," he drawled.

"I thought Gramps and Grandma were pickin' us up," Caleb answered.

"They got their runnin' around done early, so I volunteered to get you two. Wedge and Yodel wanted to come along for the ride."

Nothing could have made us happier. Caleb and I threw our lunch pails and books into the cab, grabbed the pups and climbed into the truck's bed. Wedge was determined to lick the skin clean off my face. His excitement would have killed him had he been a dog with an older heart.

"Take it easy, Wedge. I missed you too."

Caleb had his hands full with Yodel. By the time we hit the dirt road we were backed up against the cab hanging on to the collars of both dogs. Yodel and Wedge stretched their upper bodies to watch the road from around the cab on opposite sides of the truck's bed.

My time with Wedge had been forever altered. My youth and the unforeseen years of school were not factored in when I first promised him life together on our own ranch.

CHAPTER 16

The Cattle Drive

I WAS WRONG ABOUT TIME going slow. And I was wrong about Mrs. Murphy. She was demanding and unsympathetic to anyone not pulling their own weight, whatever weight they were able to pull. Like Gramps, her expectations were high, but she didn't shy away from a heavy workload herself. Her unique style made our class alert and eager.

Using fake checks and pretend bills, I learned a lot about how to budget money and balance a checkbook. I read about Indian tribes who fought for their right to live in this area. We followed up our lesson by visiting a local ranch where a major battle between the Cherokee and Utes took place. We studied early trappers and settlers who endured great hardships. Then we prepared and ate field rabbits and a rattlesnake as was described in a homesteader's diary.

Mrs. Murphy tapped into our artistic abilities by setting easels in strategic locations outside the playground's perimeter and within nature's scenic studio. She also encouraged us to read music. While playing piano lead, we experimented with her collection of instruments.

We each kept a daily journal that she collected every Friday in order to add her personal opinions and insights, something I looked forward to reading when they were returned first thing on Monday morning. Her written responses were honest and sincere. She would never humiliate or shame our efforts. I valued her opinions and trusted her advice.

Most of all, I discovered the driving force within me. Mrs. Murphy pushed each of her students only to the point where they could take hold of the reins and drive themselves. I began realizing that having a goal was very important. It gives us purpose. But to ponder and dream about it did little to put the wheels into motion. Determination, hard work, honesty and faith were key to achieving one's place of ambition. She told us, "In the end, being successful is merely being happy with what you have achieved."

The picture of my future was vivid and seemed simple enough. I wanted to own Ma and Papa's ranch and I wanted Wedge by my side the whole way. It would take a lot of money and manpower to turn it into a working ranch. Ma and Papa had made a good start of it. I wanted to have the chance to build on their vision, with a few ideas of my own.

School became a major obstacle in our everyday life on the ranch. It was a balancing act, trying to sandwich it in between morning and afternoon chores. Then came the homework which demanded the final hour or two before bed.

Wedge seemed confused with the routine at first. However, like me, he settled in for the long haul. He'd lay across my feet while I slaved away doing homework at the kitchen table. It wasn't the attention he was accustomed to getting, but he seemed content enough to just be touching me.

After the first day of school he was always in on the dropping off and picking up of Caleb and me. Usually Yodel came along for the ride too. My only time away from the little character was when my boots hit the ground in the parking lot until the minute they got back into the truck at the end of each school day. It didn't take long for him to discover I meant business when I said, "Stay!" I had to speak firmly as Gramps held him in place. The last thing I wanted was him jumping out with cars and trucks moving all over the place. "Tough love", was what Gramps called it.

Wedge would put on that forlorn look as I kissed the top of his head good-bye. It was a bit bothersome for me too, but I knew he'd be back in my arms a few hours later, making up for lost time.

While we were in school Wedge and Yodel would often join Betty with herding small groups of cattle between pastures. Al was quite pleased with the skill displayed by them. "They need more work in the patience department. Betty's a good teacher though, and they watch what she does," Al commented.

Our weekends filled up fast. Caleb and I barely had enough time to whip together a doll bed for Eva's birthday in mid September and finish the dog bed for Luke by early October. We ended up asking Ben for help with Eva's gift. It was more work than we bargained for; we hadn't counted on drilling for dowels and using wood glue, something way out of our realm. Ben did the grunt work, but he made us pay attention. There were a few times where he trusted us to saw and sand certain parts, only too aware of our limited skills.

Caleb and I breathed a sigh of relief once it was all assembled. Ben wasn't having it though. He drug out an old half filled can of light green paint and told us to "purdy it up".

"Lucky thing I found this paint, and it just happens to be Eva's favorite color. Now you two take your time and do a nice job. Your grandma said she'll make a mattress and pillow for it and, if she has time, a little quilt."

Well, what were we supposed to say? We found two small paint brushes and went right to work. Wedge even looked disgusted and circled around on a pile of straw to nap.

"This is crazy," I told Caleb. "Since when does a doll's bed take more time to build than a dog's bed? It's half the size of Yodel's bed and has taken twice the time to build."

"Yeah, I wish she could have kept Otis. Then we wouldn't have had to ask Ben for help. She just better not take this thing up to our fort. I don't want no doll bed and dolls up there to wreck it."

"Dang, I never thought of that. You suppose we could just set it up in the treehouse and tell her she'd play with it more there?"

"Yeah, that's what we could do. They can't go up to the fort without us anyway, and we're gone most of the time."

With that said, we finished painting with two smug smiles plastered across our satisfied faces.

Grandma did a little finagling and made sure Eva and Luke's birthdays were celebrated on weekends so Caleb and I wouldn't have homework hanging over our heads. She said Eva and Luke weren't aware of dates on the calendar yet and had no clue on what days their birthdays actually fell.

Eva's doll bed was a huge success. It all went according to plan and we set it up in the treehouse. Grandma finished it off with her homemade bedding. Then she propped Eva's favorite doll up on the pillow.

Caleb and I did some sweet talking. We told her how nice it looked in the treehouse and how her baby dolls love looking out the windows. It would be way too dark for them up in the fort. And besides, she would play in the treehouse a lot more. Eva agreed with us and said she would probably leave the bed there during the summer and take it up to her room in the winter. We were just glad Luke shared the room with her and not us.

Luke received the dog bed with equal enthusiasm. He liked how we painted "YODEL" on the side with the leftover green paint from Eva's doll bed. Caleb and I hauled it up the stairs and set it on the floor next to his side of the bed. Grandma made a mattress for it by sewing a cover and putting it over an old feather pillow.

Not only did early October bring Luke's birthday, it also marked roundup time. Gramps promised both Caleb and me that we could join them next fall in the high country. We would have to ride our own horses and camp out under the stars. It would take about four days of roughing-it to herd all the scattered cattle down to lower pastures for the winter and calving season.

"We'll have three good dogs to take along next year too," said Gramps. "That should make it easier on Betty and a lot faster overall."

We knew on the third day of the cattle drive the gates to the meadows on Ma and Papa's ranch would be opened for the livestock to enter. They would graze there while everyone spends the night in our cabin and barn.

For as long as I could remember Gramps, Al, Papa, Betty and, more recently, Ben took on the fall roundup and always spent the last night at our place. Ma and Grandma would set up the big tripod with the large cast iron pot steaming away over hot embers for a good part of the day. They never used a recipe. Grandma just called it "hearty hodgepodge". Soaked beans, onions and garlic would be the main ingredients. Whatever was thrown in after that was anyone's guess. Sometimes they used ham hocks and bacon pieces with corn kernels, stewed tomatoes and leftover chunks of meat. Or they'd toss in garbanzo beans, sausage, barley, celery, carrots and elk stew meat. Then there would be cornbread or hot rolls to soak up the juices. It was never the same. But, one thing was for certain, it was always good eatin'.

We were all excited about going back home to our cabin and spending the night. We'd be back on our old stomping grounds, running wild over the familiar terrain. Al and Ben always sacked out in the barn while Gramps and Grandma slept in the bedroom Ma and Papa shared with Eva and Luke. That was the one time Eva would squeeze in with Caleb and me up in the loft. Luke shared a makeshift bed with Ma and Papa on the floor in front of the fireplace. This year there would be no one sleeping in the living room or sharing the loft with the two of us.

Things got moving pretty fast. The big cattle truck was brought around from behind the barn and packed with all the essentials the men and horses would need for the next few days. Al and Ben hauled food and the pots'n'pans Grandma would be needing at the cabin. They packed them tightly into the back of the station wagon. Ben even patched and inflated two truck size inner tubes so we could play with them on the pond once we arrived. He left them with some rope for Grandma to tie to the car's roof.

Grandma had full responsibility of us and for providing all the meals in this year's roundup. Even though we would all lend our helping hands, she was bound to come up short without Ma.

The men folk had their supplies, gear and horses loaded and ready to pull out by the time the four of us kids made it down the stairs. It was early Thursday morning and Caleb and I still had to do our chores, eat and get ready for school.

Grandma woke everyone up before the crack of dawn to see Gramps, Ben and Al off. All three men were in the cab of the cattle truck. Betty rode in the grain compartment up behind the cab. Gramps sat in the driver's seat with his left arm resting on the opened window frame. He had a firm grip on the handle of his severely stained, chipped, blue enameled coffee cup filled with the black brew. His right wrist settled comfortably over the top of the steering wheel. Ben sat in the middle, leaning his knees toward Al as to keep from interfering with the tall stick shift. They, too, cradled hot coffee cups in their hands.

We all stood around waving our goodbyes. Gramps started the engine and smiled down at us. Then we heard him push down on the emergency brake and saw him set his coffee up on the dashboard. He opened his door and climbed out to kiss each one of us.

Looking at Caleb and me he said, "Now I'm leavin' you two in charge of the goin's on around the barnyard. Grandma will have her hands full with household work and gettin' ready for the weekend."

"Sure, Gramps. We'll get everything done alright. Don't worry," I answered.

Grandma gave him a final kiss and hug and told him to act his age. "I don't want to hear about you running your horse at top speed and jumping over fallen limbs. I expect to see you in one piece come Saturday, or you'll wish you never set eyes on me before."

"I'll be a good boy just this once," Grandpa snickered back. "And don't hesitate to call Tucker if you need help here."

With both of them in agreement, Gramps stepped back up into the cab. We stood watching as they rolled across the bridge and rounded the bend.

"Okay, let's get hoppin'," was the order from Grandma.

Since Grandma would be taking us to school for the next two days, Eva and Luke had to get their work done, eat and dress for the ride to Livermore.

Caleb and I would have to take on a bit more work for a couple of days, but we didn't see it as a burden. In the eyes of two young boys, the excitement of being left in charge was like adding twenty years to our youthful lives. It was obvious to us that Gramps believed we could step right into his size 11 boots.

CHAPTER 17

Together at the Cabin

Fridays always sparked energy knowing the weekend was close at hand. This Friday was one of those "heart pounding" days. Grandma had decided to take Tucker up on his offer to do the morning feeding on Saturday. It would give us a jumpstart to leave for the cabin after supper and the evening's chores.

We each packed clothes in between our pillowcases and pillows. A couple pairs of underpants, socks and a spare shirt would do it. We'd wear the same britches all weekend and swim in our undies.

Grandma promised everything would be loaded in the station wagon when she picked us up from school. We'd just have to feed and water the animals, eat our meal and head out.

I wrote all about our plans for the upcoming weekend in my journal and left it for Mrs. Murphy to read.

Grandma was sitting in the parking lot when Caleb and I ran from the school house. Luke was napping in the back seat as usual. He didn't stir, not even when Yodel stood on his back and Eva scooted in next to him. The county road had a way of putting him right to sleep, especially this time of day.

Grandma always felt better when Eva jumped in the back with Luke. Until we all got big enough to keep ourselves from banging into the dashboard every time she hit the brakes, Grandma's first reaction was to throw her right arm out across the front of us to stop any forward motion. Unfortunately, nine out of ten times it struck our neck area. It got to be such a common practice that there were times when she'd stretch that arm of hers out and no one was even sitting in the passenger seat.

True to her word, Grandma had packed everything we'd need for the next two days. She explained to Caleb and me that we would be making a quick stop at home to change our clothes and feed the animals. She thought we kids would rather get to the cabin early and cook our supper there. That will give everyone more daylight time to run around and check things out. Caleb and I agreed and urged Grandma to "step on it", a term Ben used when he'd speed up on our way to town.

We wasted no time changing into our play clothes once we got home. Grandma had Eva and Luke filling water troughs while she pitched hay for the horses and our cow, Bossy. Fortunately, Bossy was pregnant and wouldn't be making any more milk until her calf's birth early next year. The last thing I wanted to do was spend half an hour squirting milk into a bucket.

In no time at all we were running to the car with Wedge and Yodel at our heels. Grandma made sure the house and barn doors were closed tight to keep the uninvited, four legged critters out during the night. Eva and Luke got in the back seat before we ran the ropes through their open windows and over the inner tubes on the car's roof. I passed Yodel to them while Caleb jumped into the front seat. Wedge and I rode shotgun. Grandma started the car and we were on our way.

It would be the first time all of us would be together at the cabin since the afternoon our folks were buried and we picked up our toys and belongings to take to the big ranch. I was glad to have had my own time there, alone with Wedge, that night almost two months ago.

The road got pretty rutty once we headed towards the upper unit. Grandma slowed almost to a stop several times to avoid damaging the car. "The last thing I need is to break down out here right before dark with four kids."

"Awe, we can handle it," Caleb responded. "We're used to walking a lot."

"Yeah, and I suppose you can pack all our food and clothing on your backs and hike the last two miles before nightfall," was Grandma's quick comeback.

"We'll make it okay in the car, Grandma," I said. "The road levels out soon and there aren't as many ruts."

Soon we were stopped at the makeshift, barbwire gate to our land. I hopped out to open it inward across the cattle guard and flush against the fence. The car rolled onto the driveway crossing the meadow. I didn't bother closing it before I jumped back into the front seat.

We followed the road onto the culvert where Grandma paused momentarily and commented on how low the creek was. Taking a hard right, we continued up the driveway until we were past the aspen grove. We stopped as we entered the clearing. No one said a word, but all eyes were on our abandoned cabin.

"Let's put some life back into it," Grandma said cheerfully. "It looks as though it needs some noise and little running feet to perk it up."

She stepped on the gas and drove up next to the hitching post. "Let's get the car unloaded before all of you go gallivanting off somewhere. Supper just needs to be reheated, which shouldn't take long. I'll get it on the table without any of your help tonight, but I expect you to come running when I ring the dinner bell."

Caleb and I hauled our clothes stuffed pillows up the ladder to our room in the loft. Wedge seemed to remember going up once before. He tried in earnest to climb the rungs, only to make it to the second one and fall backwards onto the floor. Yodel sat watching and cocking her head sideways as if to say, "What's your problem? Don't you know you can't climb a ladder?"

Eva and Luke took their things into Ma and Papa's room on the bottom floor. Grandma would sleep in our folk's big bed next to the single one shared by Eva and Luke.

After unloading the car and hauling everything into the house, we left Grandma to her own devices. We ran around the pond first and were climbing the stack of hay in the barn when the dinner bell rang. All of us were eager to get back to the cabin and once again sit around our family table.

"My tummy is talkin' to me," said Luke.

"Really? And just what is it saying?" Grandma asked as she set the leftover roast and all its fixings in the middle of the table.

"It's sayin' to put somethin' in me right now. I'm starvin'."

"I'm so hungry I could eat a horse," Eva added.

"Yeah, well I could eat a bull moose", challenged Caleb.

"Okay, let's stop talking about how hungry you are and start fixin' the problem," Grandma suggested.

The cabin started heating up from the cook stove. But it was all of us eating around the table that warmed our insides. Unlike my earlier stay alone with Wedge, this evening our old home was filled with laughter and excitement.

Darkness and a biting chill surrounded the cabin by the time supper ended. We all pitched in to clear the table and help Grandma pop the corn and melt butter over the stove. Treats this late in the day were rare. It took several batches to fill the big stockpot with fluffy, hot popped kernels. I carefully poured a small amount of butter over each new panful that Grandma dumped into the pot. Eva was trusted to sprinkle salt on top. She had much more control over her hand than Caleb. Luke and Caleb looked on with large anxious eyes and quick fingers. Both were on the bench opposite Eva and me. They balanced themselves on their knees and did a taste test every time more corn was poured into the pot. I'm sure animals from miles around could smell the wonderful aroma coming from our cozy cabin.

Grandma topped our treat off with lemonade. We all sat around eating, drinking and talking about some of the happy times spent within our cabin walls. There were no tears or moments of sad reflection.

Grandma told us about each of our births and how Ezra seemed confused when the midwife left without taking Caleb with her. "Ezra was not quite two years old. He looked at the closed front door and then at the new baby in your papa's arms and said, 'She forgot the baby!' It's always hard for the first born to accept the fact they are no longer the only cherished child in their parents' lives."

She went on to say, "When Eva was born in the wee hours of the morning, Ezra was asleep and Caleb was up and running around, pushing his toy truck from room to room. The midwife and I came out of the bedroom to tell Gramps and Al they could go in to see the baby. Caleb ran his truck into your ma and papa's room and climbed up on their bed to see the small infant. Your papa unwrapped Eva to show everyone. Caleb was in shock. He noticed right away she was missing a very important part of her anatomy. We all laughed and your ma told him everything was okay. She explained, 'We have a girl. Girls don't have the same parts as boys. Let's just say she has indoor plumbing'."

"What about me?" Luke blurted out.

"Well now, you were a stubborn little guy. Your ma was having some trouble getting you to surface. The midwife decided we should load her in the car and make the trip to Ft. Collins. You three kids rode with Gramps and me as we followed your folks to the hospital. Al stayed to take care of the stock on both ranches. You were born just a couple of hours later and then we all came back that same day. Your ma carried you in her arms the whole way."

"And I named him Luke," I added.

Looking at Luke she said, "Yes, Ezra wanted that honor. He asked to name the baby if it was a boy, but your parents wanted to know what he had in mind first, in case it was something like Odd Ozzie or Slimy Toad. They were relieved and pleasantly surprised when Ezra suggested *Luke*. So, Luke it is."

"I think we all better get to bed. We have a big day tomorrow. I'll need some help keeping the fire going under the tripod. Those men are going to be mighty tired and hungry by the time they drive the cattle into the meadow."

"Caleb and I'll take Wedge and Yodel up to bed with us," I volunteered.

"No, Yodel sleeps by me," argued Luke.

"I think one dog can sleep in the loft and one can stay down with us," Grandma suggested.

"I'm sure glad your papa tapped into the spring up on the hillside. Nothing's worse than not having running water. I can live with kerosene lights and wood to heat and cook with, but it's having no water that would keep me from staying here. I'm not that keen on outhouses."

We all took turns around the sink brushing teeth and giving ourselves quick sponge baths. Eva and Luke jumped into their bed and patiently waited for story time. Grandma apologized for forgetting to pack a book, so she sat on Ma and Papa's bed with Caleb and me and told the four of us about her life as a little girl.

She was the fifth of six children. They had a simple and frugal life by today's standards. "Funny thing," she said, "even though we had very little growing up, we never saw ourselves as poor or deprived. There was always food on the table and a roof over our heads. The main thing was that we had each other and were grateful for what life had to offer.

"Just like my siblings and me when I was growing up, you are separated by unique differences. You have your own visions, your own tastes, and you see life differently. One thing is for certain though, your roots are the same. From those roots you will grow and branch out in your own directions. That's what makes each family tree special. No two branches are the same, therefore no tree can be duplicated."

"You mean no one else is just like me?" asked Luke.

"That's right. And no family is just like ours," Grandma answered.

"Your ma always wanted a brother and a sister. But, it just wasn't in the cards for us. That's why she insisted on having a big family, and we're glad she did.

"Now, let's say prayers and call it a day. We have a packed schedule tomorrow."

Caleb and I hugged and kissed Grandma. I ruffled Luke's hair like Papa used to do to the three of us boys after giving us each a goodnight kiss. We used to tease Papa about not messing with Eva's hair because he was afraid his fingers would get hung up in her curls. He'd just hold her face in his hands and tell her how beautiful his little girl was, kiss her forehead, then her nose, then her little mouth.

I didn't mind hugging Luke and Eva, but kissin' them was where I drew the line. Caleb followed suit and then we headed for the ladder.

Ever since Caleb was two and a half I had followed him up the ladder. Ma wanted to make sure if he started to fall I would be there to brace him. Old habits are hard to break. I waited for Caleb to lead the way. Then, picking Wedge up, I climbed the ladder using one steady hand and a heart much lighter than the last time he and I made this trip to the loft together.

I put Wedge on the rug by my side of the bed and crawled in next to Caleb. We talked about being included in next year's roundup. "I can't believe Gramps said we can go," yawned Caleb.

"He sure could use the extra hands right now," I answered. "Papa was a big help and there are more cattle to drive this year."

"Do you think they'll make it down here tomorrow?" Caleb asked.

"It's hard tellin'. I know they'll work their tails off tryin'. We best get to sleep. Grandma is shorthanded too, and we'll need to do our part to help her."

"Goodnight, Ez."

"Goodnight, Caleb."

Once again I settled my head on the pillow and gazed up through the windowpane. The treetops and mountain outside were aglow from the half-moon's reflection. Remembering back to the last time I laid on this very spot, I thanked God for allowing me to return to our cabin with Grandma, Caleb, Eva and Luke. And, feeling extremely grateful and a bit selfish, I thanked Him for letting me keep the little fur ball laying by my side.

CHAPTER 18

Unexpected Help

Breakfast was sizzling and the aroma seeped through the gap under the small loft door. Caleb sat up quickly as he got his bearings. I watched as his nose twitched like a dog's trying to decipher what was on the grill.

"We're havin' sausage," he exclaimed.

Wedge woke with a start. Somehow during the night he had worked his way up on the bed and positioned himself between Caleb and me. I guess he figured he'd slept here before so could do it again. It was easy enough to crawl up onto the mattress and weasel his way between our bodies while we were down and out.

I looked through the window and saw Jack Frost had left his mark. A thin white film of ice covered the ground and sparkled on the topmost branches, catching the morning sun rays.

Caleb pulled his pants on and began jabbering something about eggs, potatoes and biscuits. He was dressed and opening the door when I rolled out of bed.

As I pulled my pants on I thought about Gramps, Al and Ben out there for the past two nights. I remembered Papa telling us about the discomfort of being exposed to the elements, throwing together meager meals, and riding all day with only a few hours of sleep under their belts.

Ben could handle cattle drives. It was Gramps and Al I worried about. They would never admit their ages as dangerous obstacles to their wellbeing. It'll be a relief seeing them herding the cattle into the large meadow later today.

"Ezra, are you hungry? Breakfast is ready."

"Comin' Grandma," I shouted back.

I grabbed Wedge and hauled him down the ladder. He ran to the kitchen's Dutch door that led out to the back porch. Caleb stood in the entry watching Yodel chase the shadow of a flying hawk.

"How about you wake Eva and Luke up, Ez. We need to get through breakfast so we can get on with preparing dinner. I want to make plenty for those hungry men."

"Okay Grandma. I'll have them eatin' at the table in two minutes."

I took a sausage link into their bedroom. Eva was already sitting up doing arm stretches over her mangled morning hair. I held the sausage under Luke's little nose. He seemed unfazed at first. Then, opening his eyes, he said, "Whatcha doin', Ezra?"

"Does this smell like somethin' you might like?" I asked. "There's more where this came from."

"I'm outta here," Eva declared as she jumped off the bed and raced to the kitchen.

Before Luke could take a bite of the bait, I tossed it into my mouth.

"Mmmmm, that's good. Hope there's enough for you by the time I get done. See ya."

"Wait for me!" Luke shouted. "Don't eat all the sausage, you guys."

By the time I got back to the kitchen, the table was set with scrambled eggs, sausage, country hash-browns and biscuits with butter and homemade jam. I never cease to be amazed at how skillful Caleb's nose detects food. Nine out of ten times he's right on the money when it comes to what's being served.

"Thank you, Ez," said Grandma. "I don't want you kids inhaling your breakfast, but you do need to hustle a bit. We got to be ready for our cowboys when they ride in. All of you can haul firewood up from the wood pile and stack it next to the back door. The wheelbarrow should be in the barn."

"Can we go swimmin' in the pond?" asked Eva.

"You need to look outside, my dear girl. If it were any colder you'd be ice skating on the pond," Grandma commented. "Maybe it'll warm up enough to dab your feet in the water. Or you can try your luck fishing."

Caleb and I shot excited looks at each other.

"Our poles should still be in the tool shed," Caleb said.

"Yeah, and we can dig for worms," I added.

"Fresh fish for tomorrow's breakfast would be a real treat," urged Grandma. "I'll be starting the bread dough as soon as we finish eating. How would Eva and Caleb like to help cut vegetables after hauling wood?"

"Sure," both answered in unison.

"Ezra, maybe you can take Luke up to the hayloft to pitch out some clean straw. Al and Ben would really enjoy a soft spot to throw their bedrolls on tonight."

"No problem. We can handle that, can't we Luke?"

"Yep, I can do that," replied Luke.

"There won't be a big mid-day meal today. You kids can snack on left-overs and anything you see that tickles your fancy."

We all chipped in to clear and clean up the breakfast dishes. Eva got her morning hair fixing, and we set out on our first mission.

With all of us helping, we had several days' worth of firewood hauled to the cabin in a short period of time. Caleb and Eva went on to help Grandma while Luke and I opened a bale of straw to spread in one corner of the barn's loft. Ben and Al were sure to sleep soundly on the thick mattress we threw together.

Luke and I then went back to the cabin and set up a large metal tripod over the fire pit. Grandma stepped carefully down the back steps with the partially filled cast iron pot swinging by its handle. Caleb followed her with the heavy lid. She hung the Dutch oven on a large hook that was elevated by a thick chain extending down the center of the tripod.

Luke and I began gathering dry pine needles and leaves to place in the empty pit beneath the hanging pot. Once we had a small pile, I struck a match to begin the fire. Luke and I fanned the tiny flames until they were big enough to accept twigs. We built the fire up by increasing the amount of the fuel. In a short period of time we had a bed of hot embers and I let Grandma know her meat and onions were cooking.

She came out of the kitchen with a bowl of soaked beans. Eva was right behind her with a kettle of broth and a basket of spices. We watched as

Grandma added a pinch of this and a shake or two of that. She never was too good at measuring when it came to cooking. She would taste test her food and, every now and then, add more fresh or dried herbs and spices.

By late morning we were free to do whatever we wanted. All of us decided to go fishing. Unfortunately, the dogs wanted to go too. Every time one of us cast our line into the water Yodel and Wedge would jump in after it. No amount of threatening seemed to deter them. Grandma heard our frustrated yells and called them into the cabin. It wasn't long before Luke leaned his pole against a tree and called it quits. It took too much sitting still, being quiet and good old fashioned patience for his liking. Eva soon followed his example. She claimed she needed something to eat and stood her pole next to Luke's. Caleb surprised me. He never was a fella to stay in one place very long, but he seemed determined to snag a trout.

Eva soon returned carrying a couple of apples, buttered biscuits and jam, along with a bag of leftover popcorn.

"Thanks, Eva," we said.

"It wasn't my idea. Grandma made me bring you something to eat so you'll stay here and catch some fish. She's really hopin' to fry some up for breakfast tomorrow mornin'."

"Well, I'll stay here long enough to eat. Then I'm goin' to play in the barn," was Caleb's response.

It looked like if there was any fish to be had, I'd be the one getting them. Luke came down to join me when he saw I was on my own. He kept talking and I kept throwing my line in. After a little while I realized he was awfully quiet. Looking over my shoulder, I saw that he had curled himself up on a large granite rock and fallen asleep, using his right arm as a pillow.

"I guess the fish are nappin' too. It doesn't look like we'll be eatin' trout any time soon," I said aloud to myself.

My pole joined the others and I pulled Luke up to my chest. He settled his head on my shoulder as I began the slight climb back to the cabin.

Grandma saw me carrying Luke up the stairs and opened the door. Wedge and Yodel seized their chance and bolted outside.

"Lay him on his bed," Grandma whispered.

The cabin was filled with the smell of bread dough rising. It was a familiar occurrence back at the ranch house, but it had been a long time since I walked through the cabin door and was greeted by the wonderful aroma. It was bittersweet. I halfway expected to see Ma come into the room wearing her big smile and offering me a snack.

I have learned over this past year that I can't answer the question I've asked myself so many times. Someday I might know the "why" behind the reason for the loss of our folks. But for now I need to settle for gathering as many memories as I can. These walls will hold the smell of bread dough rising many more times. That I promise.

"Sorry about not catching any fish," I told Grandma.

"Oh, we'll not starve without them. I'm throwing together some cookie dough. They'll be baking in the oven soon. I'll call you all in when they're ready. Run along now and have fun while you can."

It wasn't hard to see how Ma turned out so good. As they say, "The apple don't fall far from the tree."

Wedge was waiting for me right outside the door. I walked over and put a few small logs under the bubbling pot before running out to the barn. As I entered the large opened doorway, I stopped short. I was just in time to see Eva, with a large rope knotted between her legs, jumping off the loft's ladder and swing across the barn. She had to be eight to ten feet off the ground at her highest point.

"What the heck are you doing?" I hollered.

"Look, Ezra. We found the rope Papa tied to the beam for us to use as a swing."

"Yeah, but it was wound around the beam so we would leave it alone. How did you get it down?"

Caleb and Eva shot each other guilty looks. Neither said a word for a while. Finally, Caleb spoke, "I climbed up to the loft and straddled the beam until I got to the rope. Then I unwrapped it."

"You're crazy. Do you know you woulda killed yourself if you fell?"

"Well I didn't fall, and I didn't kill myself."

Shaking my head all I could say was, "We best not tell Grandma about this."

"We weren't goin' to," Eva replied as she swung through the air.

"Watch when I go on it, Ezra," said Caleb. "Yodel goes with me. She likes it too. We tried to get Wedge to go, but he ran off."

"You can see who uses his brain," I said. "He probably doesn't trust you guys. Maybe he'll go up with me."

"After my turn," insisted Caleb.

Wedge's head followed the back and forth rhythm of the moving rope. After a little coaxing, he threw caution to the wind and allowed me to hold him while we swung the arched flight pattern several times. We all had our fill when Grandma called.

I suggested that we hang the end knot up high so Luke wouldn't see it. "He's too young to swing on it."

Luke was up from his nap and hot cookies were waiting for us when we entered the cabin. Grandma was pouring cold milk and we were taking our first bites when Wedge and Yodel began barking their heads off outside.

"What's going on?" Grandma asked in a puzzled tone.

We could hear another dog barking in the distance, then faint whistling.

"It's Gramps!" I blurted out while jumping from the bench.

"Oh my goodness. They're here early. I can't believe it!" was Grandma's surprised response.

All of us ran out to the front porch and stood listening.

"Let's go see!" shouted Eva.

"We'll go just as far as the second row of trees," instructed Grandma. "Ezra and Caleb need to hang onto the pups. We don't want them to spook the herd."

It was a mad dash past the pond, barn and corral and into the second stand of trees. Grandma ended up carrying Luke and bringing up the rear. We all huddled close to each other and watched as Al, riding point, swung a rope over his head and whistled encouragement to the lead cattle.

Gramps was coming into view as flank on the far side of the herd. My chest swelled with pride as I watched both men put all they had into the task at hand. How many men at their ages would have that much gumption?

"Who's that?" Eva shouted.

All our eyes followed her pointing finger. I looked up at Grandma's squinting eyes and realized she was clueless as to who the other flank rider was. He wore a slouched hat and appeared to have a ponytail. Then, as if to end our puzzlement, the rider made high pitched noises to help guide the cattle toward the gate's opening.

"Why, it's Vikki," cried Grandma. With a wide smile she added, "Look, there's Mark coming around the bend."

It took quite a while to funnel the cattle into the large pasture. Ben had the detested duty of riding drag. He was covered with a thick layer of dirt and had protected all but his eyes with a kerchief tied behind his head.

Once the last cow waddled through the opening, Ben dismounted and pulled the makeshift barbed wire gate closed. He removed his hat and hit it against the side of his chaps. Clouds of dust billowed up on impact. He removed the scarf protecting his face to reveal an image much like that of the Lone Ranger. The contrast between the dirt mask around his eyes and the light skin below it was comical.

Al and Gramps spotted us first and galloped over. "I hope you have enough fixin's for two more cowhands," Gramps said smiling down at Grandma.

"Of course we do. What a nice surprise seeing Mark and Vikki," Grandma responded.

Ben, Mark and Vikki came trotting up to join in on the conversation.

"Why don't you take care of your horses, and then we'll hear all about your adventures over freshly baked cookies," suggested Grandma.

"That works for me," Ben's voice rang out. "How about Caleb hop up here for a ride back to the barn. Then you can help me feed and brush Rio."

"How'd I know he'd con someone into giving free help?" Al said while shaking his head.

"Are you mad that I thought of it before you?" was Ben's smiling response.

"I'll help you Al, and I won't even ask for a ride," I offered.

"Well now, that's mighty nice of you, Ez. I think I'll just take you up on that."

"Can I ride with you, Vikki?" asked Eva. "I can help take care of your horse."

Vikki just smiled. She then reached down, pulled Eva up by her little arms and straddled her short legs behind the saddle horn. Grandma handed Luke up to Gramps and they all rode away. Grandma and I followed on foot with Wedge and Yodel leading the way.

"I'm so glad they made it back here safely," Grandma confided.

"Me too," I said with equal relief.

CHAPTER 19

Good Company

As it turned out, Mark and Vikki trucked their mounts up to the high pasture and had them saddled and ready to go when Gramps, Ben and Al showed up Thursday morning.

"You shoulda' seen those three sittin' up in that cab with all their mouths gaping. They sure didn't expect to see the sights of us waitin' for them at the base camp," Mark laughingly told us at supper that afternoon, between bites of hearty hodgepodge.

"I'd say they were in shock," Vikki added. "Seeing the looks on their faces was well worth gettin' up way before the crack of dawn."

The day turned out to be quite warm but, by evening, it had cooled off. Ben rolled enough tree rounds over for all the grownups to sit comfortably near the fire pit. All of us kids sat quietly on our familiar log, listening to the goings on of the past two days. Betty laid at Al's feet, totally exhausted from the regiment she had been put through.

"There's no way we would have made it this far today without you two," Gramps said while looking at Mark and Vikki. "These folks made arrangements with Tucker last week to take care of their livestock while they help with our cattle. Then there we go and ask him to feed for us too."

"Tucker would have loved to come," Vikki said. "But he was glad to help out by taking care of things on the home front. We all knew you three would have your hands full trying to move your stock this year."

"No tellin' what you'd be up against this late in the season, bein' shorthanded and all," Mark added.

"Well, you sure made my day," admitted Al. "If I hadn't known better, I'd of thought two guardian angels were sent down dressed and trained for the occasion."

"I bet the wad of chewing tobacco crammed inside Mark's cheek cleared the angel thing right up for you, huh Al?" laughed Ben.

"Yeah, I have to admit, it was a dead giveaway."

Changing the subject, Gramps took on a solemn tone. "This was one of those unexpected years. Anne and I had to pick up our pace a bit when our bodies didn't always want to go along. We delayed the cattle drive as long as we dared. We all know how fast Mother Nature can change her mind. Gettin' caught up there during an early snowstorm can prove fatal for man and beast."

Looking at Mark and Vikki he went on to say, "Next year we'll be back on our September schedule. We'll be takin' on two young ranch hands to help, along with their two herding dogs. The cattle shouldn't be as edgy and scattered as they were this year."

"Really? Are they from around here?" asked Vikki.

Smiling and nodding in our direction, Gramps held his cup of coffee up as if to offer us a toast, "There they sit".

All eyes settled on Caleb and me. Except for the dumbfounded looks on Mark and Vikki's faces, they were big grins of approval and a welcoming slap on the back from Ben.

"Anne thinks Caleb might be a bit young. But I assured her that I started pushin' cattle out of the brush with my dad when I was no older than him."

"I'd like to go along just to see those two in action," Vikki finally piped up when the shock of the news settled.

"You're always welcome to join us, but don't feel obliged," replied Gramps.

You can imagine how important Caleb and I felt being the topic of conversation. It was enough to stop Caleb from swallowing. He squirmed uncomfortably and put the food in his mouth on hold.

"Young blood is always a welcome sight on cattle drives," Al injected.

"That's why you welcomed me with opened arms," Ben responded with his wide grin.

Ignoring Ben altogether, Al looked over at Grandma and said, "Was that apple pie I saw coolin' off on the kitchen table?"

It was nice to have the attention off Caleb and me, as everyone laughed at Al and Ben's friendly teasing.

Eva, Caleb and I helped Grandma serve the dessert. Luke had a hard time on the stairs just practicing his eye, hand and foot coordination while keeping his own plate upright.

Ben and Mark were busy plotting a way of riding up and retrieving the trucks early. They would drop them off at the two sites, unload their mounts at the big ranch, and then take the overland route that I had traveled with Wedge and Al. They would return here sometime after dark.

Overhearing their conversation, Al suggested casually, "How about I drive you two knuckleheads up in the car, follow you down to drop off the trucks, and have you back here sittin' on those stumps in time to watch the sun sink behind the mountain?"

"Who says wisdom doesn't come with age?" Grandma said chuckling.

"It's not so much wisdom, Anne. It's common sense, something those two stepped out of line for when it was being handed out," responded Al. "You put those two heads together and you got yourself a rock pile."

Ben and Mark smiled at each other, ate their apple pie and headed for the car.

Everyone had a good laugh when Mark and Ben were back sitting on their stumps in time to watch the sun set. The big payoff was having Ben's fiddle brought back with them. Al's harmonica was easily stored inside his vest pocket where it had accompanied him on every cattle drive he'd ever ridden. We were in for an evening of toe tappin', knee slappin' entertainment.

No one was disappointed. We looked on as our two musicians fired up and disrupted the mountains' silence for quite a spell. Finally Grandma pulled the plug on the night's lively entertainment when she said it was time to turn in. Al and Ben solemnly played taps, signifying the end of the day for us youngins, as we marched off to bed.

Wedge dragged along at my side. I gathered him up under my left arm and climbed to our room. Wedge did his circling on the rug before letting out a sigh and closing his eyes. I crawled into bed, listening to the soft music filtering through the cabin walls.

The next thing I knew it was morning and there was Wedge wedged between Caleb and me. The smell of breakfast-in-the-making made its way up to us once again. I could hear Gramps and Al talking about their plans for the day. Caleb began to stir. He stretched his body to its fullest length, peeked through his sleepy eyelids at me and began his morning ritual of predicting the breakfast menu.

"Why don't you just go see what we're havin' instead of guessin' all the time?"

"You just wish you could be as good as me," Caleb replied.

"I like to eat just as much as the next guy, but I don't need to turn it into a guessin' game."

"Well then, I 'spose you don't need my help. You'll find out what we're havin' when you get there. See ya at the table." Caleb dressed without further comment and headed down the ladder.

I looked over to see Wedge's eyes inches from mine. His head had nestled under my extended arm with his nose aiming for my neck.

"We best go eat before Caleb inhales our share. I know we're havin' bacon and I'll be sure to sneak you a piece. There's no mistakin' that smell."

You can imagine my surprise when I hit the bottom of the ladder and saw crisp bacon sharing a plate with fried trout, their lifeless eyes staring right at me. Caleb hadn't guessed fish.

"Where'd you get the trout?" I asked Grandma.

"Early mornin' is the key to catchin' fish," Ben informed me.

"Vikki and Ben decided to try out a couple of poles some fishermen had left leaning against a tree. They came complete with a can of worms," Grandma informed me.

The cabin filled up fast with chatter and compliments for the scrumptious meal. Mark and Vikki took their plates to the rock hearth to eat. Ben and Al joined them in the living room, using Papa's big leather chair and part of the couch to settle their rested and renewed bodies.

"How'd you sleep last night?" came Grandma's question directed to all the barn occupants.

"It's been a while since I laid in the straw with Mark," laughed Vikki. "And it was the first time I slept with three men."

The grownups thought her remarks were hilarious. Caleb, Eva and I looked at each other quizzically as if to say, "What's the big joke?" Luke was busy taking advantage of the situation and began soaking his pancakes with more syrup while Grandma's attention was elsewhere.

All of us ran out to watch while the horses were saddled. Everyone, mounts included, was filled to the brim, rested and eager to start the last leg of the cattle drive. Grandma ran around tying cloth flour sacks on each saddle horn. "I found these bags in a bottom drawer of the cabin's kitchen. They're perfect for holding a few cookies and an apple. I'd hate to see any of you fall off your horse from starvation."

"Our horses won't be able to move if we put one more morsel of food in our mouths. We'll be lucky to lift our feet to the stirrups and swing our legs over the saddles as it is," Gramps said as he put his arm around Grandma's shoulders and walked with her to his steed.

"I'll be glad when you're all back at the ranch sitting around the supper table," Grandma told Gramps as she kissed him goodbye.

"We'll be fine. You're the one who has to rustle up the evening meal after packing, loading and unloading everything. I look to see you pass us up in an hour or two."

Turning his attention to Luke, Eva, Caleb and me, he raised his voice a bit and said, "You kids help your grandma wrap things up around here."

We all promised to lend her a hand. Luke and Eva ran to kiss and hug Gramps while Caleb and I walked over like the newly introduced ranch hands that we were. We hugged him and kissed the three-day-old whiskers that covered his cheeks.

"I'm countin' on you two to load everything into the car for Grandma. You'll also need to make sure all the cabin and barn doors and windows are closed before pullin' out."

"We'll take care of it," I promised.

Gramps turned to put his left foot in the stirrup as he swung his right leg over the saddle. Looking at Caleb and me he gave one more order. "Hang on to those dogs until we're out of sight. I don't want them excitin' the herd and scatterin' them from here to Laramie."

"Okay," was our quick reply.

We picked up both pups as Gramps reined his horse into the meadow of waiting cattle. Everyone seemed to know what to do. They positioned themselves around the herd and began yelling orders to get them in motion. Vikki broke off a tree branch to use as a waving switch. Mark and Ben swung their ropes. Al and Gramps rode point once again. The wire gate was opened wide, allowing the sea of split hooves to flow through. Betty wasted no time. She was hard at work darting at the slow movers and nipping heels.

Next year we would be a part of it all. I smiled over at Caleb and saw equal excitement from his beaming face. We had a long time to mull it over. It was a lot to look forward to. We'd be riding our saddles as hired hands, working long hours and making important decisions.

Wedge and Yodel were fighting to get down. Caleb and I held on to their collars and did the best we could to avoid being clawed by their frantic movements. Everyone walked to the gate well behind Ben and the tail end of the herd. Caleb and I yanked the gate back into position and slipped the wire loop over the top wooden pole to hold it in place.

"Well, time to get a move-on," Grandma said as she turned toward the cabin.

"First one there is a rotten egg," yelled Eva who had at least a thirty foot head start.

Grandma laughed loudly and shouted to her, "I think you mean the last one there is a rotten egg."

It made no difference. We knew what she meant. Caleb, Luke and I were hot on her trail. Luke was left in the dust easy enough, and we passed Eva by the time we got to the tree line. Caleb was harder for me to shake. My longer strides served me well jumping over fallen logs and the small creek bed. If Caleb had more length to his legs he would have been a source to reckon with. He sure could crank out some quick speed.

Luke was disappointed as usual for coming in fourth. But Grandma reminded him that she was the rotten egg since she came in last.

All of us kids hurried to pack things up. Eva and Luke were in charge of putting all the fishing poles away. I closed the barn up as tight as a drum after stashing the inner tubes and taking a few more high swings on the rope. Caleb was helping Grandma pack boxes with the little remaining food and kitchen items she had hauled to the cabin. He set each load on a small foot rug and dragged them one at a time to the front porch. When I got to the cabin there were three boxes waiting for me to help carry to the car.

"Did you close the loft window, boys?" asked Grandma.

"Yep, I did," replied Caleb.

"Then let's get loaded. I need to get home and start supper."

I stood on the porch and watched as everyone found their rightful places in the car. Wedge was at my feet when I closed the front door and walked down the steps. He jumped on my lap before I pulled the car door closed. Grandma shifted gears, eased off the clutch and slowly drove down the driveway. Through the wing mirror I watched as our cabin became smaller and smaller. The clearing disappeared and with it our first home, as the white trunks of the aspens crowded into the mirror's frame.

CHAPTER 20

Pushin' to the Lower Pasture

THE CATTLE HAD MADE GOOD time. We came up on Ben trying to eat his apple underneath the protection of his bandana that covered his nose and mouth. He waved and shouted for us to stay close behind his horse. It was like watching the Red Sea part. The herd separated as Ben led us through. They quickly refilled the space behind the car, surrounding us on all sides.

Grandma drove with caution and years of experience behind Ben and past Mark and Vikki until we reached the front where Gramps and Al were guiding the herd. Ben pulled over to let us pass. By the creases on the outside of his eyes, there was no denying his big white ivories were in full smile mode under his filthy bandana. We all waved and thanked him as he tipped his hat and skirted the outside of the walking cattle in order to return to his rear post.

Tucker had done a good job taking care of the ranch in our absence. All of us pitched in to unload the car and help Grandma begin another round of meal making for the hungry crew. Then we were given leave for an hour or so of fort time. It was there Yodel and Wedge picked up the distant barks of Betty. They stood at the cave opening and responded with high pitched enthusiasm.

"What they barkin' at?" Luke yelled out over the dogs' noise echoing off the rock walls.

I ran outside, squatted down and gathered the two pups under my arms. They were squirming with excitement when I detected the faint barking that set them off and the teeth whistling coming from Ol' Al.

"They're comin'. Let's get outta here!" I shouted. "Gramps is gettin' close."

Caleb and Luke left the cave together. Eva followed, then stopped short to tug at the large metal handle. I ran over to help her pull the massive wooden door closed. By the time the cave was buttoned up tight, Luke and Caleb were practically free falling and already halfway down the mountain. Yodel was doing her share of tumbling alongside Luke. Surprisingly, Wedge stayed waiting for us to make our move. And move we did. Eva and I shot down the embankment, determined to catch up. Wedge impressed me with his fast maneuvering around boulders and down the steep terrain. He lost his balance a few times but was quick to right himself and keep going. It wasn't long before we overtook Luke. He yelled out orders for us to slow down but, at a time like this, everyone was on their own. Anyway, we couldn't have halted our headfirst run even if we tried.

Caleb was standing for us on the bridge at the base of the mountain. He decided to wait up when he realized we had time left before the cattle entered the lower pasture. It was probably wise for all of us to hang back until Luke could catch up. Grandma would be mighty upset if he got hurt and none of us were there to help him.

Luke made pretty good time, considering his short young legs. His face showed signs of wet streaks working their way down dirty cheeks, and his nose was in need of a wiping.

"You been cryin'?" Caleb chided.

"No," was Luke's sharp reply.

"Ah, you did real good Luke. I can't believe how fast you ran and rolled down that mountain," Caleb said, trying to console him.

"You guys wouldn't wait for me," Luke sobbed.

"That's what makes you so fast," I said with authority. "If we slowed down you would too."

"Then I be faster than you guys when my legs get bigger," he said, reassuring himself.

We all agreed. We stayed with him at his pace pass the house, over the second bridge and down the driveway. We caught up with Grandma who had also heard the commotion and was quickly walking our dirt road to open the pasture gate.

"We'll get it Grandma," I shouted when I spotted her ahead of us.

She stopped and waited for us to catch up. By then Luke was dragging behind so we all checked our steps and urged him along.

"Lordy, you're a mess little man," Grandma said.

"That's because I'm so fast," he responded.

All of us laughed.

"Do you want a piggyback ride?" I offered.

"Yeah," came his tired answer.

The four of us proceeded down the road with the fifth one limp on my back. "Don't you go to sleep back there," I told him.

When no reply came Grandma looked over and said, "You might want to give him to me, Ez." Apparently, Luke's eyes were as heavy as lead. He showed no sign of life as Grandma took him into her arms and hugged him against her chest.

Caleb, Eva and I closed the gate to our road and opened the one to the large pasture while Grandma rested on the nearby stile with her three year old load. Within ten minutes we could see dust billowing and then the cattle moving at a slow pace along the fence row.

"There's Gramps," Eva yelled as she pointed out the man with the stained, sagged, once white cowboy hat.

We knew better than to run toward the herd. Instead, we climbed up onto the stile steps with Grandma and Luke. Grandma turned Luke around on her lap and urged him to wake up. She knew he'd be upset if he didn't see the herd being pushed into their winter pasture.

Luke woke quickly once he remembered where he was. He stood on the step next to Eva and began waving his arms and shouting. Quickly, Grandma told him to quiet down or she'd have to hold him again. The rest of us knew to be still and silent when the cattle were coming in.

Al took the lead. He galloped over to us and asked if anyone wanted a ride. Eva was the first to respond. He lifted her behind the saddle horn and they returned to the herd.

Luke's disappointed frown was all it took for Gramps to ride up and rescue him from the sidelines. His shift of attitude was immediate as he laughed all the way back to the moving mass of cow heads coming our way.

Wedge and Yodel were convinced the roundup team needed their assistance. The last place they wanted to be was restrained on our laps. "You gotta choice. You can stay here and behave, or we'll take you two back to your dog pen," I warned. It was an empty threat because neither Caleb nor I wanted to run them home and miss out on any of the action. Both dogs danced around a bit, fighting to escape our holds. By the time the cattle began entering the pasture they realized they were going nowhere and began settling down. Their ears were perked up and shivers ran through their bodies as they stood ready to help if released. Betty was heard bringing up the rear with Ben.

Caleb, Grandma and I stayed put while thousands of hooves streamed into the open pasture. The movement and sound of backs compressed together between the two large posts was pretty amazing. Their mighty heads were forced up onto the rumps of the cows in front of them. Al and Gramps, holding their precious young cargos, sat on their mounts near the posts on either side of the opening. Al and Eva were somewhat protected by the opened gate. Gramps and Luke backed up a ways to give the herd ample room once they entered the grassland.

Mark and Vikki made sure the cattle kept moving and, around the bend at the tail end of the herd, Ben could be seen swinging his rope at stragglers.

"I wonder where we'll be ridin' next year," Caleb blurted out to me enthusiastically.

"My guess is we'll be eatin' dirt. Ben will probably be moved up the line."

"That's called being promoted," Grandma said smiling at us. "Whoever comes after you will bump you up from drag to flank. But I guarantee that won't be for a long time. I'm afraid you'll be trying to see and breathe through the brown gritty stuff for quite a few cattle drives."

Ben whipped off his filthy bandana and yelled, "Ooh wee!" when the last hoof crossed the gate's opening. Vikki and Mark waited in the driveway with Ben as Gramps and Al guided their horses out to meet them. Caleb and I ran over to close the pasture gate while Grandma opened the other one leading to the homestead.

Caleb stepped high up on the stile and grabbed a ride back with Ben. Yodel did her best to keep up.

"Here, Ezra, take my horse," offered Vikki. "I want to stretch my legs and get caught up with all the goings on with Anne."

"Really? You'd let me ride your horse?"

"Sure. She's a good one, and she'd love to lighten her load with the likes of you."

I looked over at Grandma for her approval. "Go ahead, Ez. It beats walking."

Vikki dismounted and led her mare to the stile. I used the bottom step as a booster in order for my boot to reach the stirrup. Vikki adjusted them to my shortened height. With gentle nudging from my heels, the mare and I headed down the road. Wedge tagged along behind us.

"Her name is Poppy," Vikki shouted after me. "She loves it when you talk to her."

"Okay, thanks," I shouted back.

Gramps, Eva, Al and Luke waited for me to trot with them. The others were most likely in the corral by then, knowing how much they all liked speed. So, with jolting laughter in various rhythms, we were jostled about as we made our way to the barn.

The horses were all brushed and rewarded for their four days of service. Our loyal companions were turned out to pasture while Mark and Vikki kept their mounts in the corral. They would be loaded in their trailer and taken home after supper.

We all headed in for our big Sunday meal. The cattle drive was over.

CHAPTER 21

Gettin' Even

Visions of the next cattle drive cornered the market in my dreams. Caleb and I were irreplaceable cowhands. We played a major role with our well trained dogs gathering up five times as many head of cattle than the year before. Our horses raced up and down steep mountains following the guiding barks of Wedge and Yodel. We were heroes. Then, like the end of all good movies, the screen went blank as Grandma gently shook Caleb and me from our sleep.

"Time to get up for school," she said quietly.

"Not now," Caleb moaned while pulling the pillow over his head.

I laid there for a minute, allowing the here and now to shuffle back into my waking mind. I climbed down from my bunk and encouraged Caleb to roll out of his. There was a long road between today and the cattle drive in my dreams. There'll be a lot to learn and do between now and then. It would be up to Caleb and me to meet Gramps' expectations and earn our places on next fall's roundup.

Being Monday morning, our individual journals were waiting for us on top of each student's desk. We were free to read Mrs. Murphy's comments and were given some time to make additional remarks. My log of events had never before seen so much writing coming from my pencil. I quickly scribbled all about my weekend and how excited I was to be a bigger part of the cattle drive next year.

Mrs. Murphy walked by a few times and patted my back while whispering encouragement. Not once had she ever been a witness to such enthusiasm on the pages in my journal. When I finished I was surprised to look up and see everyone else reading silently, waiting for me to complete my entry. Mrs. Murphy just smiled. She pointed to the stack of notebooks that were turned in on top of her desk, indicating for me to add mine.

Usually we kept our written thoughts at our desks and added to them throughout the week. But this time Mrs. Murphy must have been curious about what we did over the last two days. That was okay with me because what she writes back matters. I always look forward to her remarks and thoughts, her suggestions and sense of humor.

I wasn't disappointed. On Tuesday morning we were all given a quiet period to read her feedback. She had a gift for making each of us feel important and worthy of the time she spent responding.

There was no denying she was captivated by my weekend experience. Her words brought tears to my eyes as I read. It was as if my ma was speaking through her. I could feel warmth, compassion and love from this woman who demanded initiative and personal excellence. When I finished reading her comments I looked up, only to find her gently smiling at me. Most kids would feel embarrassed, but I felt fortunate. I had a friend in my teacher.

Thanksgiving vacation seemed to come without warning. The small pool of water in the lower pasture was frozen solid. I thought of the pond next to our cabin and how Ma and Papa loved skating on it. We kids would take turns being pushed or pulled around on inner tubes, giving our folks a workout when they tied ropes around their midsections and towed us across the slick, icy surface. Bumping and laughing, we slid in every direction.

Grandma brought out the good china for our Thanksgiving meal. She let me light the tall brown candles while Eva placed a folded, newly sewn, rust colored napkin on each plate. Like Ma used to do, Grandma set a beautiful table for special occasions. Caleb rang the metal triangle hanging from the porch rafter to hurry the men along and, within minutes, three large sets of hands were fanned out in front of the fireplace.

Gramps was recruited to cut the turkey while Ben sliced the back strap from the buck he shot earlier in the month. We all found our places at the table and kept our hands clasped in our laps. Gramps proclaimed, "You can't beat a wild turkey and venison pairing to make a mighty fine meal. Don't get me wrong, Anne. The vegetables you put up from the garden come in a close second. I'm sure the Pilgrims would have loved to be able to lay out a spread like you."

Bitter cold had settled in and heavy clouds were pressing against the surrounding mountains. Eva waited patiently until Gramps finished saying grace when she pointed to the window and blurted out that it was snowing. All eyes followed her finger. We'd had a few small snowstorms pass through this fall, but none drove the flakes down with such velocity. Platters and bowls of food made their way around the long table as weather became our main topic of conversation.

"It's so nice to be sitting here with the fireplace crackling, at a table piled high with savory food and sharing it all with the ones we hold dear," Grandma said looking around the table.

I couldn't help but think of our little cabin quietly sitting alone while a deep blanket of snow thickened over it. We had always celebrated Thanksgiving there and Christmas dinner at the big ranch. It got a bit crowded at our house, but Ma said that's what made it so cozy. I'm sure Gramps and Grandma were having similar thoughts.

"I'd like to make a toast," Ben offered while raising his glass of wine.

"I wasn't aware you knew a different meaning of the word toast other than the kind you butter in the mornin'," Al said with a smirk.

"I'll have you know I've been to a wedding or two in my day," responded Ben.

"That's as close to being married as you'll ever get," Al laughed.

"Our wine will evaporate before you two stop quibbling," Gramps told them. "Let's hear what Ben has to say."

Because Grandma's mother was full Italian, she was raised with wine on the dinner table. She allowed us to have a watered down glass of wine two times a year, Thanksgiving and Christmas. With age, we were promised more wine and less water. But each year it always tasted like the same diluted stuff to me.

We all raised our glasses and looked over at Ben for his words of cheer.

"I know I've only been around for a couple of years. And I know it's the first time you have used this table for the Thanksgiving meal since before Ezra was born. I just want to give thanks for the two people who gave so much of themselves to their children." Looking at all of us kids he went on to say, "I'm thankful to have you youngins' as a part of my life. As we celebrate giving, we can't ignore all you have given us."

Grandma's eyes were full of tears and Gramps looked as though something was keeping him from breathing. Al just sat there staring at Ben with a dumbfounded look on his face. It was Caleb who broke the stillness when he lifted his glass a bit higher while aiming it in Ben's direction and said, "I'll drink to that."

All the grownups roared with laughter. The sensitive moment had passed. Glasses were tapped together and the four adults sipped their wine while the four of us youngins' tasted our watery version. Even though Luke and Eva didn't want their drinks, Grandma refused to let us two older boys help them out.

"You've had enough. You don't need to drink their wine too," she told us.

The next day was bright and white. Betty, Yodel and Wedge dove their noses into the soft mounds of snow while aiming their tails toward the sky. They would pounce on each other and run circles around all of us kids.

We built a snowman taller than me and dressed him in Gramps' tattered brown felt hat and two of his red bandanas tied together to reach around the snowman's neck. Al donated one of his old corncob pipes. Grandma rummaged through her sewing basket and found two large, navy blue coat buttons we used for the eyes. She also donated a flimsy carrot for the nose. We dug down through the snow on the driveway to find gravel that would line up together in a jagged smile for the mouth. Eva and Caleb broke dead branches off a nearby pine for the arms. Ben didn't disappoint us. He ran out of the bunkhouse with a long leather strap from Al's tooling workbench. He held it in place on the belly of our snowman by poking bailing wire pieces around it. They made perfect belt loops.

"I got one more thing to finish it off," Ben said while chuckling his way back to the ranch-hand sleeping quarters.

It didn't take but a minute before he reappeared with one of Al's rodeo buckles. Even Luke knew it meant trouble. "You goin' to use Al's buckle? Won't he get mad?"

"Probably," was all Ben said as he flashed his toothy grin.

Grandma came out and took pictures of us standing by our temporary buckaroo. Snow didn't make a habit of hanging around too long in these parts.

We all waited for the fireworks to begin when Al returned from his afternoon of hay spreading in the cow pasture. Grandma and us kids stood on the porch watching as Al stopped in front of the snowman and looked it over. With his hands on his hips and his head slightly shaking back and forth, he gave the impression that he wasn't all too pleased. He pulled off his elk gloves, slapped the side of his leg with them and said, "Well, I'll be damned." Turning, he headed for the house. We all ran inside in anticipation of what was to come.

Al entered the mudroom, removing his boots, coat and hat. Then he came into the kitchen and placed his wet gloves on the ornate metal shelf attached to the side of the hot wood stove. He poured himself a cup of coffee and went into the living room to sit on the hearth in front of the fire. He said nothing. It was obvious he was deep in thought.

The next morning Ben came in for breakfast wearing his sheep lined slippers, a long sleeved flannel shirt, his work pants and no hat.

"Good mornin'," Al said to Ben as he slid onto the bench next to me. "Did someone borrow your boots, hat, gloves and coat?"

"Yah, I lent them to that big fat cowboy out in the yard. He looked like he could use something of value since he was sportin' items of little worth."

"Good luck gettin' those 'valuable' things dry," Al told him before sipping from his steaming cup of coffee.

All of us kids couldn't wait another moment. We ran to the mudroom to bundle up and slip on our rubber boots. Without looking back, we bolted out the door to see what happened to the snowman. Ben's gloves were acting as hands on the end of the branches. From the left arm hung Ben's jacket. His hat was held by the snowman's right hand. Al had shaped the big bottom section of the snowman, giving it the appearance of two legs tapering off into cowboy boots. The only boots Ben owned were now filled with snow.

Grandma ran out with the camera again. "This is my last picture. I better make it good because I have no more film."

After breakfast Ben gathered his belongings, shook the snow from them and brought them into the house to thaw. He stuffed his boots with newspaper to absorb moisture and help keep their shape as they dried. Then he set them on the hearth. Ben hung his soaked hat and gloves on the metal fire tool rack and wrapped his coat around the kitchen chair before backing it up in front of the flames. By the looks of how wet everything was, Al must have let his creative juices flow during his waking spell.

"We can't let a little wet clothing keep us from gettin' our work done," Gramps told Ben. "You can either borrow some small sizes from Ezra or big sizes from me. I doubt Al is up to sharing anything with you."

Even Ben saw the humor in all of it. He settled for Gramps' rubber boots, knit hat, moth eaten coat, and worn mismatched gloves.

It made me wonder if it was Al who taught Papa about the "...just get even" thing.

CHAPTER 22

An Early Christmas

CHRISTMAS VACATION WAS RIGHT ON the heels of Thanksgiving, just as Wedge was on the heels of anything that moved. He showed no mercy for Betty. Finally Betty had enough. She disciplined him as only an angry mother could. He ran to me for comfort and sympathy, neither of which I would give. Al stood firm on his training techniques. Unlike Yodel, Wedge had a stubborn streak.

"That's a good trait to have if channeled in the right direction," Al pointed out. "Stubborn can evolve into determination if properly guided."

"Does that mean you're still evolving, or did you lose your guide along the way?" Ben asked innocently as he walked up behind Al.

Al made no sign of acknowledging Ben's presence and went on to say, "Some animal behavior is best to ignore, such as Wedge running to you after Betty punishes him. He'll get the message. Then there's those animals with brains the size of a horsefly. They aren't worth training because they'll never get the message." With that said, Al strode off to the barn.

"He loves me," Ben said matter-a-factly. We both laughed and went on to finish our chores.

A couple of days before Christmas, Grandma asked if anyone wanted to go to the cabin with her, knowing full well we all would. She needed to find a few things. Of course, the four of us kids jumped at the chance.

"Will we be able to get back there on the driveway?" I wondered out loud. "The road is probably covered with snow."

"Oh, we can bundle up and hike in. We'll drive across the meadow to the culvert and walk from there."

All the men had left before sunrise and would be gone for the day. Grandma wrote a note telling Gramps where we were headed while Caleb and I loaded the two small dogs into the back. Betty seemed happy to have a day to herself without harassment from her pups. Gramps insisted every vehicle have an emergency box during the cold months, so we slid that in next to Wedge and Yodel. It was actually a rectangular wooden crate with a hinged lid and a rope handle on each end. The contents included matches, a flashlight, blankets, first aid, dried food and water. It was an insurance policy in case the car broke down or got stuck. Once our bundled bodies found places on the two bench car seats, we set off for the cabin.

Surprisingly, the road to the upper unit had recently been used, allowing us to follow wide tracks through the snow. We progressed slowly up to the meadow. And there they were. Tink was hitched and stood patiently waiting in front of the sleigh Gramps' father had made. Except for special occasions, it stayed stored in the equipment barn at the ranch. The cattle truck had been used to haul the sleigh and three horses. It was the source of the tire tracks we had followed in. Gramps sat on the sleigh with reins in his gloved hands, ready to snap Tink into motion. Al and Ben were mounted and set to lead the way across the unspoiled snow.

"Are we goin' on a sleigh ride?" Eva asked while standing up behind Grandma and wrapping her little arms around Grandma's neck.

"Yes, we are. Surprise!" was Grandma's cheerful response.

Our car pulled off the road and parked next to the large truck. All four doors flew open at once. We tumbled out with great enthusiasm and ran toward the sleigh. I stopped short and returned to the car to free the barking dogs and help Grandma load the emergency box out onto the sleigh.

"Why are we taking the box?" Caleb asked as we got nearer.

"It's actually our dinner," she replied. "Gramps took the emergency items with him in the truck. We wanted this to be a big surprise."

"How come you wrote Gramps a note?" I questioned.

"Because that's what we do when we go somewhere. I knew you would think it was strange if I didn't leave one."

After we'd all scrambled into the sleigh and snuggled close together under heavy quilts, Gramps clicked his tongue and snapped the reins. Tink lifted her mighty Belgium hooves and the bells on her harness played their cheerful tune as Ben and Al guided our way. They started in on a familiar chorus, Ben raising his voice in song as Al played his harmonica. Everyone in the sleigh chimed in to sing "Jingle Bells" as it had never been sung before. It was Christmas cheer at its best, something no amount of money could buy.

Ben and Al led us in a whole slew of Christmas carols as we made our way to the cabin. Wedge and Yodel ran alongside, straying only to chase an occasional rabbit or distant deer. The untouched snow spread delicately over fallen trees and limbs. It covered boulders with artistic precision while coating the tops of each evergreen branch. The barren aspen trees were not ignored. Wisps of snow stuck to the white bark and highlighted their skeletal frames. Ice crystals hung randomly from the barbed wire fence, clinging to horse and other animal hair that the sharp prongs had snagged. It was a sight not many people live to see and a moment in time few experience.

As Al and Ben led us through the leafless aspen grove to the base of the knoll, the four of us kids gasped at the sight. There was our smiling cabin decked with holiday greenery and tied with bright red bows on each porch post. Centered high on the front door was a wreath thick with pine needles, white aspen twigs, and wild red berries. A thin trail of smoke worked its way out the chimney and disappeared into the light blue sky.

"Look, Santa came!" Luke cried out while pointing at the cabin.

"Yep, I think you're right," Gramps smiled back at him.

None of our small bodies could stay sitting with the giddy excitement built up inside us. As soon as Tink pulled next to the hitching post we jumped off the sleigh and ran up the steps. We knew Santa had been here. There were no signs of entry on the snow indicating footprints, man or animal, all the way from where we began the sleigh ride. Whoever did this had to fly over and land on the roof. It made perfect sense.

My long legs had an advantage over the others. I made it to the door first and gave it a hefty push. One surprise led to another. A decorated blue spruce stood in front of the window to the left of the fireplace. And there, across the edge of the mantel, hung the four stockings Ma had made for us. Each was spilling over with fruit, candy and small gifts. A pang of sadness wiggled its way into my big grin when I saw that two stockings were missing. As mine and Caleb's eyes met, I knew he felt the same sorrow at not having Ma and Papa with us. I patted his back and did my best to smile again, for Eva and Luke's sakes if not for ours.

Gramps and Grandma filled the doorway and voiced their genuine surprise at what Santa Claus had done.

"It appears Santa lit a fire on his way out. By the looks of it he left just a little while ago. I guess he had to hurry, seeing how there's so many kids on his list," Gramps reasoned. He looked at me and added, "You best keep that fire goin'. I'll haul the crate in while Ben and Al unhitch Tink and put the horses in the barn."

Caleb pulled the heavy screen from the fireplace while I headed out the kitchen door for more logs. Wedge met me by the woodpile with his nose to the snow covered ground. I stacked as much wood into my arms as I could and headed back to the door. It was then I noticed Wedge in the cluster of trees to the rear of the cabin. He was making an odd noise, between a cry and a nervous whimper. I opened the door and set the split logs on the bench for Caleb to retrieve and then went over to see what was causing Wedge such distress.

It didn't take long for me to put the puzzle together. Wedge stood over large, distinct human footprints in the snow. Leaning against a tall pine were snowshoes. When I looked back I could see where the shallow tracks were made right up against the cabin's foundation. Someone had used evergreen branches to try and sweep away the evidence of their visit. I noticed broken branches on the ground next to the snowshoes. I followed the deep footprints that skirted the back side of the pond. There I found horse tracks pressing the snow down into mud in a large circular pattern. Apparently, the horse was tied to the sapling while our "Santa" did his deed. Human tracks were lost at this point as the horse and rider took an indirect route toward the county road.

"Hmm, what do you think Wedge? Was it Ben, Al or Gramps? We'll keep this a secret, okay? No use spoilin' all their fun. Besides, it'll give a real boost to Luke, Eva and Caleb's imaginations. We'll just play along."

It was going to be a challenge keeping the grownups from knowing I was "onto" them. When we got back to the woodpile I picked up a piece of kindling and tossed it for Wedge to play fetch. I figured I'd make a mess of the snow where our tracks led into the brush. Wedge was the perfect partner. He ran, jumped, rolled and dove all over the evidence.

Grandma stuck her head out the back door and asked, "When are you coming in? We're all waiting on you so the stockings can be taken down."

"I'm comin'." Looking at Wedge I told him to stay away from the backside of the cabin and pond. I led him up onto the porch and opened the front door.

Al and Ben had returned from tending the horses and a huge assortment of food was spread across the kitchen table.

"I'm leaving the food out for a while. You can eat what you want, when you want," Grandma informed everyone.

"Let's see what you kids got in your stockings first," said Gramps. "We can talk about eatin' after that."

He walked over to the mantle and slipped the first stocking off its hook. "This one has Luke's name on it," he said. The youngest of us eagerly reached to take it. "And here's Eva's." They were all given out in quick order. The contents of each hit the floor in front of four kneeling bodies with eight little hands eagerly separating their goods.

"Look, I gotta pocket knife!" Caleb shouted.

"And I gotta vest!" Eva exclaimed as she unrolled the tied up leather bundle.

Luke was thrilled to receive a pop gun with a cork and string attached to the barrel. And I got my first pair of spurs. We each had a candy cane, popcorn ball, apple, tangerine, chocolate covered almonds, tooth brush, and assorted nuts in their shells. The nuts never excited us, but Ma had said that Santa was a very traditional kind of guy.

Grandma had brought cold venison topped and rolled with mushrooms, pesto and sautéed red onions. There were four varieties of cheese, homemade rolls, potato salad, stuffed eggs, apple slices, tossed salad and fried chicken. On the counter a berry pie and oatmeal cookies were lying in wait.

We all sat around the living room eating, talking and laughing. After we finished our first round of food, Ben challenged Luke, Eva, Caleb and me to a snowball fight. One against four seemed like great odds in our favor. Little did we know how accurate Ben was. What good are four arms slinging smallish snowballs against a moving target that's throwing a bull's eye ninety-nine percent of the time? Wedge and Yodel were all over the place trying to intercept the flying white bomb shells. We didn't win the fight, but we sure wore Ben out.

Ice skating on the pond was the next sporting event. Everyone but Al got in on the action. "I'm lucky these legs still want to hold me up," Al grumbled. "There's no sense in beatin' up on two of your best friends. They've been with me for all my ups and downs. I ain't about to rile them now."

The rest of us took our own "two best friends" onto the ice. We used feed sacks and the two stored inner tubes to sit on while Ben, Gramps and Grandma pulled us around. Wedge and Yodel were beside themselves trying to run on the slick surface. Wedge's overgrown paws were everywhere but under him. Yodel finally took advantage of an empty spot on Caleb's feed sack. She hopped on when it came close to her and enjoyed the free ride. Wedge, being the stubborn dog he was, ignored all the coaxing any of us made to get him onto a sack. He stumbled, slid and fell but would not stop trying to walk upright.

We were hard at it as shadows spread over our little world. The afternoon sun eased its way behind the mountains. We went indoors to eat some dessert and warm ourselves by the fire. Grandma packed up the few remaining left-overs and Gramps hitched Tink to the sleigh while Al and Ben saddled their horses. The four of us shoved our stash back into our stockings and helped clean the cabin. Caleb and I lugged the half empty crate back to the sleigh. Caleb set his end down and ran to the front so Gramps could lift him up onto Tink's back, where Luke and Eva were already perched.

As I tried pushing the crate the rest of the way, it got hung up on a blanket. When I leaned down to scoot the blanket aside, it slipped off what it had been covering. There, now partially exposed, were the two snowshoes. Only one person had the chance to retrieve them from where they leaned against the tree and then hide them in the sleigh. I smiled as I pictured our gimpy Santa taking his "two best friends" for a walk behind the cabin while everyone else enjoyed playing on the frozen pond.

I quickly covered them back up and went into the cabin to help Grandma. She was just about finished taking the ornaments off the tree. The cabin was spotless. I flattened out the embers with the poker and pulled the large metal screen back across the fireplace opening.

"What are we goin' to do with the Christmas tree?" I asked Grandma.

"Ben had a great idea. He offered to tie it up and drag it behind Rio. If it doesn't settle right with Rio, he knows Dolly would tolerate pulling the extra baggage. Then we'll set it up again at the ranch. I plan on taking the greenery, bows and wreath from the door with us too. You kids will be buried in pine and spruce on the sleigh ride back to the car."

She went out with all our refilled stockings in her hands. I began taking down the garlands hooked on the porch posts and laying them in the sleigh. I reflected back on the last week and thought about how Grandma had been gone an entire day right before the snowstorm. She said there was some holiday shopping she needed to do. Funny thing though, she didn't bring any bags into the house when she got back. Maybe she hid them, but my guess is that she was really at the cabin, getting it ready for our early Christmas. The decorations and hanging stockings definitely had a woman's touch.

When I hauled the last load of greenery to the sleigh I noticed the snowshoes had been taken from under the blanket, probably hidden in the crate by Grandma.

Ben called me back into the cabin and had me help him tug the tree through the door's opening. The trunk end was fastened with a rope long enough to reach the saddle horn and back again to the trunk. Ben's body would separate the ropes and allow the spruce to stay centered behind his horse.

That was the plan anyway. Rio would have none of it though. The high spirited horse danced around and kicked at the makeshift travois, a type of sled similar to those used by the Plains Indians when transporting their family goods.

"It looks like it's Ol' Al to the rescue again," Al said with a wiseacre tone.

The rope was taken from Ben's saddle horn and wrapped around Al's. Al pulled himself up onto his well worn leather seat and followed the indented path we'd made in the snow when coming to the cabin. Tink stepped in line and Ben brought up the rear. Rio was having nothing to do with the tree that was chasing Dolly.

The bells on the harness rang out and Al played softly on his harmonica. Most of us chattered the entire way back to the gate. Luke was all done in. It was almost dark by the time we reached the parked truck and car. The full moon cleared the tops of the trees, shedding much needed light. The snow did its part to help our night vision by absorbing and reflecting the beams cast down. Gramps took Luke from Grandma's arms and laid him on the back seat of the car without waking him. Eva took little time joining in on the slumber once she crawled up next to Luke. Caleb and I loaded the dogs and wooden crate while the sleigh, greenery and tree were piled into the truck and the horses led up the ramp.

We used everything we brought back to the ranch to decorate and celebrate again two days later. We missed our folks terribly, but felt fortunate to have people in our lives that loved and cared for us. It was a holiday never to be forgotten and a memory we could build upon. It was also the last time the eight of us celebrated Christmas together.

CHAPTER 23

The New Year

A NEW YEAR BROUGHT IN new hopes and visions for the future. With refreshed energy, Gramps and Grandma settled into their roles as parents. Grandma even thanked us during Gramps' birthday celebration for making them feel years younger. I guess taking on four grandkids had a way of jolting their hearts into motion and their brains into thinking on overtime. There was no slowing down for them now.

Mrs. Murphy must have experienced the same energy surge. She pulled out all the stops. Her demands were elevated and the workload became overwhelming at times. What used to be occasional pleasure reading became constant and required study.

"We're stepping it up a bit," she warned us. Moans could be heard throughout the classroom. Mrs. Murphy just smiled sweetly and said, "Oh, how lovely. That's like music to my ears."

True to her word, we had no homework on weekends as long as we kept up during the week. I made sure those two days were left free. Caleb and I spent many of our Saturday and Sunday hours working with Yodel and Wedge. Al was the perfect resource. He offered advice and spent much of his time steering us and the dogs in the right direction.

It was in early February when Gramps loaded up Yodel and Wedge for a visit to the vet. I knew this was coming. As a matter-a-fact, it was a might overdue. Since Caleb and I didn't have school that day, we asked to go along and Gramps welcomed the company.

The dogs were oblivious to their fates all the way to town. We remembered how uncomfortable Betty was coming home from her vet experience and feared for our pups.

Wedge was taken first. I handed his leash to the vet and surprised even myself when I looked up at him and asked if I could be with Wedge during his surgery. The vet glanced over at Gramps for his approval. I used my eyes to plead with Gramps for what seemed a small request.

I could see Gramps processing my desire to stay with Wedge. He looked me straight in the eyes as he nodded yes. "But, if it gets too much for you, you're to quietly leave. You can come back here and wait with Caleb and me."

I thanked him and glanced over at Caleb who had the "What the heck are you thinkin'?" look on his face. Wedge seemed less nervous as I walked with him into surgery.

Castration was nothing new to any of us kids. We had stood by while many calves and colts were altered, usually during branding season. It was just different when it came to my dog. He trusted and depended on me. He also comforted and, I swear, understood me. I felt as though I was betraying him. The least I could do was stay by his side and let him know I wouldn't desert him.

The vet was "well-seasoned", as Grandma would say about the elderly. He was gentle and had a way with animals. He thanked me for coming in to help and struck up a conversation that lasted throughout the entire procedure. Wedge was given a sedative and laid still with his head on my opened left palm.

Come to find out, the vet was an old friend of Al's. He actually seemed a bit surprised Al didn't fix Wedge himself.

"You mean Al knows how to do this?"

"He sure does," answered the doc. "He was in vet school with me until a bronc got the best of him. He was laid up for a while and ended up dropping out. The cost of vet school was more than he could handle, and laying around while recovering had a way of putting a stop to his money flow. It was a shame. He was one of the best."

The doc was quiet for a moment and then went on to say, "It was the same year he lost his wife and little boy to influenza."

I was shocked to learn about some of the missing pieces of Al's past. It was easy to visualize Al's quiet demeanor as he skillfully worked on animals. No wonder Gramps called him his "right hand man". There were few deaths during calving season, thanks to Al. I was saddened to learn about the passing of his wife and son. It explained the pain in his eyes when we lost our folks. He already knew how it felt to have the companionship and happiness of those you hold dear stripped from your life.

After some deep thought, I went on to mention how Wedge had struggled to live and how Al had saved him. "He breathed life into my dog when he was born," I told the vet.

"Is that'a fact?" he responded. "I'm not a bit surprised. There aren't many men like him who are tough as nails, yet carry around a heart as soft as an angel's wing."

It was similar to a comment Grandma had once made about Gramps. They both had heavy crosses to carry. They both worked through their struggles without complaining or imposing on others. Not many kids like us were fortunate enough to have two such examples in their lives.

We continued to talk as I watched and petted Wedge's head and neck. The vet was patient with my questions and took his time showing me what he was doing. It wasn't long before he was finished and asked me to carry my dog into the adjoining room where he could safely recover in a small pen.

"Would you like to come back while I work on the female pup?" he asked me. "You show quite an interest, and you're not a bit squeamish."

"I'd like that, but I'll have to ask Gramps first."

"Go do your asking. I'll clean this table up and get things ready for the girl pup."

Caleb was full of questions when I walked back into the waiting room. I told him I'd fill him in on the way home.

"The doctor is ready for Yodel, and he asked me if I would like to watch with her too."

Caleb's eyes grew as his eyebrows shot up on his forehead. "You want to watch Yodel's stomach gettin' cut open?" he asked in amazement.

Gramps sat looking at me and contemplating my request. "If you think you can handle it, go ahead. You know the way back here if you need to take a breather."

I felt so grown up as I led Yodel into the operating room. The vet bent down to pat her head and befriend her with his calm voice. He had me lift her onto the table and told me to talk to her as he gave her a shot.

She relaxed immediately and was sound asleep within a minute. Her belly was shaved and sanitized. I knew what was coming for the little girl. Memories of Betty were still fresh in my mind.

I thought the whole ordeal was very interesting. It didn't faze me in the least as I watched the vet make the incision. He explained each step and named the instruments used to accomplish what needed to be done. It was an experience I never expected and was one that made an impact on the direction I would ultimately take.

By the time Yodel was put in the pen to recover, Wedge was alert and licking his wound. He spotted me and tried to get out of the enclosure. "You gotta stay here for a while. I'll be back to get you when Yodel wakes up."

The vet was in the waiting room talking to Gramps and Caleb. He suggested the three of us run any needed errands and maybe get a treat somewhere. "It'll give the pups time to get their wits about them again."

"I think we can find ourselves somethin' to do," Gramps answered. Looking at us he said, "Let's load up, boys. There's sure to be some ice cream waitin' for us at the pharmacy. That is if you can eat ice cream on such a cold day."

We didn't have to be teased twice. We headed for the car, leaving Gramps to pay the bill. I began telling Caleb about the two surgeries. He kept shaking his head and repeating how he couldn't do what I did and still keep his breakfast down.

Gramps got into the car during the telling of the second half of my experience. "Maybe you'll follow in Al's footprints and have a knack for fixin' animals. The vet was quite impressed with the way you handled yourself."

"Did you know Al went to vet school with the doc?" I asked Gramps.

"Yep, he woulda made a great vet. But then we wouldn't have had him livin' with us. We're lucky he's a part of our lives.

"I asked Al once if he had any regrets," continued Gramps. "He said he didn't regret anything he had control over. He did everything he set out to do, even though his life took a few unexpected turns. As for me, he's the older brother I never had. He fills a void in my life. And I really believe our growing ranch would have been unsustainable without him."

Gramps didn't mention Al losing his wife and child, and I didn't want to bring it up at that time. We headed to the store to get a few things on Grandma's list and then to the pharmacy. Caleb and I were as predictable as the sun coming up in the morning. We each thought about trying a new flavor, but we walked out with our traditional vanilla and chocolate ice cream cones pushed up against our mouths. Gramps couldn't decide on any one kind, so he opted for a double scooper with the same brown and white flavors we loved. "I guess we're just content with the basics when it comes to selecting ice cream," he said as his tongue whipped off a layer of vanilla.

We headed back to the vet's to pick up our "wounded soldiers", as Gramps put it. I could hear Wedge scratching at the cage door and whimpering as soon as he heard our voices. When we entered the recovery room he was standing on his two back legs as if trying to push the door open with his front paws. Yodel was alert but laying quietly on a large pad.

"By jiggers, he looks no worse for the wear," Gramps commented on entering the room.

I immediately opened his cage and clipped the leash onto his collar. Caleb and Gramps went over to Yodel and helped ease her out of the pen. Gramps lifted her carefully, thanked the vet, and gently carried her to the car. Caleb pulled the tailgate down and jumped on it to raise the back window so Gramps could easily set Yodel on the bedding reserved just for her.

"Can I sit with her?" Caleb asked.

"I don't see why not," replied Gramps.

I settled in on the back seat with Wedge. Gramps mumbled something about feeling like one of those rich people's chauffeurs as he turned the car around and headed home.

"You're lucky you're a boy," I whispered to Wedge. He stood on my lap with his neck stretching upward in order to squeeze his wet nose into the window's inch opening. The cold blast was a real bone chiller, but it helped to keep the inside window clear of condensation and it gave Yodel fresh air in the back. Wedge just acted as though it was another day in paradise.

When we drove up to the house Al was standing by the hitching post ready to receive his new patients. He patted Wedge's head and said, "Sorry about that, ol' boy. But you sure don't look too upset about the whole thing." Then he went to the back of the car and eased Yodel out into his arms. "It's this little girl that needs some attention." He carried her to the bunkhouse where she would be given special treatment for a day or two.

Within a week all three dogs were playing together once again. And all four of us kids were spending a lot of time cutting, pasting and coloring Valentines. Caleb talked Eva into making a bunch for his classroom. She was pretty darn creative for her age. For the record, she put Caleb to shame with her artistic ability. He ended up giving her a bubblegum ball that some kid at school traded him for his cookie. She made every single one of his Valentine cards. All Caleb had to do was sign them and write a little poem on the one for his teacher.

Eva, Luke and Wedge came with Gramps to pick us up from school on Valentine's Day. When we got home Grandma was out driving the tractor while Ben and Al tossed hay from the attached wagon onto the frozen ground. The cattle followed the path of feed until they found the perfect place to stop and dine. After Grandma made a wide turn and headed our way, we spotted Yodel. She was sitting on Grandma's lap and zipped into her oversized coat. Only her furry little head was sticking out under Grandma's chin. Betty was happily running along the side of the tractor, staying clear of the large tires.

All of us raced into the house for a quick snack and for Caleb and me to change out of our school clothes. Eva was first to spot the red and white checked cloth with the decorated, leafless Valentine tree on top of the kitchen table. There were frosted sugar cookies hanging by small red ribbons, as well as chocolate truffles. The Valentine Bug even left dog treats hanging on the tree. Next to the base of it was a shoebox that had been wrapped with red paper and decorated with pink hearts. Sometime during the last day everyone had pushed the cards they made for each other into the slit on top. I know Luke was still hard at work on his when we left for school this morning, but he must have finished them in time to come with Gramps to pick us up.

We knew better than to open or take anything from the table without the go-ahead. Luke ran out the back door and to the pasture fence, yelling all the way that the Valentine Bug had come. "Hurry, you gotta see what he brought. There's enough for you guys too."

We all followed him and waited while Gramps opened the gate for the tractor and trailer. Smiles were everywhere. Ben grabbed Luke's little hand and said, "Show me what the Valentine Bug brought us."

We all returned to the house with the older folks in tow. Grandma put on a pot of coffee and heated some milk for hot cocoa. We were limited on our sweet treats before supper. That was fine with me. I liked to eat a little at a time so it would last longer. No such thing with Caleb. It was his goal to devour everything the first day. That prevented it from getting stale, so he said. Eva and Luke were better than him when it came to pacing themselves.

Al even got the Valentine itch. He made each of us something out of leather scraps. Eva and Grandma got little hearts with tooling on the front. They were threaded with leather string to wear as necklaces. Gramps got a key ring with a large leather tag attached. The word TRUCK was tooled on it. This was a bit of a sore subject since Gramps was forever misplacing his key. I got a leather collar with Wedge's name on it. Luke and Caleb shared Yodel's collar, plus they got small coin pouches for their pockets.

Ben wasn't left out. Al made a leather strip about a foot long and five inches wide. There were two holes punched and centered on the top that were connected by a leather string. It was obviously a sign. On it was the word OCCUPIED. Ben laughed immediately. Everyone else just looked at the unusual gift.

"I was gonna have it say GET LOST. But I figured, it being Valentines and all, I'd go easy on you," Al told Ben. "Since closed bathroom doors don't mean a dang thing to you, this sign might be a good reminder. I'm not puttin' money on it, but I'm hopin'."

It all became crystal clear. Everyone howled. Even Luke got the gist of it.

Ben had small mint candies tied up for everyone and Gramps had written his name on all the Valentine cards that Grandma made and also signed. There was a quarter glued to each of ours and silver dollars on Al and Ben's cards.

Caleb's and my birthdays would be the next celebrations coming up at the end of March. It had been almost a year since we moved in with our grandparents. We would always miss Ma and Papa, but I think it's safe to say that, because of the love those four distinct personalities constantly bestowed on us, we never felt slighted.

CHAPTER 24

Chicken Pox

School was something to reckon with and calving season was taking its toll on Gramps, Al and Ben. They moved around like zombies for about a week before Caleb's birthday. My birthday falls ten days after his. Ma always kept them separate and special for each of us, but it wasn't to be this time around. Caleb and I will never forget our combined celebrations.

One thing school is known for is its capability to become an incubator for germs. We did pretty well when it came to controlling the common cold, but chicken pox was a whole new can of worms. Caleb was first to introduce and share the red bumps with the rest of us. It started in his classroom and spread like gangbusters throughout the school. Caleb had been tired and complained of his head hurting. It was his agitation in bed one night that brought everything into focus. He tossed and turned until I finally snapped at him to be still and go to sleep. When Grandma entered our room to see what the fuss was all about, she found Caleb hot with a fever and his chest and back covered with red spots. It was a given that Caleb would not be going to school anytime soon.

She kept me home from class too, which proved to be a wise decision. By supper time I had lost my energy and appetite. When Grandma inspected my back and chest she found a few spots popping up. Now I understood why Caleb jerked the bunk bed and, therefore, me out of my sleep the night before. The itching was unbearable.

Grandma gave us oatmeal baths to reduce the need to scratch. She also banned all dogs from the house. They were made as comfortable as possible in their shed outside. She had a single mattress from the bunkhouse brought up for her to sleep on while caring for us.

Within three days Eva and Luke had joined the chicken pox crew. Grandma put their mattress in our room on the floor close to hers. Day and night she watched over us. She ran herself ragged keeping cool compresses on our heads and making sure we ate a little. The ice trays were kept full at all times. We drank liquids and chomped on crushed ice as much as possible to keep hydrated. She read to us a lot and did her best to keep us in good spirits. She set up puzzles, crayons and water colors in Eva and Luke's room in case we felt up to doing something.

Gramps, Al and Ben had their hands full with delivering calves from the thirty-four heifers, who were about to earn their cow status. There were also over two hundred cows in the pasture who were due to deliver. Al and Ben took turns riding out every morning to check on the cows and tally the calves born overnight. A few of them were born dead, but most were found standing with their mouths drinking in the milk from their mothers' utters.

The heifers had never been through the birthing experience before and needed closer monitoring. They were kept in the big corral behind the barn. When they looked close to calving they were brought into the barn and put into stalls. Most of the heifers delivered their calves without assistance. But, there were always those who had a difficult time. They were put into a head catch, or stanchion. Once the heifer's head was locked in, she was held captive until her calf was delivered. This is where Gramps, Al and Ben got to be our veterinarians. Grandma jokingly called them midwives.

All of us kids have watched as chains were wrapped and hooked around the front legs of the calf trying to exit the womb. When ranchers talk about "pulling" a calf, they mean just that. With the chains in place, a ratchet is used to crank, or pull, the calf from the heifer. It's tough to hear and watch the young heifer working to drop the calf. Al, Ben and Gramps had a lot of experience and used their skills to minimize the mother's pain and still deliver a healthy baby. Between the cows and heifers, they stayed busy all hours of the day and night.

Late one evening, about the same time Luke got sick, Al went to the barn to relieve Ben from his night shift only to find him sitting on a bale of hay, shivering, with a horse blanket covering his heavy coat. Al felt his forehead and said, "You're burnin' up. Why didn't you come get me? What good are you deliverin' a calf when you're too weak to stand? I have a sneaky suspicion you never had the chicken pox when you were little."

Ben just shook his head and said he couldn't remember if he had or hadn't.

Al mustered up all his strength and lifted Ben into a standing position. He half walked, half drug Ben back to the bunkhouse.

"You're a sight for sore eyes," Al remarked after removing Ben's coat and boots. He stoked up the fire and unsnapped the front of Ben's shirt. "My God, you have the worst case of chicken pox I've ever seen." He made Ben as comfortable as possible and said, "Don't get out of this bed. I'll be right back."

Al went straight to the house and woke Gramps. They agreed Al should stay with Ben as much as possible while Gramps took over Al's shift in the barn.

By this time the worst was over for Caleb and me. Our appetites had picked up some, but we were still weak from days of almost no solid foods and very little activity. Grandma looked plum tuckered out, and we hardly saw Gramps. He had moved to the bunkhouse to help with Ben and be closer to the barn. Grandma ran food out to them between caring for all of us and trying to get a little sleep herself.

Luke didn't look too bad, but Eva was a mess. She listened to Grandma and avoided scratching the annoying red bumps. Grandma worried Eva's "sweet little face" would be scarred for life.

Caleb and I helped Grandma move her small mattress and Eva and Luke's double mattress back to their room. We were both glad we were no longer in intensive care. "You're in the recovery room now," Grandma told us. Nothing felt better than feeling good, and nothing beat having our room back to ourselves.

"Can I haul Wedge's bed back up here?" I asked Grandma.

"Not until we're out of the woods," was her response.

Caleb and I assured Grandma we could fix our own food. One thing Ma insisted on was making us cook alongside her as much as possible. Breakfast was the easiest meal by far to prepare. We made bacon, eggs, potatoes and toast the first morning that Grandma gave the okay. There was plenty for any of us who had a desire to eat.

The next morning didn't go so well. The burner was too hot and we forgot to grease the pan for the first batch of pancakes. Grandma followed the burnt smell down to the kitchen and offered some helpful advice. It was smooth sailing from there. We made a few dollar sized pancakes for Eva and Luke, regular ones for Caleb and me, and huge Texas sized ones for Gramps, Grandma and Al. They all seemed genuinely grateful. Ben still had no appetite.

Caleb served Luke and Eva their pancakes upstairs in their bed, and Gramps came into the kitchen to eat his with Grandma, Caleb and me. After breakfast I volunteered to take Al's food out to him in the bunkhouse, hoping Ben would get a whiff and want some. We kept hearing about Ben's fragile condition, but nothing prepared me for the young man I saw laying in Ben's bed. He didn't look like himself. His face was a mass of blisters and his eyes were swollen almost shut below the cold compress laying across his forehead. Al was holding his head up with one hand and spooning broth between his split, crusted lips.

It was both heart wrenching and strange to watch as Al cared for him. He seemed genuinely worried. Who would have thought Ben would be on the receiving end of Al's fatherly concern? I thought of the son and wife Al no longer had. There was no doubt in my mind he carried their loss around with him tucked away silently, as I did with my folks.

Al looked up at me and nodded his head toward the table as he said, "Just set it over there, Ez. So, what did you and Caleb cook up this morning?"

"We made you some Texas sized pancakes. Maybe Ben will eat some too."

"Well now, maybe he will," Al responded not too convincingly.

I saw enough. Ben wasn't going to be out and about any time soon. His drowsy eyes followed me as I walked up to his bed. He tried to smile, but even that was an effort.

"Don't try flashin' your pearly whites, you fool. What do you want to do, crack those young whippersnapper lips of yours?" Al scolded in a tough but undeniable loving tone.

"Take care of yourself," I told Ben. "Caleb and I are feelin' real good and we can do a lot of your work. So don't worry."

He closed his eyes momentarily, using them to do his smiling. I left Al to his mending ways and headed to the barn where the animals waited for their turn to eat.

Gramps was already there throwing hay to the three heifers in their stalls. He stopped at the last one and watched momentarily. I joined him and could see right away that the heifer was in distress.

"Help me get the girl into the stanchion, Ez. She's havin' a hard time of it."

Together, Gramps and I coaxed the heifer out of the stall and into the triangular pen. She was scared and in a lot of pain. Once her head was clamped in place, Gramps and I waited by her tail end for signs of the newborn. With each contraction the heifer bellowed. The time seemed to drag by before we detected two hooves followed by thin little legs. Gramps was quick to apply the chains. He asked me to help him tug to free the calf. We both put all our limited strength into pulling. There was little, if any, progress. Gramps allowed the ratchet to take over. He cranked and the poor heifer yelled out as the calf's nose appeared, then its entire head, the neck and shoulders. Finally, with amazing speed, the rest of its body dropped to the ground.

Al surprised us by coming in as the calf did his freefall. He helped Gramps wipe away the mucus from the calf's nose and mouth. He stuck a straw into one of the nostrils to activate breathing. There was no response. Gramps touched one of the opened eyes and got no reaction. The calf had been dead for some time inside the heifer. Gramps said he'd haul the little carcass to the draw. I saw how exhausted both men were and offered to take it myself.

"Do you think you can handle it, Ez?" Gramps asked in a defeated tone.

"Sure. I'm guessin' Caleb will give me a hand. I'll run up to the house and get him."

Within the hour we had pushed the wheel barrel (used to transport stillborn calves) over the back bridge and south, away from the river. Each of us grabbed a back leg and drug it to the hollow. We threw it into the dead draw, or pit, where our dead animals were dumped. There was no sense burying them. The coyotes and bear would have them dug up and devoured in nothing flat. It was nature's way.

A week and a half after the first signs of the pox showed up on Caleb, the worst was over. All of us kids were back into the routine of doing a few chores, eating better and playing. The pox sores were disappearing and Ben was sitting up at the table in the bunkhouse spoon feeding himself. Eva's face was clearing up nicely, but a few spots on her tummy would tell the tale for the rest of her life. The three people, who had the chicken pox as youngsters and didn't go this round with us, looked the worst. They were beat down by lack of sleep, work overload and worry.

By that time nineteen calves had been born, two of which never took their first breath. One of the cows had been found standing over her stillborn calf the day after we lost the one born to the heifer.

I started thinking about all the school work I missed and began to fret. Grandma asked what was weighting my shoulders down and I told her I was bound to be buried in school work when I returned.

She laughed and said, "I forgot to tell you. Your teacher called last week and said the chicken pox had spread like wildfire throughout all the classrooms. They decided to close the school down for two weeks until the epidemic was under control. Because of it, you'll be getting no vacation come Easter."

Everything looked a lot brighter after hearing the news about school. My appetite went back into full swing and the dogs were allowed into the house again. Wedge was beyond excited as he followed his bed and me up to our room. Betty got her customary spot in the mudroom back, and Gramps said Yodel could sleep with Luke and Eva.

Caleb was never one to glance at the calendar. His birthday came and went without so much a peep from him. I mentioned the fact to Grandma and she said it would be best to delay it until everyone was up for celebrating.

It had been almost two weeks since we all sat at the supper table together. Grandma, Caleb and I spent the whole morning making a special meal. Grandma asked the two of us the night before what we wanted for supper. We wasted no time making our desires known. Our stomachs were ready to take on the flavorful foods Grandma could rustle up and pass our way. The table was set for eight and Eva had Luke help her make an arrangement in the center of the table using pine cones and evergreen branches. It looked like Christmas instead of the end of March, but Caleb and I held our tongues. Grandma raved about the beauty of it all and acted as though she didn't notice the off season decor.

The menfolk entered the mudroom, removed their hats, boots and coats, and washed up before coming into the kitchen. I didn't know who looked worse, Al or Ben. They had both lost weight. Their faces were sunken and pale, but their eyes were full of life. Ben gave everyone a half smile as we found our places around the table. It was the Sunday right before my birthday. Gramps offered a prayer of thanks that each of us felt deeply. Life was good again. We were all anxious to use our renewed strength and restored vigor.

The meal was perfect. Ben ate very little, but as Al put it, "Baby steps, just take baby steps, Ben."

I had a feeling we were fixin' to celebrate a birthday or two. And sure enough, Grandma had baked and decorated two cakes. Gramps carried the chocolate one out of the pantry and Grandma followed with a vanilla. Both were lit with candles, ten on mine and eight on Caleb's. Everyone sang to us and promised gifts at a later date. No one had time to make anything or shop for us since the chicken pox entered our home. That was okay with Caleb and me. We really hadn't asked for anything. The dinner set for eight was enough. Combining the two birthdays was a great idea. It was "just what the doctor ordered".

CHAPTER 25

Mrs. Murphy

THERE WERE THREE MORE TRIPS to the dead draw by the time calving season ended. One included a seasoned cow. Gramps used the tractor to remove her carcass from the pasture so that it wouldn't encourage wild critters to come in with the cattle.

Incredibly the old cow's calf survived, barely. Had the cow died a week earlier, one of the stillborn calves' skins could have been grafted onto the little feller. He'd have a good chance of being accepted and cared for by the dead calf's mom. The men of the ranch have all skinned dead calves, stretched their hides over live ones, and cut slits by the armpits and groins to slip the legs through, fitting them with temporary overcoats. Keeping the grafting in place for one day was all a calf needed to smell like the newborn he wasn't. If the mother accepted him as her own, life for everyone would be much easier.

As it was, Al assigned Ben the task of mothering it. "You might as well make yourself useful now that you can stand upright again," he told Ben. "I'll show you some tricks to keepin' it alive. The main thing is feedin' it. You'll have to use some of Bossy's milk. I doubt she'll take on another mouth, being the ornery cuss she is. You milking her will produce plenty for the little orphan, with ample left for her own calf."

It might have been a job given to Ben, but all of us wanted to help with the bottle feeding. Bossy was kept in a small corral next to the barn, where she had access to one of the inside stalls. She loved her calf, but she loved her grain more. It was easy to milk her while she ate. Her calf nursed from the opposite side of where Ben sat on his stool and squeezed the warm white substance from Bossy's teats. He then poured the contents of his bucket into a quart milk bottle and topped it off with a large rubber nipple.

The four of us kids took turns feeding Orphan, the name inspired by Al. Orphan would stand rigidly on all four of his lanky legs and tilt his head up to receive his meal. He wagged his tail back and forth like a dog's while he gulped the warm liquid. White foam would develop around his mouth and drip down to the straw bedding. He'd empty the bottle and then butt at it for more. We would give him our fingers to suck instead. That pacified him for a short period of time, and then he'd go on an all out butting rampage again. Luke and Eva were quick to jump up on the stall rails to avoid being smashed against the wall. Caleb and I were more inclined to turn Orphan's shenanigans into our own private rodeo. Wedge and Yodel threw fits trying to get in to us. They could hear the hootin' and hollerin' and fought with all they had to be a part of the action. Ben usually let us play a bit before telling all of us to climb out of the stall.

Caleb and I headed back to school and our old daily routines were in full swing. We dug our heels in and faced the ending months of classwork without much enthusiasm.

Easter vacation consisted of one extra day tacked onto the weekend. That worked for us. We took what we could get and considered ourselves fortunate as we recalled our chicken pox episode.

After returning home from church on Easter Sunday we found eggs we had decorated the night before spread all over the yard and treehouse. It was obvious to me the Easter Bunny did the deed. It was also clear that he was getting old. Most of the eggs were in plain view, not at all hidden the way they had been in the past.

Since there was no green grass to pick in April, Luke, Eva, Caleb and I set our straw stuffed baskets on the kitchen table as we left for morning services. Now they were filled with candy and lined up on the porch swing. Betty, Wedge and Yodel were locked in the dog pen, which told me the bunny may be old but was no dummy. They would have sniffed out all the hidden eggs and made short order of the goods in our baskets. The bunny was pretty sneaky too. He waited until all of us church goers were gone and Al was busy trimming horse hooves to fill our baskets and hide the eggs.

Also on the swing were four smaller wooden boxes with rope handles. They too had straw bedding with candy on top. But the candy wasn't homemade like ours. They were what the stores sold. Each box had a name on it. Caleb and I read them aloud, "Gramps, Grandma, Ben and Al."

Ben's huge smile was back. And he used it in a big way when he said, "Well now, we got ourselves one busy bunny hoppin', or perhaps gimpin', around here."

Gramps and Grandma seemed equally surprised and tickled. We couldn't wait to see the look on Al's face when he discovered what the Easter Bunny did right under his nose.

As we all stood on the porch anticipating his reaction, Grandma rang the dinner bell to reel Al in. He didn't disappoint us. It's not often you get to see Ol' Al laugh out loud. Oh, he'd put on a smile often enough. But laughing was not part of his character. It looked to me like he was trying to keep a grin in check as he walked up the back steps. When he saw us and what was on the porch swing, he couldn't help but chuckle. Ben, Grandma and Gramps broke into uncontrollable laughter. Al wasted no time joining in on the robust behavior. The four of us kids looked at each other smiling in a bewildered sort of way. The Easter Bunny sure had a knack for making kids happy, and adults goofy.

The days were getting longer and warmer. Rain replaced the cold snaps and snow. Greenery budded on the bare branches. Summer was finally knocking on our door. School was coming to a close and I promised Wedge a season full of my companionship. He wouldn't have to drop me off and pick me up from school for the next few months. Everywhere I went, he'd get to go with me, except for church on Sundays, of course.

Grandma kept telling Caleb and me to stay focused on school until the end. But the closer that got, the more day dreaming I did. There was so much for a boy and his dog to do around a ranch. Summer visions tugged at my imagination and stimulated my mind.

Grandma helped us make some goodies as a thanks to our teachers. She then had us write notes to include with our small gifts. Caleb wrote a poem to his teacher. It was short and really funny. My thank you card was serious and longer than any I had ever written. I wanted to make sure Mrs. Murphy knew how much I appreciated her driving force. She raised the bar without ever raising her voice. She challenged each of her students to reach as high as we could and, from where I sat, it looked as though everyone did.

Mrs. Murphy stayed consistent until the end. I'm sure I wasn't alone in thinking how nice it felt to make it through her class intact and with good grades. It was a type of earned pride many of us would carry throughout our lives.

Although I had been preoccupied with visions of summer, the last day of school proved to be a mixed bag of emotions. Mrs. Murphy made certificates for every student. Each of us walked to the front of the classroom to receive our customized award and get our journal back for the final time. She called me up last. My certificate simply said, "Most Likely to Achieve His Goal".

She smiled at me with tears filling the brims of her eyes. Blinking set them free and she hugged me as though I was her own child. I told myself to be strong, but strength has a way of melting down to expose a fella's heartfelt emotions. My feelings were on display. I made no effort to shrink away. I was grateful to the woman who challenged, prodded and understood me. I was proud of who I was and what I was determined to accomplish with my life. I owed a part of that confidence to Mrs. Murphy.

Gramps and Grandma brought Eva, Luke, Wedge and Yodel to pick us up. They were all standing outside Caleb's classroom when the final bell rang. They thanked his teacher and then we went in my room to thank Mrs. Murphy. At last Mrs. Murphy was able to meet the main topic of my journal entries. Kneeling down, she asked Wedge to shake her hand, which he was more than happy to do. She stroked the top of his head and down his back saying, "So you're Wedge. I'd recognize you anywhere. You and Ezra will have a great time traveling life's road together. I have no doubt where you two will end up."

Then looking over between Luke and Caleb she spotted Yodel. "And that makes you Yodel, the little girl with the big personality."

Everyone laughed. I hugged Mrs. Murphy one last time, as did Grandma. We all headed out the door for home and to begin our three months of summer vacation. I had a tight grip on my filled journal. It was more than a keepsake. It was a link to the past and to my future.

I gave a quick glance back and saw Mrs. Murphy standing in the same spot, following us with her eyes. I offered a small wave and she gave back a big smile.

That was the last time we saw each other. She surprised everyone by retiring and moving to another state to be near her grandchildren. Like Caleb, Eva, Luke and me, her grandkids were lucky to have such a strong-willed, determined and loving grandmother.

CHAPTER 26

Ridin' Drag

Gramps waited until school was out before branding the calves. He was last in our small area of ranchers to do so. Once again Gramps, Ben and Al helped other locals with branding their cattle and, in return, they all ended up at our ranch to lend us a hand.

Grandma had planned a big feed and barn dance after the last calf was set free. All the women helped prepare food for the occasion. Jake, a whiskered old cook from a neighboring ranch, also pitched in by barbecuing a whole lot of tasty steaks on Gramps' homemade barrel grills.

Caleb and I were on deck for running the hot branding irons to the men who tackled and pinned down the calves. The male calves were castrated and all were vaccinated and ear tagged. Gramps kept a close record on what calf came from which cow as well as the bull who sired it. Few, if any, of the calves were named. The brands served to show ranch ownership. Their age and other information that went into their identity was traced through the number on their ear tag.

It was hard to believe another year had gone by. Here we were again, dirt flying, calves bawling and the stench of burning hides permeating the air. It's an endless cycle ranchers are roped into in order to eek out a living. The funny thing is, I didn't see one man or woman there who would want it any other way, leastways they never appeared discontent.

When the final calf was released the men headed for the bunkhouse. Ben had rigged up a couple of outdoor showers next to the back bunk door. The water was piped in straight from a garden hose, which meant it bypassed the water heater. But, the grimy cowhands didn't appear to notice. In fact, they seemed to welcome the cold stream hitting their sweat drenched bodies. They stood on wooden pallets with a small fence to give them privacy. Anyone walking by could glimpse over and see soapy water lathering down their heads and chests. Then the scene would pick up again from the knees to their feet.

Caleb and I were thankful for the warm water spraying down on us from the bathroom shower. Gramps was waiting his turn right outside the door when we opened it. He had paid his dues for many years with the cold shower routine behind the bunkhouse.

"Hi, boys. You beat me to it. This old body has had its share of shock. I don't need to upset my heart anymore by standin' under a spigot of ice cold water."

It was my guess Al used the bunk's indoor shower. His heart was a lot older than Gramps'.

The food was fit for a king, as usual. It was the tradeoff and worth all the grime, sweat and wretched smoke our bodies endured throughout the day. The long buffet was draped with a variety of colorful clothes. Under them were the thick planks of wood we helped haul a few days earlier from behind the barn. They were set atop bales of hay, which made solid legs and a perfect prop for all the food on display.

Grandma clanged on the dinner bell. It didn't take long for the hunger pangs to kick in and help guide our famished bodies to the waiting food.

The sun had enough for one day and began sinking behind the mountains. The evening had cooled off nicely. Everyone sat around on benches, stumps and hay bales eating and talking about the cattle moving back to the upper unit. Caleb and I gave it no thought until we heard our names mentioned.

"Hey, Dave. Are your two oldest grandsons goin' along this time?" one of the cowhands asked.

I knocked Caleb's knee with mine to get his focus off the food he was shoveling into his mouth and to pay attention to Gramps' reply.

"Well now, I haven't asked them yet, but I figure they can handle drag together, at least up to the cabin," came Gramps' response. "We can spend one night there before pushin' them to the high pastures. It's not like the fall roundup where we have to hunt down all the strays. I think we'll give those two dogs a try as well. Al thinks they'll be okay and this would be a good time to see how they'd do."

We just stared at each other a moment before gulping down our forks full of food and smiling. In one day we had gone from running branding irons to riding drag. On top of that, Wedge and Yodel jumped from being in training to being working dogs.

We both looked over to where Gramps was sitting. He winked at us and said, "How about it boys? Do you think you'd like to do a little cow pokin'?"

I said, "Sure!" as Caleb nodded his head in agreement.

Ben started rosining up his bow and Mark showed up with his guitar. Everyone was ready to squeeze out their last reserve of energy for what was panning out to be a real leg shaking night.

Moments like that had a way of sneaking up on me. Not seeing Papa standing up there next to Mark and tuning his guitar too was hard to swallow. Al pulled his traveling partner out of his pocket and headed for the small platform inside the barn.

Afternoon and evening showers were common around this time of year. The dessert table was set up in a clean stall. We had all done a good job of hauling wood shavings from the small mill out back. Our barn floor had been covered days ago in preparation for the dance. Al made sure he hosed it down a bit right after dinner to keep the fine dust settled under boot stomping feet.

The music started on a high note as Ben electrified the air with "Dixie". Al and Mark joined in. I doubt any group with twice the musicians could have stirred up half as much enthusiasm as those three.

Caleb and Eva were perfect dance partners. They picked up on all the moves done by the older set. Grandma grabbed me and Gramps picked Luke up. Wedge followed me into the mass of hoppin' legs but promptly decided to rejoin Yodel on the sidelines. The barn was filled with movement, laughter and song.

Another branding was done and another cattle drive would soon take place. The thought of it put a surge of high spirited energy into my dance steps. Yep, growing up has its perks.

Gramps put Caleb and me on the fast track after that branding. Everywhere we went Yodel and Wedge followed. For three days Caleb and I were up, fed and mounted by 7:00 a.m. I rode Tink and Caleb was assigned to Moses. We helped to merge all the cattle into the front pasture where, once again, the gate opened and hooves would begin moving to the high ground.

By midweek the stage was set. Mark and Vikki showed up before dawn with horses saddled and loaded in the back of their cattle truck. They had insisted on helping and being eyewitnesses to the debut of the two new hired hands. Our four horses were readied and tied to the hitching posts until breakfast was finished. Grandma woke Eva and Luke up to eat and see us off.

The morning air was crisp and cold as Tonto did his part to move the day along. The lightened sky had faded all the stars by the time Caleb and I led our horses to a nearby fence so as to boost ourselves high enough to reach the stirrups. We rode side by side behind Ben. Luke and Eva walked with Grandma, trailing the seven of us horsemen.

All but Al and Gramps entered the pasture to start pushing the cattle out. Grandma closed the gate leading to the homestead and once again positioned herself with Eva and Luke on the stile. The cattle crowded together and moved as one up the driveway with Gramps and Al riding point. Betty stayed with them. Normally she was in the back with Ben, but she had the rare privilege of being up front so the two rookies could work out all their beginner kinks on their own. Betty was disciplined and experienced. The cattle up front had nothing to fear unless Gramps or Al sent her after them. If need be, she could be taken to the back of the herd to straighten out whatever Wedge and Yodel bungled.

Caleb and I were last to exit the pasture. Grandma got off the stile and walked over to close the gate behind us.

"We'll pass you two on the road in a couple of hours. You did put the food I set out into your saddlebags, didn't you?"

"Yep," we both answered.

"Those canteens should have enough water in them to last until you get to the cabin," she continued.

"We're good, Grandma," I assured her. "Don't worry about us."

"Just take care now. Ben is within yelling distance if you need help."

"Yeah, and don't fall off your horses," Luke added, almost falling off the stile with laughter.

We nudged our horses and waved goodbye. Although Tink and Moses were built to haul much heavier loads, we felt pretty darn big as we rode away with the sun's light hitting the lower half of our faces beneath the shade of our brimmed hats.

Yodel was the spittin' image of Betty. She was good at rerouting the cows on Caleb's side of the road and keeping them moving at a good pace.

Wedge was less inclined to accept the slow reaction of the cows. They got his message quick enough, but their legs didn't move at an acceptable speed for his liking. He would spin around and take a double shot at their hocks until they scampered back to the road in bad humor. After a few scoldings, he showed more restraint and followed Yodel's example.

It wasn't long before we decided to pull our kerchiefs up over our noses. The dirt was unmerciful. It crept into every crease of clothing and clung to every exposed skin pore and strand of hair. Within an hour we had taken off our coats and tied them behind the saddles' seats where bedrolls usually go. We were just starting to dip into our saddlebags when Grandma's station wagon slowly crept up behind us. It was the first car we had encountered and we weren't sure what we were suppose to do.

"Are we gonna guide them through the herd like Ben did?" Caleb asked me.

The answer came immediately when we heard Ben yell, "I'll come get your Grandma through. You two just keep the cattle movin' and out of the ditches."

Eva and Luke had their heads poking out both backseat windows. They were asking us a lot of questions and urging Grandma to get closer.

Ben made his way back along the fence row. He asked us how we were getting along and if we could still see through the dirt in our eyes. Then, with his usual big grin, he pulled his kerchief back up, turned Rio into the back of the herd, and made the path clear for Grandma's car.

Under Grandma's orders, Eva and Luke got quiet. They waved to us as they passed and we watched from a different perspective as the herd closed in behind them. The car looked like a floating island in a rolling sea of cowhides and bobbing heads. We lost sight of them as they climbed the road and disappeared around the bend.

Caleb and I were lucky. We could talk to each other. Ben was on his own a fair distance in front of us and well behind Mark and Vikki. I told Caleb about my dream to take over our cabin and expand the ranch like Papa and Ma had planned; he thought that was a great idea.

I found out he'd been giving his future some considering too. His idea was to stay on and help Grandma and Gramps with the big ranch. It was just like him to think of others first. Of course, I'm almost sure having Grandma around to cook his meals probably entered his mind.

Yodel and Wedge continued to do their part to keep the cattle from stopping to nibble on the weeds along the roadside. Every time we crossed a bridge they detoured to run down and quench their thirst. By the time we spotted the gate to our land, they were pretty much all done in. Their tongues were hanging out and they resorted to barking at the wandering cows instead of dashing after them.

We could spot the front ranks once we got on the straightaway near our destination. Tink and Moses knew the end was near. They both perked up as if wanting to finish the day's job and get over to the familiar barn where a meal of oats, hay and water would be waiting. We could see the pasture filling up with our herd. Ben, Mark and Vikki were stationed across the road to divert the cattle through the opened gate. Caleb and I took on some renewed energy when we realized how close we were to completing our first day riding drag. Our dogs also proved worthy.

As we pushed the last cow through the pasture's opening, the three sent up a loud cheer. Mark and Vikki rode over and patted both of us on our backs. Ben dismounted to close the gate and, before getting in the saddle again, he walked over to each of us and shook our hands. "You two did a fine job. Your dogs did their part too. Your Grandpa knew what he was talkin' about when he said both of you show good judgment."

We could only respond with a simple, but sincere, "Thanks".

I didn't need to look over at Caleb. I knew he was about to burst with pride, same as me. We kicked our horses' sides and galloped over the culvert, following the road to our cabin. Moses and Tink were more than accommodating. They were happy to put on a little speed after being held at a snail's pace for so long.

Yodel and Wedge were reunited with Betty. They sensed our urgency and ran ahead as if to lead the way. After skirting the cabin, we caught up with them along the pond's edge. All the dogs were jumping on and licking Eva and Luke. They were probably excited to see bodies down at their own level and not sittin' high on a horse. Luke and Eva were equally delighted to be on the receiving end of such affection. The two of them had just come through the wooded creek bottom where they left Grandma, Gramps and Al. The men had dismounted and were leading their horses on the narrow path behind Grandma.

Caleb and I met up with Gramps, Grandma and Al at the barn. We eased ourselves down from our saddles and dropped to the ground. The solid earth under my feet had never before felt so good. All I wanted to do was eat and go lay down. Caleb's expression and sigh indicated he was thinking along the same lines. We both knew our desires were on the back burner. Moses and Tink had to be tended to first.

Ben, Mark and Vikki rode out of the creek bottom as Gramps and Al pulled our heavy saddles off for us. There was no way Caleb and I could have gripped the saddle horns and seats in order to lift them from such big horses, especially Tink. When it came to feeding and brushing them, though, it was our responsibility. Everyone was busy in the corral taking care of their own four legged mounts.

Yodel and Betty were nowhere to be seen. But Wedge was underfoot, following every move I made. I think he was interested in wrapping things up so I'd give him the praise and attention he rightly deserved.

Gramps took Caleb and me under his arms as we walked to the house. He was beaming with pride and asked us if we were up to pushing the cattle the rest of the way. No amount of saddle sores or tired bones could have kept us from going. We were given a job to do and we were determined to see it through.

Betty and Yodel were spread out on the porch somewhere in doggie dreamland. Wedge flopped between them, minus the usual circling-before-bedtime routine.

We knew tomorrow's ride would be half the distance of today's. We also realized we'd need to eat and climb up to bed early. Our bodies were drained, but our hearts were full. Caleb, Wedge and I were fed and saying our good-nights before dark. We climbed the ladder and were asleep as soon as our heads hit the pillows. Wedge didn't even have the strength to sneak into our bed during the night.

It thunder stormed overnight, but we hardly noticed. The rain dampened the road and kept the dirt in its place. Caleb and I enjoyed a morning of fresh air without having to wear kerchiefs over our faces. The dogs seemed rejuvenated too. Wedge tried his usual double-take on a few hocks, but retreated when I showed him who was boss. He sensed my displeasure and reluctantly backed off.

Al had trained the dogs and me well. He had never resorted to physical abuse or yelling. He told me once that one's voice is a powerful tool. "Most dogs, and some people, understand and react to a person's tone," was his exact comment.

Grandma pulled up soon after we reached the upper sections of land. She brought sandwiches for all of us and took Mark and Ben down to pick up the cattle trucks. All of us, dogs and horses included, would get a free ride home.

We got a taste of what was in store for us on the next cattle drive. Caleb and I thought we knew what we'd be up against. We couldn't have foreseen what was to come, nor could we have prepared ourselves.

CHAPTER 27

Loyalty

SUMMER WAS BUSY AS USUAL. Grandma had one more child to sew school clothes for this year. Eva wouldn't let playing teacher rest. Poor Luke got the brunt of it. Caleb and I had no desire to partake in anything resembling a classroom, pretend or not. Eva toted her small tablet and crayons to the treehouse and up to the cave. It really cut into Luke's cowboy time with us. So we finally told her to teach her doll and stuffed animals the ABC's and let Luke be. It didn't take long before the educator in Eva went on vacation somewhere. We got our sister and little brother back, and on our terms.

All of us spent a lot of time in our cave and hiking. There wasn't a Mr. Olson this year to ruin my summer, and I didn't fear heading back to school thinking I'd be facing a tyrant for a teacher. Both of last summer's threats to my well-being proved to be important pieces fitting into the irregular shapes that would make up my life's puzzle.

Howdy got a load off his mind too. Eva and Luke were his only wranglers since Caleb and I continued to ride Tink and Moses around the ranch in preparation for our next cattle drive. We helped Ben mend fences at the upper unit, which allowed Al to stay back with Gramps and lend a hand with ranch projects. It was a constant chore fixing stretched or broken barbed wire and replacing posts due to heavy snow drifts, elk and age. Because of downed fences, we'd find cattle from other ranches in with ours and vice versa. No one was bothered by it. They'd all end up with the rightful owners after the fall roundup.

Wedge was my constant companion, but Yodel was content to go with whoever showed an interest. Betty usually stayed with the old timers. She would fall into step beside Al or Gramps whenever they headed out the back door. She was a quiet and faithful servant, eager to please her masters. However, her gentle ways covered up and suppressed a ferocious survival instinct. It laid dormant within her, yet was quick to spring into action if need be.

Such was the case one morning in early July when Gramps called her to ride with him out to a fallen tree down on the southern tip of our little valley. Al and Ben were busy repairing a leaky roof and promised to join up with Gramps later.

Betty jumped into the bed of the truck and balanced her front legs on top of the tool box right behind the cab. Gramps drove off down the bumpy pasture road with his working partner's head reflecting in the driver's side mirror.

It was just another day on the ranch. Eva and I were hanging up the laundry, Grandma was picking garden vegetables with Luke, and Caleb was the gofer, getting this and that for Al and Ben who were on the chicken coop's roof. About fifteen minutes after Gramps left we heard a rifle shot. The deep boom echoed off the canyon walls and between the mountains to where we were working. Everyone froze momentarily before Ben broke the spell by jumping from the roof and running to the bunkhouse. Al clambered down the ladder and hobbled quickly to his old pickup. The motor was running by the time Ben appeared with two rifles.

"You all need to get in the house and take those dogs with you, "Al ordered.

They drove off at a speed both Al and his truck were not accustomed to traveling. We did as we were told and ran to the house. Grandma tried to calm us down by bringing out some snacks and offering to play Chinese checkers with us. Every so often she would glance out the living room window. It was obvious she was watching to see if there was a sign of Gramps or Al driving back.

Finally, Grandma stood up and said, "Here they come!"

We could see the two pickups jolting back and forth over the rutted road. It looked to me like Ben was sitting in the back of Gramps' truck. Grandma led all of us out to the driveway where we waited for their arrival.

I was right. Ben was sitting on the opened tailgate. As they drove past us we could see Betty laying across his lap. Her head was bleeding and her body was soaked with blood. It covered Ben and was dripping onto the tailgate. We followed the truck until it stopped. On closer inspection we could see her right ear had been cut open and she had, what appeared to be, a deep gash on her hip. She was alert and anxious to get down on her own, but Ben held her firm and spoke softly to her.

None of us said a word as Al got out of his truck and went with Gramps toward the bunkhouse to open the door and make way for Ben. Grandma knew she needed to gather up some bandages and start sterilizing the surgical instruments Al would need to patch our faithful girl.

Gramps always kept a veterinary supply box in the bunkhouse and he pulled it down from its shelf as Al sprayed and cleaned the tabletop and Ben gently laid Betty down. She looked as though she didn't understand what all the fuss was about. "I'll have to sedate her just to keep her still. I'm hopin' her wounds look worse than they are. They'll need to be cleaned and then stitched. Infection will be her worst enemy."

Gramps added, "She won't be as pretty, but then pretty is as pretty does. And it was one beautiful sight seein' her come between me and that mama bear."

Eva and Luke had enough and left to see if Grandma needed any help. Caleb sat on Ben's bunk while I stood next to Gramps, opposite the table from Al.

"I think I'll clean up a bit and change my clothes," Ben said as he grabbed a shirt and pair of pants off the wall peg and disappeared into the bathroom.

Grandma brought in a pan of operating instruments that she had cleaned and left to soak in rubbing alcohol. She asked if Al needed anything else before leaving to watch over Eva and Luke.

There was nothing shaky or aged about Al's steady hands. Betty laid perfectly still soon after she was given the shot. Al proceeded to wipe the area around her hip wound. It was as he predicted. The deepest cut had not reached the bone, but muscle tissue had been severed. He spent little time inspecting the damage. He seemed to know exactly what needed to be done. I was surprised when he started explaining what he was doing. Then I realized it wasn't for Gramps' benefit. Al was speaking to me. He told me to come over to his side of the table in order to get a better view. As I moved nearer I noticed Caleb stand up and close in behind Gramps.

Betty's ear took little attention once her hip was sewn and bandaged. Al asked me if I wanted to clean the dried blood that had formed around her sliced ear. Fresh blood began oozing again once the crusted clotting was removed. Al disinfected the wound and began the stitching process. I watched as he worked his way down her dark velvet ear.

"Two more should do it," he said. "How would you like to finish it off, Ez?"

When I looked up at Gramps he simply shrugged a shoulder and raised an eyebrow. It was my decision and I decided to give it a try.

Caleb watched at a distance with squinted eyes and a crinkled up nose. It obviously wasn't his idea of fun, nor did he seem to want any part of the task at hand. After one stitch he volunteered to fetch Betty's bed from the mudroom. She'd be staying in the bunkhouse under Al's watchful eye once again. The two stitches went in easy enough. Al inspected my handiwork and complimented me on a job well done.

Wedge and Yodel spent the entire time right outside the bunkhouse's screen door. They sat quietly and seemed to sense the urgency of their mother's condition.

Gramps told us all about the bear incident during supper. Apparently, he drove up to the fallen tree and noticed a mother bear and her cub scampering into the woods. What he didn't see was the twin cub hiding under some large branches that were laying across the ground.

"My common sense told me to take one of the rifles from the rack behind my head, but I wouldn't listen. I figured my hands would be full with my saw and tools. I hauled what was needed to the far side of the trunk and was just about to start working on it when I caught sight of the cub. Immediately, I started to retreat back to the truck when an angry, grunting mama bear tore out of the brush. I didn't have a chance in a million to climb over the upturned trunk and get to safety before she'd overtake me. I thought for sure I was a goner."

All eyes were on Gramps and our ears were hanging on every word.

"Then, out of nowhere, Betty sprang into action. She flew over the fallen branches and met the bear head on. It gave me the time I needed to retrieve the rifle. Betty had been takin' quite a beating and I was afraid she'd be my unintended target. I prayed a loud shot into the air would untangle the angry females. It worked. The cub ran off and its mama made tracks right behind it."

"Poor Betty," Eva said.

"Yeah, she was pretty tore up. But she hobbled over to me to check if I was alright. I tried to see the damage done to her but could only tell that she was bleedin' pretty bad. Then I heard Al's old truck comin'. I hugged her and told her that help was on the way."

"A quick lookover told me she had no mortal wounds," Al said, adding to Gramps' explanation. "We just wanted to get her back here before she lost too much blood."

"Will she be okay?" came Luke's concerned voice.

"Yep, she's a trooper. Chances are she'll walk with a little getty-up in her step. But, take it from me, that won't stop her from bein' useful. Give her a few weeks and she'll be up and at it," Al assured us.

Once again, I was called upon, this time to remove Betty's ten-day-old stitches. I liked feeling useful in a way that helped animals. Al lent me any book off his shelves I wanted to read. The words were a bit complicated, but Al simplified the content by putting it into layman's terms. He encouraged me in every way a person would patiently guide a child he loved.

August came and Betty moved back to the mudroom. Her ear healed almost without a scar. Her leg wasn't as fortunate. The evidence of a wound was minimal, but the slight stiffness in her walk would always be with her. Like Al, she didn't let a little limp stop her from earning her keep.

CHAPTER 28

Summer's End

SUMMER MARCHED RIGHT ALONG. GRANDMA was working overtime trying to make shirts for Caleb and me as well as dresses for Eva. The person trying on the dresses was a lot more excited about school starting up than the two shirt owners. The only thing Caleb and I looked forward to when summer ended was the fall roundup.

There were just a couple of weeks left before we headed out the door with our lunch pails in hand. We busied ourselves with chores, playing bandits in our hideaway cave and riding Tink and Moses. Howdy was a kid's pony. He served us well when we were little, but now our traveling needs were those of young men. And, two practically full size cowhands need to ride big horses. Tink was larger than average and Moses was no lightweight, but that's what made them perfect for us. They allowed for lots of growing room.

Eva and Luke loved having Howdy to themselves and I'm sure he was relieved to feel only four small feet dangling from his sides. Caleb and I resorted to the stair stepper Ben made for us to use when saddling our mounts. We showed Eva how to saddle Howdy and she got pretty good at lifting the heavy weight onto his back and cinching the wide strap. However, the first few times she attempted to get up into the saddle it would slide over sideways. Howdy would turn his head and look back at her as if to say, "Better luck next time".

Finally, I walked over and gave that old boy a good punch with my knee into the side of his fat belly. When his air released I pulled the cinch tighter.

"There you go. I guess he thought he could pull one over on you," I told Eva. "You have to let him know who's boss."

We all rode together almost every day. Yodel and Wedge were happy to tag along and protect us from all the dangerous animals, bandits and wild Indians that lurked within the dense forest and behind the granite boulders.

The ice cream maker was brought out one last time for the year. Ben and Al rested on the porch, tired from a long day of work, and played a few tunes. The coyotes voiced their high pitched approval as we all sat around eating the frozen dessert.

"How'd you like to learn the harmonica, Ez?" Al asked between songs.

"Sure," was my quick response.

Al wiped the mouthpiece dry with his shirt and explained to me where I'd find the high and low notes. "You make music by both blowing out and sucking in. It takes a while, but you're not afraid of workin' at somethin' until you get it right. Any time you wanta' practice just let me know. You can keep it until tomorrow night, since you'll have more free time than me."

"Now, ain't that just about the sneakiest way to get out of playin' more music?" Ben snickered.

"No one's stoppin' you from screechin' on that old fiddle. I figure I'd let Ezra give it a try. He could play as good as you right now," Al calmly answered.

I did give it a try. Ben slowed his pace to give me a chance to follow. I was pretty bad, but everyone clapped and cheered me on.

Gramps got up and said he was turning in for the night, and we all took his lead. I thanked Al one more time for allowing me to use his harmonica. Grandma followed us upstairs to read both sets of bedtime books. Her routine never changed. While Eva and Luke were settled into bed, Caleb and I would clean up and head to our room. Grandma would then continue by reading a more advanced book to us two older boys. Prayers were last and we always said our thanks for everyone and everything that made our lives so good. Grandma kissed us goodnight just as Gramps came in to do the same. We had one day of freedom left and we were determined to make the most of it.

There was nothing I really liked about going back to school. The worst thing was leaving Wedge. I tried preparing him for our separation by giving him the countdown every day for the last week. His response was always the same. He'd stare at me with those big brown eyes, tilt his head to the side and perk his ears forward looking as though he understood. Then he'd get up and wag his tail as if to say, "Okay, that's then. Let's make the best of now."

Gramps did his part to make sure we had no idle time in which to mope around. He piled on the work until our mid-day meal. We were free to run wild after that, and run wild we did. Grandma even allowed Luke another no-nap day.

It was to the cave we went. Grandma said she'd rustle up some oatmeal cookies and ring the dinner bell if we wanted to come down for nutritional fortification. We discussed having to go back down on our way up the mountain. Then we did the democratic thing and voted three to one that Eva would return to the house and pack the goods back up to our fort.

When the bell rang, Eva headed out to retrieve the cookies and, of course, milk. You can imagine how surprised and disappointed we were when she returned sometime later with one cookie apiece and a look of contentment. Grandma thought it only fair that she and Eva get what was left of yesterday's dessert. They each sandwiched the ice cream between two cookies and washed them down with cold milk.

"Grandma said there wasn't enough ice cream for all of you. Besides, it would have melted by the time I got back up here. She also didn't think the milk would have stayed cold and carrying six cookies instead of three would be kinda heavy for me," Eva told us with a sly smile.

We each got a second cookie after dinner that night. It was a little irritating watching Eva eat her third one for the day. Grandma said she froze the rest for our school lunches that week. I suppose starting school did give us at least that to look forward to.

Caleb and I accepted our class promotions the best we could. Eva, on the other hand, acted as though she had waited her whole life for first grade. The next morning, all but Al, Ben and Betty piled into the car. Wedge was familiar with the routine. He seemed to know school would separate us once again.

I had a man teacher for the first time. He was new to the school, so there was no reputation that preceded him. I was convinced, after having Mrs. Murphy, that no teacher from then on could unravel me. She prepared me well. I missed not seeing her but, like she used to tell us, her presence would be felt. And it was. She followed me into my classroom and stood over me throughout my hours of homework.

We would have a little over a week and a half of school before taking a few days off. Not even sitting in a classroom every day could dampen our spirits. Caleb and I thought cattle drive, ate cattle drive and dreamed cattle drive.

By Eva's sixth birthday everything was packed and stored in the cattle truck for trekking to the high country. Grandma double checked our sacks of warm clothing and added wool blankets to our sleeping bags.

"Two nights up there will put hair on your chests if you're not careful. Since you're a might young for that, you'll need to be prepared and not give it any reason to grow," she advised.

Eva's birthday was celebrated the night before we were to head up country. Caleb and I learned our lesson last year and chose to make her something that wouldn't need help from someone else. We had a hard time deciding what to do for her. It's next to impossible to be creative with each other's gifts when none of us seemed to have many wants. Luckily, Caleb asked to have a section of blackboard that had been broken and sitting in his classroom. Gramps hauled it home after dropping us off at school. Al trimmed the jagged edge and Caleb and I built a wooden frame for it. Grandma took Luke to town with her to buy some large chalk and black felt material in order to make an eraser out of a block of wood.

Eva was so excited to get a large chalkboard from her two older brothers and was equally grateful to Luke for the chalk and eraser. She recruited him once again to be her live student.

The spring roundup was still fresh in our minds the next morning when Grandma came in to gently shake us from our sleep. Unlike getting ready for school, we were quick to dress and eager to eat and begin our day.

It was dark outside and no stars were twinkling in the sky. When I looked down from our bedroom window I could see Ben handing Gramps the last of the food supplies we'd be needing for the next two days. They had done a fine job rigging up the little tack shed behind the truck's cab. It would offer protection and shelter from unpredictable weather.

CHAPTER 29

The Fall Roundup

Gramps wanted to put Caleb and me in back of the cattle truck along with our gear, the tack and the dogs. There would be plenty of room for us to travel in comfort. However, Grandma wouldn't hear of it.

"I will not allow you to stick those boys in the back. I will drive them up if need be," was her finger shaking threat.

Gramps knew better than to ruffle her feathers. He meekly reconsidered and said we could ride up front; he'd make room.

Caleb and I were baffled over how five of us could fit on one seat until we were told to load up under Gramps' direction. Caleb sat on Ben's lap in the middle and I sat on Gramps. The driving was turned over to Al, probably because his lap was on the frail side.

Grandma waited until we were all in place before pouring five tin cups of coffee, each half full in order to avoid accidental spillage. Luke and Eva were there to hand her the mugs as she poured hot brew from the pot. Caleb and I were given the last two cups. She had gone heavy on the milk with ours.

The truck was shifted into gear and we were on our way. My stomach was twitching all over with excitement. No doubt Caleb was experiencing the same fluttering sensation. The long awaited day had arrived. Other than having to sit on someone's lap, we felt pretty darn big.

The morning was warmer than what I remembered it being last year. Of course, it was later in the season back then. Not long after my observation, Al commented on the cloud cover and how it helped to heat things up a bit. "I just hope it doesn't decide to cut loose. Nothin's worse than huntin' down cattle in the rain. It's hard enough to grab some sleep on a good night. It's nearly impossible in bad weather."

Mark volunteered to help us again. Gramps only agreed if he, along with Ben and Al, could return the favor the following week. Mark didn't have as many cattle as we did, but he'd be shorthanded without Vikki. She was in a motherly way and out of the saddle for a while. Instead, she offered to help Grandma feed everyone once they moved the cattle down to the cabin.

Our headlights landed on Mark waiting at his gate. Al stopped long enough for Mark to load his horse and then climb through the tack door behind the cab. He was glad to sit in back with the dogs. He would have more room than the five of us. He also didn't have a grandma telling him where he had to ride.

"You boys finish that coffee before we get to the rough part of the road," Gramps told us. "I want to stay as dry as possible before the rain hits."

We drove past the driveway to the cabin just as the sun began rising above the dense clouds. "I don't like the looks of it. Hopefully, the rain will hold off until we get all the cattle down from the mountains and onto the big meadow," Al commented.

Grandpa was also thinking about the weather. "You boys can always sleep in the cab and the rest of us will take turns watchin' the herd and catchin' a few winks in the tack space."

"We can help too," I insisted.

Caleb was quick to agree. The two of us had been preparing ourselves and counting the days for this moment. No amount of rain could dampen our spirits.

"We'll see," was Gramps' short response.

"Here we are," Al said as we pulled off the road. "Looks like word got out in the cattle world. They're startin' to band together to decide who will be in the lead once we open the gate."

Gramps had me jump down from his lap to open the post and barbed wire gate. Al pulled through the opening and parked alongside the large wooden cattle shoot. I quickly closed the gate to keep the oncoming cattle from escaping. The side door to the stock truck was slid open and the horses were taken down the shoot's ramp one by one to be tied along the small boarded corral.

"We'll be ridin' in pairs at all times." Gramps informed us. "Mark and Ben will take Betty with them. Her leg will give her some problems by the end of the day, so go easy on her. Al and Ezra will have Wedge." Looking at Caleb, he went on to say, "You and Yodel will be goin' with me. My guess is we'll be gettin' thunder and lightnin' soon. All the horses and dogs can handle the weather. Be sure of what you're doing, and don't take any unnecessary chances. We can always come back later and hunt down stubborn strays."

"Hopefully, they'll all be rounded up and down here before one drop of rain hits the ground," said Ben.

"You need to dry the wetness from behind those big ears of yours," Al mused. "Every ounce of me says the rain is close, and it's no Sunday mornin' spring shower. Let's get mounted and get this done."

All of us had slickers tied to the back of our saddles. Food was in every saddlebag and a canteen of water was slung around each saddle horn.

Gramps seemed most concerned about Caleb, being so young and all. They followed the base of the mountain and left the rugged climbing to the rest of us.

No sooner had we started in our designated direction when a distant thunderclap boomed through the air. Al led the way up a well used trail. Tink followed closely with little, if any, guidance from me. Wedge never left my sight. He seemed to realize the importance of our mission. Lightning and thunder took their turns delivering powerful strikes against the high wilderness. Wind decided to add to our predicament. The noise level was beyond any I had ever encountered, but it was only a warning before nature's full attack.

Al yelled for me to get my slicker on. Both of us turned around in our saddles and unstrapped the canvas, oil cloth dusters that Gramps nicknamed the "cowboy's trench coat". With some effort, we pulled them on and flipped the large collars up under our hats. We dipped down the embankment of the North Fork of the Poudre River. The water was low, typical for this time of year, and easy to cross.

Within an hour, we stumbled upon a group of cows huddled together in a small ravine. Al indicated me to circle around to the far side and send Wedge in to begin moving them toward him and the trail.

I pointed and Wedge responded to my cue. He ran in and hit his mark. His quick action was followed up by several repeats on the heels of those refusing to cooperate. The reluctant cattle began moving, leaving the shelter provided by a cut bank.

They weren't the only things moving. The rain drops that had been promised by the unrelenting heavens came pelting down. Impact was from an angle, forced by the severe wind. The water came with such ferocity that it bounced at least a foot off the surfaces it hit.

I had ridden in many thunderstorms, but this was the angriest yet. The clouds opened on us with a vengeance. I could no longer see or hear Al. Only a few rear-ends of the cattle that were directly in front of me could be seen through the thick sheet of rain. We were traveling in a downward direction and, as far as I could tell, north toward the large meadow. Fear started creeping in. Strangely, I remembered what Ma and Papa used to tell me about talking to myself at times like this. I found my mind saying over and over, "I can do this. I know I can do this."

Al made sure the cattle followed the descending path as Tink and I pushed them along. Wedge had never before worked alone. He must have been aware of the urgency of his job because he was persistent with his snapping jaws. As the cattle became more cooperative, Wedge became more subtle in his approach.

Tink took her time. How she could see was beyond me. My hat served as a shield for my eyes, but she had no such protection. Slowly, she felt her way. I gave Tink her head and put all my trust in her surefooted experiences along steep mountain terrain. Wedge stayed close to her back feet, careful not to interfere with their progress.

It seemed to take hours before I felt Tink level off at the base of the mountain. The wind and rain had no intention of backing away. Rivers of muddy water gushed down every incline. Pools of water spilled from my hat each time my head tilted forward. The cattle were nervous and bawled their discontent.

Tink came to a halt and I realized some of the cows stood still in front of us as if refusing to move. Wedge was in no mood to stop the procession. He ran around Tink and sprang onto a few of their unsuspecting haunches, the only thing exposed above the deep mud. He looked like no creature I'd ever seen. The muck and water turned him into something resembling a giant sewer rat. His stubborn determination was enough to spur the cattle onward.

When our trail dived down into the Poudre I figured we were home free. But then again, nothing's really free. The storm placed yet another punishment on us. There was no way I'd let Wedge try to swim that current. He was a little confused when I ordered him to stay up on the bank while Tink and I worked our way along the river's edge. We were standing in a shallow rush of water when I called him to come. He was about shoulder height to me when I leaned over as far as I could and grabbed the scruff of his neck. He let out a yelp as I lifted him safely onto the saddle. His large paws dangled across my lap and over each side of the saddle. With one arm securing him, I gave Tink a nudge with my heels.

"Let's go girl!" I shouted over the river's roar and persistent rain. We turned into the current and crossed behind the last two cows.

Al must have been holding his boots out to keep them from submerging. Tink was a much bigger horse than Dolly and my legs were much shorter than Al's. The water came right below my stirrups. I was sitting pretty comfortably, considering what we were going through.

Tink got the brunt of it. She took her time, finding her footing as she crossed. The cattle had done a good job of trampling, slipping and eroding the saturated bank. Tink chose a spot that hadn't been torn up and eased us out of the brown churning river.

Al had apparently held the cows until we were safely behind them. They were all standing around looking at each other as if their hooves were stuck.

"You're one heck of a cowboy," I heard Al yell to me. To my surprise he had ridden back and was only a few feet away. "It's easier goin' from here on out. We'll be in the meadow once we clear this patch of trees. You might want to let Wedge down now. I was hopin' you'd find a way to carry him across. He probably could have made it, but he'd be a ways downstream before climbin' out."

Leaving the forest canopy was the only indication I had that we made it to the pasture. The small group we drove down joined the others with their tails to the storm and heads hanging down.

"Let's see if anyone else has made it back," Al yelled to me through the incredible noise of the storm.

I followed him through the slush to where the stock truck had been parked. Ben and Mark's horses were tethered inside the corral and the side door was wide open, revealing both men leaning opposite each other within the door's frame. Betty sat between them at their feet.

We rode up alongside the truck when Al called out, "Any sign of Dave and Caleb?"

"Nope. We haven't been here long ourselves," Ben yelled back.

Al dismounted and led Dolly to a nearby fence post. He gestured for me to follow. I didn't climb down off Tink until I joined Al and used the fence rail as a step ladder. Then I bent over and gathered Wedge into my arms. He was shivering and his little heart was beating faster than a scared rabbit. I hugged his slippery, mud soaked body and told him how proud I was. He had done a fine job. His quick little tongue warmed both my cheek and my heart.

We made it back safely.

CHAPTER 30

Sheep Creek

It felt good to get out of the pounding rain. We learned that Mark and Ben had driven down six head of cattle. We added eight to the count. Betty looked as rough as Wedge and her limp was more pronounced than usual, although she did her best to leave the protection of the truck and return to work.

The wooden slats did little to prevent rain from blowing in through the side panels. Luckily, the truck was parked on an incline that let the water run down and out the back end. It was a good thing Gramps had attached a tin roof to protect the traveling tack room from summer rains. The noise echoing off the tin was deafening. He hadn't banked on being in a storm of such magnitude.

No one had eaten anything from their saddlebags. We all agreed to open the metal food cache and help ourselves to some lunch. I noticed everyone kept their eyes focused on the blurred view outside the sliding door.

An hour dragged by without any break in the weather. Al was out of character. His normal calm was overpowered by subdued stress, obvious to the three of us. Ben tried to break the tension by giving Al many opportunities to chide him with friendly sarcasm. Al didn't oblige. He seemed to be miles, or perhaps years, away. I sensed a deep sadness hovering over him, the smothering type of uneasiness and dread that sometimes comes before bad news. Mark and Ben glanced at each other and then at me. I didn't know how to respond to Al's behavior either.

I sat on the floorboards petting both dogs and remembering what the vet had told me. Was Al thinking about the wife and child taken from him so many years ago? Did he sense and fear something was terribly wrong now?

"This rain has got to let up soon," Mark said. "When it does, Ben and I will see what's takin' them so long."

"If anyone goes, it'll be me," was Al's quick response. "We'll give it another half hour."

I spent the longest thirty minutes of my life sitting on that rough wooden truck bed, running my hands down the filthy wet backs of Betty and Wedge. No one had much to say. Al didn't leave his post by the door. He squinted tirelessly trying to detect two riders and a dog.

No one had a watch but guessing the allotted time was typical for a man like Al. He turned and looked at all of us and gave a briefing on which direction he'd be going.

"I'll be back in an hour or so. Maybe they'll be here by then. There's no sense in everyone being spread all over tarnation in weather like this. Hopefully the clouds will wring themselves out soon and we'll be able to see beyond six feet."

I stood up and walked over to Al. Looking straight into his kind eyes I said, "Let me go with you."

He stood quietly collecting his thoughts. Then he put one hand on my shoulder, gave it a little squeeze, and kindly responded, "I don't think your Grandpa would want you out in that mess any more than what's necessary."

"This is necessary," I countered. "Caleb's out there too. The more eyes lookin' for them the better."

Al looked over to where Ben and Mark sat on the toolbox. Then he looked down at me. "We'll take it slow. You stay right with me and do exactly as you're told. Havin' Wedge along might be helpful too. He's keen on hearing and might be able to pick up on somethin' that we can't detect. I don't want Betty comin'. Her leg is causin' her some pain right now."

Ben stood up and argued, "There's no reason for two of us to sit here waitin' like lumps on a log. Mark's a big boy. He can handle stayin' here alone. Ezra's right. The more eyes lookin' for them the better."

"Oh hell. We might as well take the entire herd with us. Then look at all the eyes we'd have searchin' for those two," Al responded with disgust.

"I take that as an 'Okay'," Ben said smirking.

"Stay close," was all Al said before turning to walk down the stock ramp.

Ben told Mark to honk the horn if Gramps and Caleb got back while we were out. "Hopefully, we'll be able to hear it over all this racket."

The three of us pulled ourselves up onto our drenched saddles. None of the horses seemed all too anxious to move through the pounding rain. Their legs were bogged down by mud sucking holes each time a hoof made contact with the saturated earth. Al had me ride behind him and in front of Ben. We left the corral with Mark standing in the shelter of the doorway holding firmly to Betty's collar.

Wedge had gotten his second wind and kept pace with Tink to the far side of the meadow. As we neared the North Fork of the Poudre, the roar of rushing water put the fear of the devil in me. The dense brown water was cluttered with nature's debris. It had come out of its banks and grabbed at everything in its path. Nothing it touched escaped the violent water's wrath.

Al stopped and waved for Ben and me to ride up alongside of him. "If they're on the other side of this mess, they'll be there for a while. Even if the rain stops, the water won't be low enough to cross for a couple of days. I'm thinkin' we might ride up to where Sheep Creek and Cornelius Creek feed into the North Fork. Dave would look for shelter if he crossed over. There's an old hunter's cabin on the other side next to Sheep Creek. It's worth checkin' out."

We fell back into formation and rode parallel to the swollen river. Before reaching the tributaries we stumbled upon a cow and two heifers. Al signaled for us to leave them be. Wedge had his own plan. He shot out after them before I had a chance to call him off. They were shaken from their trance and moved slowly in the direction of the herd. I yelled for Wedge to come back, but the raging river and the deluge of rain kept him from hearing me. Ben came to my aid with his piercing toothy whistle. The high pitch was enough to rupture an eardrum. It was also enough to bring Wedge back.

The rain was starting to let up. It had no intention of stopping, but we were happy to get whatever relief we could. Al spotted Cornelius Creek merging into the North Fork. Sheep Creek would be the next tributary a short distance away.

Sheep Creek was half that of the North Fork. However, crossing it was still out of the question. It had been some time since the creek held that much water. Trees and shrubs had been uprooted and were forced along by the swift current. Luckily, the water at this point was within its banks.

It was a short distance further when Ben and I rode Tink and Rio up to where Dolly stood. Al was pointing to a little cabin behind some aspens. It was butted up to the base of a steep rock mountain on the other side of Sheep Creek.

"There it is," he said.

He sat quietly as if pondering what to do next. Then a big smile spread across his face and tears wailed up in his eyes. "Well, I'll be damned. If that ain't smoke, then I don't know what is."

Ben and I squinted toward the old rock chimney. There, rising to meet the angels, was a thin wisp of gray haze.

We rode as close to the creek as we dared and began shouting over the water's fury. There was no response from Gramps or Caleb. Then Ben told us to cover our ears while he let out another piercing whistle.

"If they can't hear that, maybe Yodel will," Ben said, quite pleased with himself.

Within a few seconds the door flew open. Yodel ran out onto the porch barking, followed by Gramps and Caleb. We waved again, receiving hearty responses in return.

Wedge was beside himself seeing them on the other side of the creek. He jumped around at the water's edge as if contemplating swimming across.

"Ez, call your dog before he does somethin' stupid," ordered Al.

I yelled for Wedge to come to me. He was a bit hesitant and even ran back and forth along the bank. With one more stern command he came obediently and stood next to Tink.

Gramps yelled over to us to tell us they were doing fine. They had eaten all that was in their saddlebags and were good for a few more hours.

"He's doin' better than us," Ben commented. "They're warm and dry at least."

"Oh stop your snivelin'. You'll be dry with a belly full of food soon enough. The warm part will have to wait a while, but you'll survive," said Al.

It was good to hear the old Al was back.

Al continued talking, "We'll wrap the food from our saddlebags in a bandana." Looking at Ben he went on to say, "Then we can tie it closed and you can show us what that outfielder's arm can do. If you happen to throw it with any accuracy, we can use the same method to get them whatever they need."

We did just that. All the snack food Grandma made for us was dumped into Al's bandana. He tied the ends tightly together and handed it to Ben. Dismounting, Ben trudged to the creek's edge and threw it between some trees, right onto the cabin's porch steps. Caleb had his hands up in the air and was jumping for joy. Both he and Gramps ran down to retrieve the bundle.

"Thanks!" they both shouted over the river's roar.

"We'll bring you dinner in a few hours," Al yelled to them.

Ben got back on Rio and we all vigorously waved our goodbyes. The rain had almost stopped as we rode side by side away from the creek, going directly to the truck. We talked about how we could fill one of the canteens with some of the beans Grandma sent, wrap a few biscuits in a pair of Caleb's clean socks, and stuff a couple of steaks inside two tin cups. We could put all of the food in the pillowcase that Caleb had used to pack his clothes for the trip. We'd tie it up tight and throw the whole thing over the creek. It all sounded like a great plan. They would be safe for the time being.

Al and I agreed to sleep in the cab of the truck and the other men could make do with the compartment behind it. The four of us would spend tomorrow adding strays to the herd from this side of the river. It'd be a long night, but nothing that could compare to the length of that day.

CHAPTER 31

Merciless Water

MARK HAD DINNER STARTED BY the time we got back. He'd attached a canvas lean-to on one side of the truck and draped another outside the ramp to form a wind break. A nice campfire was going, with rocks supporting the grate and a big pot of beans simmering in the center. Grandma had insisted on keeping a supply of dry firewood in the storage area of the cattle truck for all our cattle drives. She knew Gramps pretty well. He would feed himself and his crew cold meals otherwise.

Betty barked our arrival before Mark saw any sign of us. He looked a little confused with all of us returning in good spirits and no sign of Gramps or Caleb. We didn't say a word to him about our findings until we gathered around the fire to get warm.

"So, what about our two lost souls? Did you see them?"

"Yep, we saw'em," Al answered.

Mark looked at each of us waiting to hear more information. All he got were three smiling faces and Ben's request for food.

"Okay, this is what's goin' to happen. No one will get a bite of anything until you tell me where Dave and Caleb are. I can't imagine you being happy as newborn colts if they were stuck out in the rain."

The three of us exchanged glances until Al finally said, "I'm as hungry as an ox, and you got me by the horns. So I guess I'll fill you in on where we left 'em."

Mark handed each of us a tin plate and a fork. We sat under the tarp eating hot beans and steak while Al told all about Gramps and Caleb holding out in the old cabin along Sheep Creek.

Ben volunteered to take them their dinner along with some grain for the horses. Since he had a strong throwing arm, we all thought he was the best candidate for the job. Mark wanted to go along just to check out their accommodations.

After dinner we threw some food and clothing together in one sack and horse feed in another. Al found an extra slicker and used it to wrap Gramps' and Caleb's sleeping bags. He tied a rope firmly around the bundle to keep it in tact and waterproofed. Ben and Mark set out to make their delivery while Al and I cleaned up the dinner mess. No one would lose a night's sleep by watching the cattle. With the river up so high they would stay right where they were, pinned down between the high water and fence.

Al and I rode around the herd once just to make sure all was well. The tired cattle huddled together in one large mass, with their backs to the wind, trying to insulate themselves from the elements. We returned to the truck, unsaddled our horses and fed them. Then we hung up our chaps and called it a day.

The rain reduced itself to a drizzle, making the river's noise more enhanced as it ricocheted off the mountains and roared across the large meadow. A cold wind settled in once the sky darkened. Mark and Ben made it back before total blackness set in for the night.

"They were glad to get the supplies. Dave was really happy about the sleepin' bags. Caleb was happier with the food. I'm sure we made points with the horses too," Ben said while warming his hands over the fire.

We stayed up a little longer talking about the day and adding wood to the blaze. Mark commented on how it was a good thing the truck wasn't needed for a few days. The ground it sat on was too wet to try moving such a heavy load.

Al reached through his thick coat and pulled out his harmonica. "Do you want to play a tune?" he asked me.

"I'm not so good," was my reply.

"Well now, playin's how you get good," urged Ben. "Come on. Mark has never heard you."

I took the harmonica from Al's outstretched hand. Slowly, I moved it across my lips with cupped hands, bending the notes and coming up with a close facsimile of "Home, Home on the Range". It was a crowd pleaser, a small crowd pleaser, but enough for me. All three of them recognized the tune and sang along. When I finished, they clapped their approval and voiced their surprise at my ability. It was the only song I had practiced. I handed the harmonica back to Al and he took over.

After a short time everyone headed to their sleeping spots. Mark claimed the top of the large storage box, leaving Ben and Betty with the tack room floor. Al and I climbed up into the truck's cab. He sat behind the steering wheel and gave me the rest of the seat to stretch out. I argued, saying we each should have half. But he wouldn't hear of it. Wedge had plenty of room on the passenger's floorboard. He turned his circle and rolled into a ball with an exhausted sigh before Al and I quit arguing about our sleeping arrangements. It would have been a real challenge if Gramps and Caleb were here to bed down. The last thing I remembered was saying goodnight to Al and giving Our Lord thanks for a safe day.

The morning brought with it a bright sun. It peeked between large gray clouds and teased us with a little heat. The river had gone down below its banks, probably three feet lower than the night before. But it was still much too high to cross.

Ben took on the duties of head chef and cooked up a fairly good breakfast of bacon, eggs, grilled toast and black coffee. We threw the leftovers onto a tin plate and tied another upside-down plate on top of it. Some coffee was poured into an empty canteen. Then all of us rode to make the special delivery to Gramps and Caleb.

Betty's leg seemed much better. Her limp was back to its normal slight hitch. She and Wedge jumped over puddles as they kept stride with the four of us. They had the morning off from work and seemed eager to take advantage of their freedom.

We were all amazed at the reduced height of Sheep Creek. The water was still traveling at a quick clip, but had receded by about half. It wasn't much higher than the Poudre when Al and I crossed over with the cattle.

Gramps and Caleb were out in the sunshine with their backs to us watching Moses and Gus eat grass in the small area between the creek and the cabin. The horses had been allowed to graze with only ropes tied around their necks. Their sleek bodies shone like our greased down hair on Sundays. Apparently, they had been tied under the lean-to next to the cabin the day before, which kept them hidden from view.

Movement under a cluster of aspens caught my eye. Three strays were busily munching the beaten down grass. Obviously, Gramps and Caleb had found them and pushed them to the cabin. They must have been hidden behind some boulders, seeking shelter from the storm, when we came earlier.

Yodel sounded the alarm that we were approaching. Betty and Wedge answered her call by running to the water's edge and barking. Gramps and Caleb waved to us and moved close to the bank in order to make themselves heard. Caleb hung onto Yodel while Gramps hollered his plan.

"We've been watchin' the water and markin' it with a stick. It's gone down a lot from just an hour ago. I think we'll cross over later today after it drops some more. I'll need Al or Ben to come and help with the strays. The rest of you will need to start pushin' the herd toward the gate. I want to get them down to the cabin before nightfall."

Al yelled to Gramps that he'd return later to ford the swift river. Ben threw their breakfast over and we all waved goodbye.

We noticed on our ride back that the cattle needed no probing. They were already in position to head down the road. Those that had been separated earlier that morning were now mingling with the masses.

"It looks like all we need to do is clean up camp and pack things tight in the truck. The grass has been trampled into the mud and they're not goin' to settle for chewing their cuds much longer," said Mark.

"Yep, they're ready to move on. The faster we get Dave and Caleb across the creek, the faster we can get outta here," Al responded.

It took very little time for all of us to pack things. We busied ourselves with small jobs until Al thought enough hours had passed. I rode along with him back to Sheep Creek. He agreed to let me go as long as I stayed on our bank. He said it would be "cheating the hangman" riding back and forth over high water for no good reason. They really didn't need my help or Wedge's this time around.

The creek was at least a foot below the last stick Gramps wedged among the rocks along the inside bank. Moses and Gus were saddled and tied to a couple of trees. Caleb was sitting on the porch step when Yodel spotted us and signaled our approach. Caleb jumped up and called out that we had arrived. Gramps' tall silhouette soon filled the cabin's doorway. He came out onto the porch, turned to close the door and picked up the sacks of supplies we had thrown over to them. Together they walked down to the horses where Gramps tied one of the bags to Moses and the other to Gus.

Al thought it best for me to hitch Tink to a tree and hold Wedge while he rode over to assist Gramps. I did as I was told and positioned myself on a large rock directly across from the widest, therefore shallowest, part of the creek.

Wedge fought my hold until Al made it to the other bank. He finally realized I had no intention of freeing him and sat obediently with his ears perked forward. We watched as Gramps boosted Caleb up to the stirrup and spoke to Al. Al nodded in agreement and headed over to the grazing cattle, taking Yodel with him.

Wedge began jumping around when he saw his herding partner spring into action. I held tight as he barked and thrust himself forward over and over again.

The cattle were heading toward the designated crossing just as Gramps and Gus entered the water. Caleb was close behind. They took it slow, allowing their horses to find footing. The water in the center was the most treacherous, both in depth and speed. Gramps had Caleb keep Moses' head close to Gus' rump on the upstream side. He looked back constantly. His calm voice never stopped speaking to Caleb.

The water rose to their knees and then lower thighs. As they neared the center of the creek, Gus and Moses began drifting down stream. Their hooves had lost the rocky creek bottom and were now forced to swim. Caleb held the saddle horn with both hands and fought to stay in the seat. Gramps turned himself enough to grab onto Moses' bridle.

Suddenly, Gus found his footing and Moses was just a step behind. Gramps released his hold on Moses and each of the horses picked their spot on the muddy bank where they determined to climb out of the current. They heaved themselves up onto the shore with much more enthusiasm than when they entered.

I released Wedge and ran for Tink. By the time I got back to the crossing, Moses and Gus were shaking river water off so hard that Gramps and Caleb were vibrating in their saddles and grinning from ear to ear. Gramps praised Caleb for his bravery and appeared genuinely relieved to be across.

Then all eyes were on Al, who wasn't wasting any time getting the small group of cows pushed along without compromise. They moved their heads back and forth as if refusing to abide by Al's demands. Yodel was just as insistent as Al. She barked and nipped at them until they had little choice but to plod into the murky water.

Al dismounted and called Yodel to him. He picked her up and slowly pulled his old, tired body onto Dolly's strong back once again. Just as I had held Wedge on the North Fork, Al laid Yodel across the tree of the saddle and his lap. They started following the same crossing as Gramps and Caleb.

As soon as Al, Yodel and the three strays made it to our side, we'd be joining Ben and Mark and the cattle would leave the upper unit on their trek to my family's cabin. It was safe to say we'd be entering our pasture just before sunset. The road was bound to be torn up after the heavy rain, but at least Caleb and I wouldn't be eating dirt behind all the moving hooves.

At the center of the creek the cows became buoyant, same as the horses had done. They were pushed with the current a short distance until they could regain footing. Then the last one, a young steer, started to panic. He tried to turn midstream and return to the opposite shore. Al was not having it. He used his free hand to wave his hat and yelled out some colorful words, as only he could. Caleb and I were laughing at the comedy of it all, until we noticed the grim expression on Gramps' face.

The steer was crazy with fright and bawled his terror of the bottomless creek. He turned into Dolly and a wild clash of hooves stirred beneath the water's surface. Al used his leg to try and push the panicked animal away from Dolly. It looked as though he had the upper hand when, with a stunned expression, he tried to yell something. His pitiful cry was cut short and lost in all the commotion. Al's strained face jerked back as one of his gloved hands grabbed his jacket's lapel. He hunched over as if in pain. Yodel was released and seemed to welcome the chance to jump from the chaotic upheaval. The steer hooked his head around Al's leg and pulled him down from his saddle.

Wedge caught sight of Yodel floating downstream and ran to her aid. He threw himself into the rushing water and swam out to her little head bobbing through the rapids.

Gramps kicked Gus and they tore downstream from the struggling cattle. He had his lariat in his hand as rider and horse plowed into the churning water. He was yelling Al's name as Dolly and the steer came towards him, fighting for their lives.

We caught sight of Al's arm reaching up out of the water as if to grab something, anything, in order to pull himself up for air. Gramps lashed out at the steer as though the rope was a whip. Finally the steer passed Dolly's hindquarters and proceeded to get its footing on the opposite bank. Dolly followed the rest of the cows up our side of the creek, riderless.

Gramps stayed in the creek desperately looking for Al. It was too much for Caleb and me to absorb. I finally looked at Caleb and told him to run Moses down along the creek and help the dogs once they reached something they could climb out on. "Don't get in the water. I'm sure they'll make it over. Just follow them," I told him.

Then I too unlaced my lariat from the saddle and looped one end onto the saddle horn. I rode down parallel to Gramps. That was when I caught a glimpse of Al's jacket several feet downstream from Gramps.

"There he is!" I yelled while pointing to the familiar coat.

Gramps looked over at me with those determined blue eyes. He said nothing as he slid into the cold water. Gus fought his way to the water's edge and climbed out of the churning nightmare. Gramps settled into the rapids, keeping his head above water. When he saw what looked to be Al, he began swimming and working his way to the partially submerged jacket.

I got off of Tink and led her along the creek's edge at a pace equal to that of Gramps. He reached the coat and found Al was still inside.

Quickly, he turned him over until Al was looking up to the heavens. I gasped at his face, void of color or expression. Gramps wrapped his arm around Al's neck.

Gramps broke my trance when he yelled for me to throw a rope. Without hesitation, I threw the free end of the lariat. My aim was true. It landed upstream within reaching distance. Gramps grabbed it and looped it around his free hand, creating a tight noose. I began backing Tink up in order to pull the two men to land.

Gramps never loosened his hold until they were out of the swirling depths. He found the rocky bottom and readjusted his grip by placing his hands under Al's arms. I halted Tink and pulled him forward a couple of steps to slacken the rope's tension. I ran down and helped Gramps heave Al onto the bank. He scrambled up next to him and checked his vital signs.

I knew Al was gone. I'd seen the vacant eyes of death before. Glancing down at his whiskered old face to his slightly opened mouth, I began feeling the impact of what had just happened. One glove had come off revealing a hand with years of hard work etched into it. I touched his cold fingers and looked up at Gramps.

Gramps took his hand from me, trying to feel for a pulse. He opened his jacket and found Al's harmonica in the pocket over his heart. Gramps laid his head on Al's chest, hoping to find some sign of life.

I felt helpless watching Gramps trying to will breath back into the old body. He finally stopped and looked up at me. Our tear filled eyes met until I covered mine with my hands and sobbed. Too exhausted to stand, he raised himself to his knees and pulled me into his wet embrace. Our arms entwined and we both cried uncontrollably.

For some time he rocked me back and forth, squeezing me against his chest and trying to get words of comfort to come out of his mouth.

Suddenly, two wet dogs ran up on us. They began licking our salty cheeks and rearing up on our backs. Gramps pulled away and finally put a sentence together. "It was too much for his old heart. He died, Ez, doin' what he loved. You gotta remember that."

Gramps stood and wiped his hands across his tired face. Softly he said, "I'm goin' to cover Al with his slicker. There's no point in havin' Caleb remember him this way."

Caleb had Moses in a trot when we spotted him coming. Gramps and I began walking in his direction. On his saddle horn Al's hat hung by its stampede strap. Caleb saw it washed up against a rooted tree not far from where the dogs climbed out of the water.

"I found Al's hat," he shouted.

He rode a little closer with his big boy grin plastered across his face. He looked in Gramps' direction and said loudly, "Looks like you lost your hat too."

"I lost more than that," Gramps replied as he turned back to look at the covered body of Ol' Al.

Caleb's eyes looked beyond us and settled on the covered body laying on the matted grass. He then looked back at me. My red streaked face and bloodshot eyes confirmed the obvious. Glancing back at Gramps' battle weary expression, his moment of shock turned into reality. He shook his head back and forth as he yelled, "NO!"

Gramps walked over to Moses and reached to pull Caleb down from the saddle. Caleb fell into his arms and went limp with emotion. Gramps held him for as long as it took Caleb to empty his sorrow.

I turned away and began walking toward the three riderless horses waiting loyally for their orders. The ground was a blur and my legs didn't feel as though they were attached. Wedge seemed to understand my grief. He followed at my side, but with a reserved nature not typical of him.

Dolly, being a quarter horse, was much smaller than Tink. I was able to reach the saddle horn and pull myself up onto the saddle without help. Once I got on her I rode a short distance to Tink and Gus. I took each of their reins and led them back to Gramps.

"Can you ride okay now?" Gramps asked Caleb in a low voice.

Caleb nodded his head. Gramps helped him back onto the saddle and told him to keep Moses right there until he got Al.

I dismounted from Dolly and went to offer my assistance. It wasn't needed. Gramps picked up Al's worn-out body and cradled it in his arms for a moment, away from Caleb's view. He draped Al over Dolly's saddle and tied the slicker over him in several places. He turned to me and asked if I'd bring Gus to him. I led both our horses over so he could give me a boost up onto Tink.

Once we were all mounted, Caleb and I began pushing the stray cattle back to the herd with Gramps and Al bringing up the rear. I turned around and asked Gramps about the steer across the creek.

"He simply said, "Leave him."

CHAPTER 32

Lettin' Go

Mark and Ben were ready to begin the march down to the lower unit. Everything was packed up tight and they were pressing the herd toward the gate when we arrived. Ben caught sight of us first. He sat unmoving for a moment and then, slowly, walked Rio in our direction. Caleb and I said nothing as he passed us. We just looked into his eyes. He knew full well the loss we felt. He continued back to Gramps. I could hear his deep voice but couldn't make out the words. Nothing else was said by anyone all the way to the gate.

Ben's hat had been pulled low and tears slid freely down his unshaven face. He rode over to talk to Mark and they both returned together. Gramps asked Ben to take point and Mark and Caleb to ride flank with Betty. Wedge would not stay in the rear without me, and there was no way he was patient enough not to harass the cows riding a forward position. That left me in the back of the herd once again with Wedge and Yodel.

I knew Gramps would be no help with the cattle. He was consumed with so much grief, the worst kind of pain. He'd lost an old friend, one who had been working at the ranch since before Grandma and Gramps were even married. He was like an older sibling who helped and watched over him most of his life. He stood up for Gramps at his wedding and stood down when Gramps had the final say in ranch decisions. There was a mutual respect and a deep bond between the two men.

The air turned cold and wind whipped through the mountains. Once the gate swung wide, the cattle moved through with little persuasion. Everyone did their part to keep the herd moving. I followed the last of the cows through the entrance, with Yodel and Wedge springing into action. I looked back at Gramps leading Gus with one hand and Dolly with the other. He pulled the barb wire gate across the opening and placed the fastening hoop down over the fence post. He leaned against it and looked out toward Sheep Creek. As if to gather the strength he'd need to walk through each day without Al, he remained motionless for quite a spell.

I realized how ironic life can be. There stood a man full of emotional grief, yet was showing no signs of physical discomfort. Neither did his water drenched clothes and hatless head indicate the deep sorrow he was suffering. His heart had taken on a burdensome weight once again. This time his comrade of strength was not there to support him.

No one had much to say. We missed Al's yell from a distance, directing the cattle back on course. The dogs worked harder to pick up the slack. Betty could be heard doing her part, while Yodel and Wedge barked their orders from the rear.

I looked back a few times and saw Gramps following a short distance behind. His head was always tilted down as though life had been snatched from within him too. He seemed so lost at those moments. Perhaps seeing him like that is what put strength in me. I stopped crying and began thinking about all the things Al would want me to do and all the times he'd want me to remember. My emotional load felt lighter. Al would always be with me.

The first leg of the cattle drive was soon over. We made it to our pasture right at nightfall. No one was there to greet us. The path through the wooded area between the meadow and the barn was flooded. We stayed mounted as the horses followed each other single file through the standing water.

We tended to the horses in the corral while Gramps went inside the barn to take Al down from Dolly's back. I took responsibility for Gus as Ben went in the barn to retrieve Dolly. When Ben came out to the corral he asked me to go fetch Grandma. "Don't mention Al to her, Ez. That's somethin' your Gramps needs to do."

Mark took over my horse duties and I walked toward the cabin with Wedge. Light shining through the windows reflected off the pond and I could see that water had overflowed onto the wide walking trail. Wedge didn't think twice before plodding through the large puddle. It was deep enough to reach his belly, so I knew my boots were in for a soaking.

I walked slowly up the porch steps and told Wedge to stay. I opened the front door and was quickly greeted by everyone. Grandma ran over to me with the look of relief and a smile sweet enough to melt the heaviest of hearts. She gave me a huge hug and asked when everyone else would be coming. I said nothing as I looked around the room. They had waited dinner for us. The cabin was filled with the aroma of well-seasoned elk stew that included an ample amount of onions, garlic and vegetables. Hot rolls were waiting on top of the stove.

When she released me my eyes were full. As bravely as I could, I said, "Gramps wants you to go with me down to the barn."

Her face paled as her smile disappeared. She held both my cheeks in her shaking hands and said, "Where's Caleb? Is he okay?"

"Yes. He's helping to feed the horses."

I looked over to Eva, Luke and Vikki sitting on the hearth and waiting for more information. I turned away and took Grandma's coat down from a peg beside the door. "You'll need to wear rubber boots," I told her.

She took the wrap, slipped on some galoshes and followed me out the door. We walked silently down the trail and through the flooded pathway to the barn. I left her in front of the closed doors and returned to the corral.

Everything was just getting put away for the night. Ben, Mark and Caleb were hanging up the bridles and readying to head for the cabin. None of us spoke a word as we walked past the barn doors and heard Grandma crying while Gramps' deep voice tried to utter comforting words. Betty stopped outside to wait for Gramps.

Vikki was sitting between Eva and Luke on the couch reading to them when we entered the cabin. We gave the rug in front of the fireplace to Wedge and Yodel while we hung our coats and hats. Normally the aroma of Grandma's cooking would stir our hunger pangs, but no one seemed interested in eating.

"Where's Gramps and Al?" asked Eva.

Vikki got up and walked over to Mark. He hugged her and guided her out onto the porch. Ben put on a forced smile and asked Luke and Eva what they'd been doing all day.

Caleb and I went to wash up. We closed the bathroom door behind us, looked at each other and started crying. "How come all the animals made it to safety and not Al?" Caleb choked out, trying to whisper.

"I don't know. I can't believe he's gone."

"Why does God keep taking the people we love so much?"

Again, I had no answer.

We heard Mark and Vikki enter the house, followed by Gramps and Grandma. Quickly, we washed our faces with cold water and tried to put on a brave front when going back into the living room.

Gramps asked everyone to sit as he stood by all three dogs laying comfortably in front of the crackling flames. His coat had been removed and hung over the metal poker that leaned against the rock fireplace. His wet wool shirt steamed across his broad back from the wood's heat. We all looked into his strained eyes. Grandma sat on the leather footstool by his side. Her face was streaked from tears and she stared unblinking at the sleeping dogs by her feet.

Eva and Luke must have sensed the seriousness of it all. They cuddled up to Ben on the couch and said nothing. Mark and Vikki stood behind them while Caleb and I shared Papa's large leather chair.

Gramps looked directly at Eva and Luke when he said, "We lost Ol' Al today. My guess is his heart failed him. He was easily pulled down into some high water by a frightened steer. I'll be takin' his body to town tonight in the car and will be late gettin' back. We have a herd to move, so all of you need to be up before sunrise. Get yourselves some food and sleep. I'll see you in the mornin', dark and early."

With that said, he went to the bedroom to change his clothes. Grandma wrapped a warm scarf around his neck and walked him out onto the porch. Ben followed, offering to go along, but a quick "No" ended the conversation. Instead, Gramps agreed to let him back the car down to where the pond's overflow began.

Grandma insisted on everyone eating a hot meal before retiring. She also gave her bed to Mark and Vikki. She would curl up in Papa's large chair for the night. Between Ben and her, they would keep the fire going.

Eva sat crying in Grandma's arms as Luke cuddled to them looking totally confused. He wasn't old enough to grasp the idea of never seeing Al again. He knew the news was bad, but the concept of "forever gone" hadn't quite taken a hold on him.

Caleb and I decided to each take a roll and a small bowl of stew up to the loft. Wedge seemed content sleeping next to the fire with Betty and Yodel. His big feet were twitching and jerking as if cows were getting the best of him in his cattle dog dreams.

We crawled into bed and both looked out our little window that faced the pond and barn beyond. The partial moon had come up and was casting its bright reflection on the pond's still water. We could see the station wagon backed down as far as it could go. The rear window had been raised up and the tailgate pulled down.

In the distance we could see Gramps carrying Al's bent body, like a parent would a sleeping child. He walked through the water as if it weren't there and up to the back of the waiting car. He and Ben exchanged a few words as Gramps laid Al gently in the back. Ben closed the tailgate and upper window.

Caleb and I took the whole scene in with the calmness of two grown men until Ben turned around and hugged Gramps in a mutual expression of suffering. They appeared to be crying, showing no sign of humiliation. They pulled away as Gramps patted Ben's back. He left Ben standing at the tailgate while he walked to the driver's door and lowered himself behind the steering wheel. Ben stood motionless, watching Gramps take Al away. The car drove up past the cabin, through the aspen grove and out of sight.

Caleb and I laid down with heads next to each other on our pillows. Looking up at the pine ceiling, we spoke quietly of Al and the times he altered outcomes with his calm and knowledgeable presence. Through tears I disclosed the secret of Al's past. Caleb listened attentively as I spoke of his young wife and infant son dying during the influenza epidemic. And I explained why Al had a shelf full of animal husbandry books in the bunkhouse. When

I finished pouring out what little I knew of Al's history, Caleb simply rolled over and buried his head in his pillow, trying to muffle his hurt. Eventually, he fell asleep.

I started to doze off when another cry sounded from the bottom of the ladder. Wedge had woken and realized I'd gone to bed without him. Quickly, I scrambled to get my noisy pal before he roused anyone else.

While stepping down the rungs, I noticed Grandma and Ben sitting on the hearth with coffee cups and speaking in low tones. They seemed oblivious to my presence or Wedge's whimpers. I gathered him into my arms and struggled back up the ladder. I didn't bother to put him in his own bed. He'd end up next to me by morning anyway. His soft fur and warm body brought the comfort I needed. Thinking back to the night of his birth, I actually smiled. Al had lived a long life and, because of him, others were allowed to live theirs. Wedge was his gift to me. I would forever be grateful.

Morning snuck up on us. Caleb's appetite and nose worked together to put his body into motion. His movement was enough to waken Wedge and me from our deep sleep.

"Ezra, get up! We gotta eat and saddle Tink and Moses."

Although the sun wasn't up, the smell of sausage let us know a new day had started. We fed Wedge our uneaten dinner from the night before and headed for the kitchen. Caleb and I confessed to each other that our appetites had returned.

Mark, Vikki, Ben and Grandma were sitting around the table doing the best they could with their breakfast. As soon as we slid onto our benches, their tones became lighter and somewhat cheerful. All of us spoke of pushing the herd home. No one mentioned Al. Eva stumbled in from her night of sleep to join us, just moments before Luke ran into the room.

Apparently, Gramps had gotten back a few hours earlier. He'd already fed the horses and readied everything for the day's drive to the ranch. We heard the stomping of feet on the porch as Gramps tried to rid his boots of mud before entering the house. He opened the door slowly, peering in to see who was up and about.

"You take those boots off and come in here," ordered Grandma. "There's no way I'm gonna let you put one foot in a stirrup before getting food in your belly."

Gramps looked like a scolded school boy. He sat on the bench next to the door in order to pull his boots from his feet, then walked over to join us at the table. Luke was on him like a bee on a blossom. He held Gramps' scruffy face between his dimpled hands and kissed him. Not to be outdone, Eva wiggled her way over to him. Standing up on the bench beside him she wrapped her arms around his neck, kissed his cheek and said, "I love you Gramps."

It was the perfect remedy. The daily morning ritual made by Eva and Luke pulled Gramps back into the world of the living. He smiled and returned the love they were accustomed to and expected. Caleb and I were drawn into the conversation about plans for the day. Gramps was breaking through the barrier. He was the grandfather and boss all of us knew.

Towards the end of our meal we noticed headlights bumping their way along the driveway and reflecting off the cabin walls. It sounded like a truck pulling a horse trailer. Ben excused himself from the table and went out to the porch. Company at the cabin was rare, especially at such an early hour. We could hear men talking and it wasn't long before the door opened with Ben and Tucker stepping over the threshold.

Gramps had stopped by the ranch on his way to town the night before. Tucker, who had once again been overseeing things for us while we were at the cabin, was just finishing evening chores when Gramps arrived. He learned of the incident and decided to lend a helping hand with the cattle as well. Tucker figured Vikki could drive his truck and horse trailer back to our ranch where, when we arrived with the herd, he'd reload his horse and return home in time for dinner and his own chores. Tucker also suggested the trailer not go back empty. Dolly and Al's gear could be hauled to the ranch in it, making a much safer and easier ride for Gramps. Everyone was extremely grateful to add another skilled cowboy. I was particularly happy to have Caleb riding drag with me again.

The sun was just clearing the mountains to the east when we all headed for the barn. Grandma sent food for our saddlebags and promised to catch up with us shortly. The morning was crisp, the sky clear, and a mist was rising from the saturated ground. A thin layer of ice had settled over the pond during the night. The aspens were showing signs of frostbite. Such cold snaps would soon transform the fluttering leaves into patches of bright yellow mixed among the dark evergreens. The season was short, but majestic enough to become embedded in a fella's memory for an entire lifetime.

The water that spilled over the narrow road next to the pond had receded. We were able to walk on a muddy ridge, skirting around the flooded areas. Coming up to the barn, we were all pleasantly surprised. We knew Gramps had fed all the horses, but seeing them saddled and tied to five separate fence posts was quite a treat. Dolly stood bareback and fastened to the hitching post. Al's saddle was draped over a top fence rail with his hat hanging from the horn. It was to be the first cattle drive in forty-two years that Gramps would finish without Al.

CHAPTER 33

A Tough Decision

CALEB AND I WERE TOO absorbed with loss to feel the pride we had once anticipated when pushing the last stragglers into the ranch's lower pasture. Grandma was not at her usual spot on the stile with Eva and Luke. Gramps, Mark and Tucker waited on their horses to block the driveway while Ben stood at the gate ready to swing it closed. Caleb, Ben and I followed the other three to the barn, ending three relentless days.

It had been less than two years since we'd made our home at the big ranch. I felt as though I had aged tenfold. All of us had been knocked down by death's mighty fist. Fortunately, if our hands were too small or weak, there were stronger ones ready to grab hold. We were taught at a young age that palms up were to be used for a lift, not a handout. If no one was there to help, we'd need to press our palms to the ground and push ourselves up. This was one of those "pushing up" times.

Dolly had already eaten and been left to roam in the corral. She perked up on our arrival and greeted us at the gate. Tucker thanked Gramps for the dinner offer, opting instead to head home before he even fed or unsaddled his horse. It was understandable. With ranch life comes tremendous responsibility. His mare was loaded into the trailer and they were rolling out of the yard by the time we were dragging our saddles to the tack room. No one was in a race to the house. We helped each other until everyone was ready to head in for our meal.

Caleb and I were exhausted when we entered the mudroom. I was yanking my boots off when Caleb elbowed me and pointed to Al's hat hanging on the peg that once held Gramps'. Then we watched as Gramps stopped short before going into the kitchen and faced the hat. He stood still as if contemplating on what to do. We were surprised when he removed it from the peg and placed it on his head. He seemed pleased with the perfect fit. Putting it back on the wall, he continued to pass through the door.

Al's hat was the only tangible thing Gramps kept for himself. He said it was like having Al watching over him.

Five days later, Vikki gave birth to a plump little boy. Had he been born with a mustache he would have looked just like Mark. They named him Mark Alan, but most folks went on to call him Al.

Ol' Al was buried alongside his wife and child. Apparently, Gramps and Grandma had visited their gravesite several times over the decades. They said three of Al's rare trips to town every year were predictable. Flowers could be found on the combined tombstone for each of their birthdays and again on Al and his young bride's wedding anniversary. Once again, the four of us stood alongside our grandparents and Ben while prayers were said over a freshly dug grave. Here was another who had been taken from us. Yet, in life, he had given so much.

More than a week passed before Gramps and Grandma went out to sort through Al's belongings. In his few worldly possessions, Grandma found a journal. It appeared not even his sleepless nights were spent wasted. A lot of thought and gratitude had gone into the carefully handwritten pages. Much like my own journal, he wrote of everyday existence in our mountain refuge. It was about a life most people couldn't relate to, or would even want. Because he was around during the raising of our ma, he mentioned how thankful he was for her choice of husbands. He wrote words of praise and respect about Gramps and spoke of the strength and inner beauty of Grandma. The loss of his wife and child was referred to only once. They were remembered with reverence after the death of our folks. His concern and love for the four of us kids was evident. He had even taken time to write about his late night ride with Wedge and me to the cabin. And his thoughts about Ben were not only humorous, but full of reflection. Interestingly, he felt Ben was much like himself.

Al had few material needs. So it wasn't a big surprise to find a small fortune under his bed, stacked neatly in a closed, homemade box. On top of the money was an old sealed envelope with "Dave" printed neatly across the front. Gramps' hands shook as he tore through the top edge. Like Al, the note was simple and to the point. It said, "Spend it as you see fit."

We didn't see evidence of Gramps spending any of Al's money for many years. However, Gramps did pass Al's few earthly goods on to all of us, the ones he loved so much. The first item handed out was Al's harmonica. It's been tucked into my shirt pocket, right over my heart, every day since. Eva was given the privilege of keeping Dolly. She was the perfect choice. Her caring ways and love for the horse was evident from the start. Luke was ten when he inherited Al's saddle, which he used later in riding competitions. Caleb was fourteen when Gramps presented him with Al's rifle. I received his collection of animal husbandry books later, after graduating from high school and announcing my intention of becoming a vet. Al's prized rodeo buckles were framed and remain on display in the living room.

Ben wasn't left out. He still drives Al's old Studebaker truck.

Grandma keeps the most precious item of all on her dresser, next to the wedding picture of her and Gramps. Al's journal serves as an uplifting collection of wit, wisdom and common sense.

Caleb and I haven't missed a single cattle drive over the years. Along with Wedge, we worked our way up to riding flank when Eva and Luke were hired on as drag. Yodel stayed with them and was content to work alone.

Caleb and I moved into the bunkhouse two years after Al died. We gave Ben some much needed company and Luke no longer had to share a room with Eva.

My interest in doctoring animals was aided by Al's small library of books as well as Gramps' handed down "knowledge through experience". Wedge was my constant companion with the exception of attending church and school.

Like Al, Betty had lived a full life. She never shied away from hard work and she left behind two amazing dogs who learned from her example. When

I was nineteen, she died peacefully in the room where she gave birth to her nine pups.

Thanks to a portion of Al's savings, I was able to go on to college. Together, Wedge and I faced a world of cement sidewalks, crowded streets and bunched up buildings. He spent long hours in a small rental house, waiting for me to return from school or my part-time job. He fought desperately to rid himself of the leash he was forced to wear when we went for walks. It was a life neither of us liked. I knew it was a means to an end, but there was no way Wedge could understand. All he knew was that he was with me. He'd sacrifice his freedom to share what little time we had together.

We went home as much as my schedule allowed. Wedge would reunite with Yodel and run until his legs nearly gave out. We'd hike to the fort or I'd ride Tink while he scouted a new trail for us. A few times we crossed the mountains to sneak up on our deserted cabin, just as we had done with Ol' Al that long ago night. I would light a fire in the fireplace and have his full attention while I told him about all the plans I had for the place, once it becomes ours.

Caleb chose not to take the college route. He was living his dream right at the big ranch. He was the burst of energy Gramps needed, welcomed and had once possessed himself.

Gramps and Grandma offered to give Luke and Eva each a small section of land, the same as they did for our folks. It would be payment for the years they worked to help keep the ranch viable. The agreement was, that if either chose to sell, only a family member could buy.

This was done at the same time our folks' property was promised to me. However, true to everything my grandparents stood for, I had to complete at least two years in vet school and pay a portion of the cabin's value to my sister and two brothers. Even though they wanted no part of taking my money, Gramps insisted I earn my ranch. I wouldn't have had it any other way.

It was my second year in vet school when I noticed a dramatic change in Wedge. His hearing became severely impaired and his energy had been sapped out of him. I took him to the ranch for Easter and a well deserved vacation. He scared me one day by wandering off for no apparent reason.

Calling his name proved unsuccessful. His hearing was too far gone. Caleb helped me search for my old buddy, only to locate him on the other side of the river. He seemed confused as to where the bridge was in order to find his way back across the high water. When we returned to the ranch house with Wedge, Gramps suggested I attach a small cow bell to his collar. It would help me locate him should he lose his way again.

Yodel had also shown signs of old age before her unexpected death a few months earlier. She'd retired from ranch work a year after Gramps purchased two heeler pups. She spent her free days in slumber or walking around the barnyard. Yodel wasn't one to stay in the house during the day by a warm fire. So as it turned out, the harsh winter took its toll on her one cold afternoon. Luke stumbled across her little body curled up in the hay.

I spent that night on a bottom bed in the bunkhouse. Ben and Caleb had no problem drifting off to sleep. Wedge was snuggled against my chest as I stroked his head and thought back over the years. Tears dripped onto my pillow as I buried my face in his soft shoulder. He stretched his old legs and pawed at my cheeks. There was only one thing I knew I had to do.

The next morning I woke the old boy and took him to the main house. A light was on in the kitchen. I climbed the back steps slowly so Wedge could keep up. He stayed by my side as we entered the mudroom. I looked down to the corner where Wedge was born and, in a flash, relived the moment Al took him from my hold and breathed life back into his tiny lungs. All was quiet except for the low murmur of Grandma and Gramps talking quietly at the kitchen table. When I stuck my head through the kitchen door they seemed surprised. Both sat staring at me with fingers still hooked through their cups of coffee. They said nothing as they read my face.

Grandma broke the silence with her soft voice. "Pull a chair over, Ezra. I think you have a tough decision to make."

I picked Wedge up and sat across from them. Wedge's head was almost level with mine as he straddled my lap. It'd been years since I'd cried out to them. When my tearful eyes met theirs I was reminded of how many times they had felt my pain. Grandma reached over to clasp my free hand.

Gramps' filled eyes met mine as he said, "We know, Ez. Wedge has little time left. He has seen you through many years of joy and sorrow. His heart has always been with you, but you know his place is here in these mountains."

My lip quivered as strength failed me. I brought Wedge's wiry old face up to mine as I sobbed out the words, "I'm leaving him here. I couldn't bear to go back to our little house someday after school and find him dead. I'm afraid he'll be all alone when it happens. He deserves better."

"There are just a few weeks left until summer. You can come back and be with him then." Grandma wiped her eyes and continued, "Because all of you will be here, I'm planning a late seventy-fifth birthday party for Gramps, since it always falls during calving season. Then we can move all of your belongings to your cabin."

I smiled at the realization that Wedge and I were going home to our own place. Hopefully, we'd sit together on the front porch and watch as our small ranch witnessed the change of seasons.

CHAPTER 34

Home

EXCEPT FOR THE LAST WEEK of college, I was able to get home for a day or two over the weekends. Wedge and I shared mutual enthusiasm when we reunited and experienced the same sadness when we had to part. Final exams dictated where I had to be. Knowing I was nearing the home stretch kept me focused. I was anxious and eager to return to the ranch for Gramps' birthday celebration and stay with Wedge through the rest of the year. I was prepared to put school on hold during the fall so Wedge and I could be together for as long as he needed me. Nothing would ever separate us again.

Gramps had begun to recognize signs of demise and took time away from ranch chores to ensure Wedge wouldn't be alone. He rigged up a saddle cushion on which Wedge settled for one last ride. The two of them journeyed together over the mountains, alive with spring and new life, to the cabin. My longtime companion spent his final day with Gramps, lying next to him in the sun while Gramps chiseled Wedge's name into a modest sized stone.

That evening Gramps was holding Wedge's old gray head in his lap as they sat on the couch before the fire. Gramps was speaking softly to him when my little buddy cried out for the last time. He had been staring up into Gramps' blue eyes before he yelped, as if to say goodbye. The hand Gramps had been using to soothe Wedge's limp body reached up to close his lifeless eyes.

It was important for me to hear all about the death of my closest friend. The phone call I feared came late the following morning. Gramps did his best to answer the questions I was unable to ask. His voice broke several times and there were a few pauses in the one sided conversation. When he finished, all I could muster up in response was, "Thanks, Gramps."

I missed being back with Wedge by two days.

My head rolled to one side as my hand fell off the armrest of Papa's leather chair. My eyes snapped open, taking in the familiar cabin interior. I sat for a moment, reflecting on my dream-walk through the years. I had come full circle. I mentally gave thanks for the people who influenced my life and inspired me to "climb the ladder with both hands". Then I thought again of Wedge, my four legged friend who never complained of long training hours, hard work or time spent alone.

Now, turning my attention toward the front window, a creased paper on the small side table catches my eye. I lean over and retrieve the written message, immediately recognizing Caleb's blocked handwriting on the unsigned page. It's a poem. He has become known as a poet-of-sorts around these parts and has made a name for himself with his wit and humor. After reading the first stanza it becomes apparent this did not fit into the typical Caleb mold. The words are heartfelt and his intentions sincere. They are words I'm unable to utter, an insight into my emotions.

Looking up, I gaze through the dusty glass to where Wedge was, so lovingly, laid to rest. He had played a big part in getting me here. This is where the road we traveled together finally brought us.

Shadows cast down by the trees indicate hours have passed since my arrival. Soon I will be joining family at the big ranch. We'll unite to observe another loss and lift our spirits with reflections of life's gifts received. I'll spend the last hour collecting all of my things from the bunkhouse and bringing them home to our cabin at the end of the road.

I look around and know these walls will hear laughter and music again. They will comfort, protect and, God willing, witness new life. Future generations will climb that ladder and gaze out at the stars through the small loft window. They too will give thanks and ask for the strength needed to handle whatever life sends their way. With any luck at all, one of them will be comforted by the warmth, love and devotion of a sleeping puppy snuggled softly against his proud chest.

SITTIN' BY THE GATE

GRAMPS TOOK US BOTH IN
NEITHER KNOWIN' WHAT WAS IN STORE
ALL THOSE WONDERFUL DAYS WE SHARED
WHAT I'D GIVE FOR JUST ONE MORE.

RUNNIN' THROUGH THE HILLS
PLAYIN' TAG IN TALL GRASS
NEVER THINKIN' THOSE DAYS
WOULD COME TO PASS.

IF EVER THERE WAS TROUBLE
YOU WERE RIGHT BY MY SIDE
NEVER WANTING TO SEE ME HURT
I WASN'T THERE WHEN YOU DIED.

I KNOW YOU'RE SITTIN' PATIENTLY
UP BY THE GATE
ONLY GOD KNOWS HOW LONG
YOU WILL HAVE TO WAIT.

Acknowledgments

I MUST ACKNOWLEDGE THE STRENGTH of character and moral compass in my husband, David, and the encouragement, artistic abilities and unique personalities of our children: Ezra, Caleb, Eva and Luke. They are my life and the soul of this book.

A special thanks goes to my good friend Sherry Marine. Without her positive feedback and careful critique, this story would have been filed away. Thanks to my sister, Linda Fessenden, who, as close siblings do, gave thoughtful advice and kept me on track. I would like to praise Nikole Morgan for capturing real ranch life through her spontaneous photography and to Meghan Gray for designing the book's cover. I am also grateful to Eric Holland who got me through the self-publishing process. A big thank you goes to Luke and his firsthand experience with ranching. He proved to be an invaluable resource and his unfailing optimism urged me forward. Not forgotten is cheerful, blond, blue eyed Ben, a past student who had faith in my desire to author a book.

In Memory

of my loving and determined mother, an orphan who knew all about the pain of loss and traveling on life's bumpy road.

www.ingramcontent.com/pod-product-compliance
Lightning Source LLC
Chambersburg PA
CBHW051821040426
42447CB00006B/316